PRESS WATCH

Wilt: Just Like Any Other 7-Foot Black Millionaire Who Lives Next Door

The Levy Caper

Journalism Today: A Changing Press for a Changing America

David Shaw

PRESS WATCH

A Provocative Look at How

Newspapers Report the News

MACMILLAN PUBLISHING COMPANY

NEW YORK

Macmillan Publishing Company
866 Third Avenue, New York, N.Y. 10022
Collier Macmillan Canada, Inc.

Library of Congress Cataloging in Publication Data
Shaw, David, 1943–
Press watch.
Includes index.
1. Reporters and reporting—United States.
2. Journalistic ethics—United States. I. Title.
PN4867.S465 1984   070.4′3   83-24832
ISBN 0-02-610030-4

10 9 8 7 6 5 4 3 2 1

Designed by Jack Meserole

Printed in the United States of America

Macmillan books are available at special discounts for bulk purchases for sales promotions, premiums, fund-raising, or educational use. Special editions or book excerpts can also be created to specification. For details, contact:
    Special Sales Director
    Macmillan Publishing Company
    866 Third Avenue
    New York, New York 10022

For Ellen, who was my best editor
as well as my best friend, my lover,
and my wife

Author's Note

The material in the introduction to this book is based, in part, on a speech given by the author at the University of Hawaii on March 8, 1983. The individual chapters are reprinted with the permission of the *Los Angeles Times*, where they were originally published, in substantially the same form, during the years 1977 through 1983.

Although all interviews were conducted at the time each story was originally researched, each chapter has been edited, updated, expanded, and provided with a separate, new introduction to place it in a broader context; to provide personalized, behind-the-scenes information; and to yield the greatest possible benefit and pleasure to readers interested in the performance and function of a daily newspaper today. The epilogue is entirely new material written specifically for this book.

Contents

PRESS WATCH

Introduction:
On Arrogance and Accountability

I spend quite a bit of time in airplanes, and since the only thing worse than trying to sleep on an airplane is eating on an airplane, I tend to carry a lot of books on board.

On one cross-country trip last year, I took along Irving Wallace's novel, *The Almighty*. Wallace is not my normal fare, but my late wife, Ellen, had even loftier literary tastes than I do— she tended to prefer Lord Byron, Virginia Woolf, and Lady Mary Wortley Montagu (whoever that is) to what she called the "vulgar" popular novels that are written, she insisted, by "hydrocephalics," exclusively for "dental hygienists." So when she saw me unobtrusively slipping the Wallace book into my suitcase, she gave me the sort of scornful glance that she normally reserved for people who scrawl graffiti on the walls of buildings or cut in front of her on the freeway.

But I took the book with me anyway. And I read it. And it was almost as bad as Ellen had predicted. But it was not altogether a waste of my time.

I read the book primarily because I knew from the reviews that it was about a newspaper publisher, and I knew from the book jacket that Wallace is "one of the five most widely read authors in the world today" (the others, I assume, being Matthew, Mark, Luke, and John—although I'm not quite sure where that leaves Benjamin Spock and Harold Robbins). As a newspaper reporter—and particularly as a newspaper reporter who specializes in writing about the men and women who own, edit, write, and read newspapers—I figured that when one of the world's most popular novelists writes about a newspaper publisher, I'd better see what he has to say on the subject.

Who knows how many millions of people will learn all they ever know about newspapers from Irving Wallace? Who knows when I might bump into someone at a cocktail party and have to explain that, no, the publisher of the *Los Angeles Times* is not one bit like that guy in *The Almighty*.

No indeed.

The protagonist in *The Almighty* is a power-mad, megalomaniacal, second-generation newspaper publisher who makes such observations as, "There's not enough hard news around, exclusive news. Usually, my competitors have the same thing to sell that I have. But we here want our news alone. Since it's not around, we might have to invent some of it."

This publisher, Edward Armstead, decides that the best way to attract attention to himself and his newspaper, the *New York Record,* is to hire a band of European gangsters, arm them, finance them, and give them various "assignments" over a period of weeks. The assignments are not stories, of course, but crimes. Incredible crimes.

Armstead promises to pay these gangsters millions and millions of dollars to steal the Dead Sea Scrolls. And to kidnap the king of Spain. And the pope. And the secretary-general of the United Nations. And, finally, this brilliant newspaper publisher has his personal gang engage a Japanese pilot—a man whose life has been filled with shame because he didn't have the courage to complete a kamikaze mission during World War II—and arrange for this man to crash a stolen Cuban jet fighter into Air Force One over the Atlantic, thus killing the president of the United States and all his fellow passengers.

Since Armstead himself plans these terrorists acts, he can write the story of them exclusively for his paper even before they actually happen. Then, the instant they do happen, *voilà,* an exclusive for the *New York Record.* Needless to say, this stunning series of exclusives lands Armstead on the cover of *Time* magazine and—well, I don't want to give away too much of the story. . . .

I realize that the portrait of a newspaper publisher drawn by Wallace is not a very realistic one—to put it mildly. But I didn't react as defensively to that portrait as do most journalists when it is suggested that not all the giants in our profession are candidates for sainthood.

Surely no profession whose pioneers include the names of Hearst and Pulitzer and McCormick can recoil with horror when someone says that the power of a newspaper publisher is sometimes used to advance something other than the common good. Their frequent good work—and their even more frequent encomiums to each other—notwithstanding, newspaper publishers are not invariably paragons of virtue, universally beloved and respected for their commitment to the commonweal.

Indeed, I remember reading that Hiram Johnson, the governor of California from 1911 to 1917, once said of Harrison Gray Otis, the founder/publisher of my own newspaper, the *Los Angeles Times:*

"He sits there in senile dementia with gangrene heart and rotting brain, grimacing at every reform, chattering impotently at all things that are decent, frothing, fuming, violently gibbering, going down to his grave in snarling infamy . . . disgraceful, depraved, corrupt, crooked, putrescent—that is Harrison Gray Otis."

This description, although a bit more richly written than Irving Wallace's portrayal of Edward Armstead in *The Almighty,* is probably just as hyperbolic. But as I was reading Wallace's novel, I suddenly realized—somewhere over Utah, as I recall—that Wallace was mining familiar ground; since the heady, halcyon days of *All the President's Men*—when Jason Robards played Benjamin C. Bradlee playing Jason Robards, and two young reporters named Woodward and Bernstein became household names—fictional journalists have been depicted in one outrageous, compromising, unethical situation after another.

Journalists have often been the subjects of movies and books and plays, of course, but recent characterizations bear little resemblance to the rogues and romantic figures of *The Front Page, Foreign Correspondent,* or *His Girl Friday.*

Journalists depicted on the silver screen today are more likely to be rotten than roguish or romantic. Wallace's Armstead is certainly the most despicable of these characters, but examples abound, the most well-known being the reporter in *Absence of Malice.* In that film, reporter Megan Carter illegally wore a concealed tape recorder during an interview. She had a love affair with a man she was writing about for her newspaper. She betrayed the confidence of at least one of her news sources and callously invaded the privacy of another. And she was so eager to rush into print with a story about a murder investigation that she blindly allowed herself to be used by a ruthless prosecutor to blacken an innocent man's reputation—without making the slightest effort to investigate the prosecutor's story or to learn his motive (and without making more than a token effort to get the alleged suspect's side of what was actually a phony story).

Even though *Absence of Malice* was written by a former newspaper editor, many journalists thought it was egregiously unfair to journalists. No reporter would do what Megan Carter did, they said, and if she did, no editor would let her get away with it. I agree that the character played by Sally Field, like the character of Edward Armstead in *The Almighty,* was a bit overdrawn. I can't imagine a newspaper the size of hers in the movie not having at least one reporter or editor or even copy messenger who would have at least suggested, however tentatively and perhaps even unsuccessfully, that she might be doing something unethical.

But I think most journalists overreacted to *Absence of Malice.* I found their protestations that "It can't happen here" almost as hollow as I found similar protestations after reporter Janet Cooke lost her Pulitzer Prize and her job at the *Washington Post* for writing a story about a nonexistent eight-year-old heroin addict. And I wondered, with Janet Cooke still fresh in our minds, why we in the press were so determined to insist on the unassailability of our virtue.

The answer, I think, is fairly obvious. Like lawyers—and doctors and politicians and athletes and movie stars and everyone else I know—we don't like to be criticized.

The press—individually and collectively, personally and institutionally—is fond of saying that what separates us from other institutions in our society is the First Amendment. And we are quick to wrap ourselves in the protective cloak of the First Amendment at the first hint of criticism. I sometimes think that the phrase "chilling effect"—as in "This will have a chilling effect on the ability of the press to fulfill its First Amendment obligations"—is routinely administered to all journalists, by injection, along with their first press cards. But the First Amendment guarantees only that we are free to publish, *not* that we will be free of criticism for what we publish. The press is a powerful institution that, at its best, acts as a surrogate for its readers, shining the light of public scrutiny on those other powerful institutions (and powerful individuals) who occasionally abuse and misuse—or just misconstrue—the public trust.

We observe. We monitor. We report. And by so doing we sometimes hold others accountable for their errors of commission and omission. But who observes us? Who holds us accountable when we abuse or misuse or misconstrue the public trust?

In other words, Who Watches the Watchers? The brief, oversimplified but honest answer is that no one does. And no one should. We should watch ourselves. Carefully. Constantly. Critically. Publicly. And we don't do that, at least not in the sense I think is necessary. That's one big reason why characterizations such as those in *Absence of Malice* and *The Almighty* often find a receptive audience.

Like many other journalists, I was invited to a preview screening of *Absence of Malice* before it was generally released in late 1981, and I can still vividly remember a conversation I had at a dinner party immediately after the screening.

Everyone, naturally, was talking about the movie, and I was busy deploring the unethical behavior of Megan Carter. But a young woman, the first nonjournalist I spoke to at the party, asked me, quite ingenuously, I thought, "But don't all journalists do that?" This exchange took place perhaps six or seven months after the Janet Cooke affair became public, and I suspect my dinner partner may have been influenced by the news reports on Janet Cooke.

But Janet Cooke did not shape public opinion all by herself. The whole affair only confirmed what many of our readers—not too many, I fervently hope—have long suspected about us: We cannot altogether be trusted.

In 1963, when I took my first full-time reporting job, I worked for a small daily newspaper that had a feature similar to many of the time: a daily "Man in the Street" interview. Everyday the paper's lone photographer and its newest reporter would visit one of the nearby shopping areas to interview (and photograph) several shoppers and passersby on some issue of current concern. The next day, six one-paragraph interviews (and six one-inch-square photographs) appeared in the newspaper.

The first few times I drew the "Man in the Street" assignment, I was excited by the friendly, ego-gratifying reception we invariably received. People would spot us in the distance and come racing toward us, virtually begging to be interviewed and photographed. But this was before Selma and Watts, before Berkeley, before Tet and My Lai, before Martin Luther King and Mario Savio and Bella Abzug, before free love and free choice—in other words, before the press began to report, on an almost daily basis, all the civil rights marches, antiwar protests, campus demonstrations, feminist rallies, sit-ins, teach-ins, love-ins.

It's become almost a cliché to say it now, but the young people of that time were challenging the values and standards and traditions of the establishment generation, and most members of the establishment generation not only resented the challenge, they resented the press for reporting it. Time and again we in the press heard that if only we would go away, deny the demonstrators our front pages and our cameras, they would shut up, go home, and start submissively listening to mom and dad and the teacher and the preacher once again. We didn't go away, thank God. Neither did the protesters. Nor, alas, did the issues they raised—as witness the continuing threat of nuclear war and the continuing problems facing the poor and the black and the brown and the continuing (if somewhat diminished) discrimination against women in our society.

But I don't think our readers came to resent us—and, in many cases, to dislike us and mistrust us—solely because we were messengers bringing bad news. I think they also resented and disliked and mistrusted us because of the arrogance with which we brought them the bad news (in fact, any news). And that arrogance is still with us today.

Indeed I think the arrogance of the press may be one of the greatest problems we, as an institution, face today. Too many members of our profession seem to agree with a *Wall Street Journal* editorial of almost sixty years ago that said:

"A newspaper is a private enterprise, owing nothing to the public, which grants it no franchise. It is therefore affected with no public interest. It is emphatically the property of its owner, who is selling a manufactured product at his own risk."

I believe in a free and independent press. I think the First Amendment is the best guarantee America has against tyranny and totalitarianism. The Bible says, "Ye shall know the truth, and the truth shall make ye free," and I am convinced that a vigilant, independent press is the best, the only, way for a people to know the truth, the only way for them to be free.

I believe wholeheartedly in the First Amendment assurance that the press must not be held legally accountable to the government; that way, ultimately, lies tyranny. But I also believe wholeheartedly that the press must be held morally accountable to itself and to the society it serves.

That accountability is multifaceted, but most journalists respond only to the most visible of those facets: their responsibility to report the news fairly, impartially, and comprehensively, "without fear or favor," in the words of Adolph S. Ochs, an early publisher of the *New York Times*. That is an honorable and by no means modest objective, and I quite frankly think more journalists, and more newspapers, are performing this basic, essential job better today than ever in our history. There are not nearly as many good newspapers in this country as there should be, but I still think that for all our flaws, newspapers collectively (and, in particular, the half-dozen or dozen best newspapers individually), are more accurate, more insightful, more complete, more ethical—in a word, *better*—than ever.

They are also more responsible. And more responsive. But they are not nearly responsible and responsive enough. Too often they remain, as I said earlier, arrogant and unwilling to be held morally accountable, even by members of their own staffs and their own profession.

For far too long, journalists have operated on the assumption that we don't owe anyone anything—except, of course, the Truth. If we do our job—if we report, write, edit, and publish accurate stories—we figure that's all anyone can ask of us.

People have every right to ask much more of us. They may ask us, for instance, why we published a certain story on a certain page on a certain day, and why we didn't publish another story. And why certain information and certain photographs and certain headlines were or were not handled in a certain way. But I have a better idea. Why do we wait for someone to ask us? Why not tell the readers first?

I am constantly appalled by how little most otherwise-intelligent, well-informed people know about how a newspaper actually functions, about what its objectives and limitations and traditions are, about its structure and its decision-making procedures.

I am confronted by this ignorance time and again at parties when guests learn I am a journalist and begin asking well-meaning but utterly ignorant questions about the most fundamental aspects of newspaper work. Even worse, I hear these questions often when I speak informally to college journalism classes. I have actually encountered senior journalism majors who think the chairman of the board of the company that publishes the *Los Angeles Times* comes to the city room each day and dictates the tone, selection, and play of every important story.

There are several reasons for this misconception. One is that, in generations past, at many newspapers, my own included, the vested self-interest of the publisher did often dictate news play. Another reason is the pervasive cynicism many young people now have toward the media. But the main reason may simply be that we've never explained ourselves.

Until relatively recently, about the only time newspapers wrote about themselves was when they won a Pulitzer Prize or when the publisher's son got married or his wife was placed in charge of one important social group or another or, heaven forbid, when the newspaper was sued for libel. Anything short of a threatened lawsuit, of course, and the paper would bury the correction back on page thirty-seven, among the ads for corsets, jock straps, and athlete's foot powder. We felt we didn't owe anyone an explanation or an apology, so we seldom explained or apologized. Worse, perhaps, we never wrote about ourselves the way we wrote about anyone else.

In part this was arrogance; in part it was the social graces of the gentleman's club. But, for whatever reason, for too many years the press was a powerful institution dedicated to the critical examination of every other powerful institution in society— except itself. As Abe Raskin, former labor editor of the *New York Times,* wrote in the *New York Times Magazine* in 1967,

"The press prides itself—as it should—on the vigor with which it excoriates malefactors in government, unions, and business, but its own inadequacies escape both its censure and its notice. . . . The real long-range menace to America's daily newspapers lies in the unshatterable smugness of their publishers and editors, myself included."

For the most part, that complaint is as true today as it was in 1967. Sure, there is now a National News Council, an independent body that monitors and reports on media performance. And there are formal, written, professional codes of ethics—not only at the organizational level of the American Society of Newspaper Editors and the Society of Professional Journalists but also at an increasing number of individual daily newspapers. And at about twenty-five American newspapers there are ombudsmen who write in their own papers about their readers' criticisms.

Big goddamn deal.

The National News Council? Most newspapers don't bother to publish its findings and most people outside the profession (and a great many inside it) don't even know it exists. The *New York Times,* the best and most authoritative newspaper in the country, doesn't support the council financially and doesn't respond formally when the council has a complaint against it. Worse, the *New York Times* prints only brief stories (or no story at all) when the council issues its findings. Because of its low visibility the council has trouble raising the money necessary to do its work. As the *New York Times* itself observed last year, the council is "struggling to stay alive."

Twenty-five ombudsmen on American newspapers? That means there are only about 1,700 daily papers without ombudsmen—and the editors of most of those papers, if they've thought about the ombudsman issue at all, probably feel much as one prominent editor told me a couple of years ago, after firing his ombudsman and deciding there would be no replacement:

"An ombudsman is just window dressing. Any editor who

can't make value judgments on his own and make them correctly is in the wrong job.''

But suppose the editor, an excellent editor—intelligent, ethical, a good judge of news and people alike—just makes a mistake. Suppose further that he doesn't think he made a mistake.

Tough. You don't like it? Write a letter to the editor. Same guy, right? Too bad. Case closed. As Abe Raskin wrote in 1967, ''Of all the institutions in our inordinately complacent society, none is so addicted as the press to self-righteousness, self-satisfaction, and self-congratulation.''

If you want proof of that, all you have to do is read the newspaper trade publication, *Editor & Publisher,* every week. One week last year, for example, *Editor & Publisher* printed a half-page cartoon that perfectly illustrates this attitude of perpetual self-congratulation. The cartoon showed a skier—labeled ''Press''—skillfully and determinedly weaving his way downhill, between flags labeled ''Attacks on Confidential Sources'' and ''Hard Line White House News Policy'' and ''Press Abuse in Poland'' and ''Pressure on 1st Amendment Rights'' and ''Freedom of Information Cutbacks.'' At the bottom of the slope were two admirers, with one saying, ''There's a guy with guts!''

So what can be done to overcome this attitude, to effect the changes necessary to make the press see that it is in its own best interest to hold itself morally accountable for its actions?

I yield to no one in my respect for those reporters and editors who have had to struggle with subpoenas and demands for confidential notes and names—often at great personal and professional sacrifice. Theirs is a valiant and invaluable struggle, and all of us—as journalists and as citizens—have benefited from it.

As I've said, I don't want any legal pressure exerted to make the press more responsible. Neither do I think news councils, ombudsmen, or codes of ethics should be mandatory. But I do think it's time for newspapers to take action themselves, individually, as they always insist they like to act.

About eight years ago, William F. Thomas, the editor of my paper, the *Los Angeles Times,* decided to act. He was concerned, he told me, that the press was the one uncovered story of our time, and he asked me if I would like to write full time about the press the way I had written about a wide variety of other subjects over the years.

Bill said he did not want me to be an ombudsman. An ombudsman, he said, is "just one voice, speaking for himself or herself, on the editorial page or the op-ed page." He wanted a reporter, writing in the news columns of the paper, carrying the full weight of the paper.

Although much of what my job is today has gradually evolved, without either Bill or me talking much about it, its basic structure has remained relatively stable. In my job I am a reporter first and a "critic" second, and I am not a critic in the sense that someone is a "book critic" or a "film critic" or a "restaurant critic." I do the kind of reporting I have always done: For each story, I interview 80 or 100 or 150 people; I read every relevant article or publication I can find; I spend whatever time the story requires; I travel wherever the story takes me; then I synthesize and analyze what I've found and I try to write a comprehensive story that includes my own judgments. I try to point out our flaws and strengths, to give the reader some sense of just how and why a newspaper does what it does.

Generally, I tend to emphasize our flaws—"our" meaning those of the *Los Angeles Times* in particular and of newspapers in general. Why emphasize the negative? Overall, because the newspaper industry spends a good deal of time and effort—and money—championing itself, whether by lobbying Congress, writing editorials on First Amendment issues, or promoting itself in newspaper and magazine advertisements, on billboards, television commercials, and (in Los Angeles) in movie theater commercials. Since many editors and publishers risk whiplash from patting themselves on the back so vigorously and so frequently, I think I should write about the other side of our business—the mistakes we make and the inadequacies we display. As far as my own newspaper is concerned, well, it is an excellent paper—one of the two or three best in the country, most journalists would agree. On some days, it is the most interesting—though rarely the most comprehensive or the most authoritative—of all the newspapers I read. But it does make mistakes—many of them—and it has seemed to me from the beginning that my credibility would depend on how I addressed those mistakes. So—to the chagrin of many editors at the paper—I try to avoid doing stories on subject areas that I know in advance the *Los Angeles Times* excels in covering. I would rather write about those areas in which we do poorly.

Actually, I was a bit reluctant to take the job when Bill first proposed it. I had always avoided specialization and feared I would easily grow bored. I was intrigued, though, and asked if I could think about it overnight. When I came back the next day I said I had a number of concerns—fourteen to be precise. Among them were:

- Would I have the right to reject story suggestions from editors?
- Could I quit after a year, without prejudice, if I so desired?
- Would I select my own stories?
- To whom would I report and submit my stories?

Foremost among my concerns, however, was the one I discreetly listed as number nine:

- Will I have complete freedom to select stories and, within those stories, make judgments, regardless of how sensitive the subject or whose personal or corporate ox is being gored?

Bill assured me I would have the freedom I sought and would report directly to him. But he also reminded me that I would continue to be a reporter, not a columnist or an ombudsman, and that he would be my editor. He would not censor me, he promised, but he would edit me. "No reporter goes unedited," he said.

I agreed. Without qualms. Bill had been the metropolitan editor of the paper when I was hired, and I had worked closely with him on many stories before he became the top editor. Even as editor he had asked me to do an occasional story. I had found him the best editor I'd ever worked for, both in terms of large conceptual questions and in wielding a pencil as a word-by-word, line-by-line text editor. Most important of all, he was a reasonable man and a man of his word. He told me he would not have to agree with my judgments and conclusions for them to be published; he would just have to agree that I had made a reasonable case and had supported it adequately.

I didn't foresee any problems. And I, we, haven't had any. Every story I've written has been published largely as written (and, in substantive terms, almost exactly as written). We've never had an argument, and I've never had to make a compromise that involved my principles or my independence. I have agreed with most of his editing—although not always at the time he did it— and even when I've disagreed, I have understood and conceded the legitimacy of his viewpoint.

With rare exceptions, Bill's editing and his criticisms have involved structure rather than substance. I mention in the introduction to the chapter on restaurant critics that he told me to cut those stories considerably, and that directive has been by far the most common—though the cuts have never been as major as in that story. He'll tell me to tighten up a story here and there. Or he'll say I should try to combine two stories into one. Or he'll say he doesn't think I really need two "sidebars" (those short newspaper stories that sometimes accompany and expand upon one element of a larger story on the same topic).

Many of Bill's questions and criticisms are characteristic of the traditional editing process: "This isn't clear." "Is this correct?" "Isn't this more detail than the reader wants?" "This is awkwardly phrased."

On the first story I did in this job, Bill thought I was too "strident" in my judgments, in large part because I had not found the right "voice" for my new position. I understood immediately what he meant, looked at the pencil marks he'd made in the margins of my story, and fixed the story to our mutual satisfaction in a matter of minutes.

On a couple of other occasions, Bill said he didn't think I had adequately represented his side of a particular argument. I agreed to quote him to that effect so long as I didn't have to water down the argument on the opposing side. No problem. That doesn't mean Bill has agreed with everything I've written. Far from it. On several occasions, in fact, he's told me, "Dave, I think your conclusions on this [story] are horseshit." But he's published them anyway because I had made a legitimate case for my "horseshit" conclusions. Once I even quoted another editor as saying Bill's own judgment in a certain matter was "nonsense . . . stupid." That observation ran, unedited.

I can remember only three times in my nine years on this job when Bill and I have actually disagreed vigorously on one of my stories. The first involved a story I wrote about another paper, the *Los Angeles Herald Examiner*. In that story, I said that the most avid sports fans in town preferred the *Herald*'s sports sections to our paper's. Bill said I was dead wrong. All his friends, he said, liked our sports section better. But his friends, I pointed out, played golf "and golf isn't even a sport." He laughed—and capitulated.

A couple of years later, I suggested a story on the phenomenon of chain newspaper ownership. I wanted to personalize the story, to build the story around a profile of Al Neuharth, the flamboyant and controversial head of Gannett, the biggest newspaper chain in the country. Bill said he didn't particularly want to read or to publish a profile of Neuharth. But, as usual, he told me to go ahead if I was determined to do so. I was. And I did. And when I turned my story in to Bill, he read it and said, "Well, I told you I didn't want to read a profile of Neuharth."

I had written a two-part series: the first part was primarily a profile of Neuharth; the second carried through that theme but included a great deal of information on Gannett and on other major chains. I told Bill I thought that approach made the story more readable than would a more issue-oriented approach. He agreed. But he said he thought I was underestimating what he called "the intelligent interest of our readers in the serious aspects of our business."

Bill said he thought I had a great deal of new, interesting information on newspaper chains—their strengths, their weaknesses, their strategies, and their dangers—near the bottom of the second half of my story. That material, not Neuharth's colorful personality, should be the focus of my story, he said.

I didn't know then—and don't know now—if he was right in terms of attracting readers to the story. But I couldn't very well argue with him. If you write a serious story and your editor tells you to make it sexier so people will read it, you can stand on principle and refuse to trivialize your serious journalism. But if your editor tells you to emphasize serious journalism and de-emphasize personality, what principle are you going to stand on?

I restructured the story as Bill wanted.

Bill knew I hated to lose all my good Neuharth material so he grudgingly (but graciously) suggested I write a short, separate sidebar on Neuharth to accompany the main stories.

"Then," he said, "if you're still not happy, why don't you try to write a Neuharth profile for *Esquire* or someone."

Everything came out fine. I included some of the Neuharth material in my main story for the paper, put most of the rest in a sidebar, and did indeed write a Neuharth profile for *Esquire.*

The most serious disagreement Bill and I have had involved stories I wrote on how newspapers handle obituaries. As I originally wrote it, the story contained two major parts and one sidebar. The first major part discussed general newspaper treatment of obituaries and contained a great deal of information on the *New York Times* (in particular), the *Washington Post,* and, to a lesser extent, several other papers. The second part dealt almost exclusively with the *Los Angeles Times,* and it was very critical of the paper.

Not surprisingly, Bill told me, "I don't much like part two."

He had two objections: (1) I had written too much about the *L.A. Times;* that was not my charge. (2) I was wrong in some of my judgments.

Bill said he wanted me to considerably shorten what I had written on the *L.A. Times*—to make that segment of the story about the same length as what I had written about the *New York Times* and *Washington Post*—and to incorporate that abbreviated part two in my original part one. He also thought I should reconsider some of my judgments in light of his own explanation of why the *L.A. Times* handled obituaries as it did. I said I realized I didn't usually write so much about our paper, but I reminded him that I had done so previously when circumstances warranted. I explained why I thought circumstances again warranted a long look at the *L.A. Times.* He still disagreed with my reasoning and my judgments, but he conceded that I had a defensible position. The story would run. He did, however, want me to make clearer in the story why I found our treatment of obituaries "unique" and, hence, worthy of a story. He was right; I should have done that in the first place. He also wanted me to include a statement from him on the *L.A. Times*'s philosophy on obituaries. Fair enough. I made the changes and my story was published.

I like to think the freedom that made possible the publication of the obituaries article—and my other stories—has enhanced both my credibility and that of the *Times.* I don't know how to measure it, but I do know that public reaction to what the *Los Angeles Times* has been publishing on the media has generally been quite good. People seem to feel that a newspaper willing to publish a discussion of its flaws on its own front page can be trusted to report honestly on other issues as well. Response within my profession has been mixed, however. Many reporters, editors, and even publishers say they admire my work. But some clearly don't like it. Or me. And some refuse to cooperate with me. It took me two months last year, for example, to persuade Rupert Murdoch, publisher of the *New York Post* (among many other publications), to grant me an interview. Murdoch rejected my letters, ignored my telephone calls, and only agreed to an interview when I flew across the country and confronted him at a cocktail party. But he is not alone: The man who was then editor of the *New York Times Book Review* refused to even take my phone call when I wanted to interview him for a story on best-seller lists several years ago. The editors of *Time* and *Newsweek* refused to let me sit in on the weekly meetings at which they discuss future cover subjects. Then there's Walter Cronkite. *TV Guide* asked me to write a profile of him. At first he refused to give me the time I thought necessary to do the job right. Grudgingly, he relented. And when my story was published—a story that was so unremittingly favorable to him I was almost embarrassed—he complained that I had quoted him using words like "goddamn" and "son of a bitch." He seemed to suggest that he hadn't used such language. I pointed out that he had indeed—and I added, "And Walter, I didn't even quote you on all the 'cocksuckers' and 'motherfuckers' you used."

End of complaint.

But Walter sure knew his audience. I received about a thousand letters on the story—a remarkable response for such a story—and the vast majority pilloried Cronkite for his language and said they felt betrayed.

Reporters and editors at my own newspaper have also, on occasion, been less than pleased with my work. When I took my job, Bill promised that I would have the freedom to do the job as he and I agreed it should be done. He has kept the promise. And many other editors and reporters at the paper have been very supportive. But some editors, and some reporters, have taken exception to much of what I've written. One editor complained to the publisher about one of my stories and didn't talk to me for a year, even when we passed in the hallway. Another editor wadded up one of my stories and threw it in his trash basket and asked me if I thought the paper ever did anything right. Another editor, a good personal friend, wrote me a letter to say he was "terminating our personal relationship" after one of my stories made him and his department look bad. A few reporters have been equally hostile.

These personal experiences have demonstrated anew to me the acute sensitivity—and rampaging hypocrisy—of many in the press. It's okay for us to criticize other people, they clearly think, but no one should be allowed to criticize us.

Despite these minor, periodic problems, though, I am enjoying my job enormously. That's why I've kept it eight years longer than I originally agreed to. And I have no plans to give it up soon.

Is the *Los Angeles Times* approach the best way to address the problem of press arrogance and insularity? I don't know. But it is one way. I'd be delighted if there were other newspapers with reporters doing the same thing, or different things, just so long as they were doing something. But they're not. The twenty-five ombudsmen and the occasional serious pieces in the daily newspapers and alternative weeklies are not enough.

Public opinion polls consistently show that people trust us less and less, and our own personal experience should tell us that they like us less and less. There are many complex reasons for this, but I think our refusal to examine our shortcomings is an important one.

Is there hope for a more open press—in every sense of the term? I am not optimistic. But there was also a time, not so very long ago, when I despaired of seeing fair, reasonable corrections policies in most newspapers. Now many newspapers have begun to publish regularly—indeed daily, in a prominent or consistent position in the paper—various corrections and clarifications of their errors and oversights. Just last year, the *New York Times* began publishing periodic "Editors' Notes," an attempt to rectify or amplify what the paper's editors consider to be "significant lapses of fairness, balance or perspective" in the paper.

This is a small but significant step toward the "moral accountability" of the press. There are other small, tentative steps in the same direction. CBS News now has an ombudsman, and ABC periodically broadcasts its "Viewpoint" program that contains criticisms of its own news programs.

But more, bigger, steps are needed.

I realize there are dangers in self-criticism. CBS News did an internal study of one of its controversial programs not too long ago, and the study—much of it critical of CBS—was ultimately subpoenaed in a lawsuit and ordered divulged by the court. That is not likely to encourage CBS or any other news organization to indulge in further self-criticism. But news organizations *must* take that risk anyway.

Many of us in the press are fond of quoting Thomas Jefferson's famous line, "Were it left to me to decide whether we should have a government without newspapers, or newspapers without government, I should not hesitate to prefer the latter." Some of us forget, however, that Jefferson also said, "The man who never looks into a newspaper is better informed than he who reads them, inasmuch as he who knows nothing is nearer to truth than he whose mind is filled with falsehoods and errors."

We in the newspaper profession also tend to overlook another pretty fair writer and social observer, Dr. Samuel Johnson, who wrote in his own newspaper more than two centuries ago:

"A newswriter is a man without virtue, who writes lies at home for his own profit. To these compositions is required neither genius nor knowledge, neither industry nor sprightliness; but contempt of shame and indifference to truth are absolutely necessary."

The vast majority of the newspaper reporters, editors, and publishers I know are not lacking in either virtue or industry;

they are not indifferent to truth but rather dedicated to the pursuit of it. Most have knowledge. A few may even be geniuses.

But not one of them is perfect, and not one of their newspapers is perfect, as they would be the first to admit. Privately. But it's time we all began to admit that publicly—to rebuild the bond of trust that once existed between newspaper and reader. The only way to do that is by replacing arrogance with accountability. We must stop acting as if what we do everyday is either an arcane secret, too complex for the reader to understand, or a state secret that's none of the reader's business. We should tell you how we function and why, and how we sometimes malfunction and misfunction. That is why I wrote the stories on which this collection is based. That's why I wrote this book.

1

THE FRONT PAGE

When I first suggested to William F. Thomas, the editor of the *Los Angeles Times,* that I take a look at the front pages of major daily newspapers around the country to see how similar (or different) they were on any given day, he said he thought I'd be wasting my time.

'Not much story there, I'm afraid,'' he told me. ''I can probably guess what you'll find. The major papers will usually have just about the same three or four big foreign stories and . . . two or three big national stories everyday. We'll probably each have one or two different, strictly local stories and maybe one different story that's . . . a feature or something [other than a story tied to that day's news].''

I told Bill he might well be right. But I wanted to take a look anyway. He agreed. That was—and is—how we've worked. Most of the stories I write are based on my own ideas. I go to Bill for approval, and he usually shares my interest and enthusiasm for the idea. But not always. Sometimes he points out the flaws in my suggestions, and I have to agree that he's right—there's no story there. On three or four occasions, Bill has made his objections or criticisms and I have said I still thought I had a good idea. In those cases—and my idea for a story on front pages was such a case—Bill's attitude is, ''Okay, you're the reporter. Go report the story if you think it's there. But remember: I'm the editor. If the story doesn't work, I won't run it.''

So far, every time I've gone ahead on that basis, the story has worked out, and Bill has liked it and published it—on page one. That's exactly what happened with my story on front pages. In fact, my findings in that story surprised even me so much that instead of just working as I usually do—turning my story in when it's complete, without making any interim progress reports—I told Bill the preliminary results of my research before I started writing. He was stunned. So were the other top editors I spoke to, at the *New York Times,* the *Washington Post,* and elsewhere. I found that, day in and day out, the front pages of the nation's major daily newspapers had far less in common than even their own editors had thought. Was that an anomaly? I don't think so. My study covered five months' worth of front pages—not exactly a small sample. And I've made spot checks since then. The results have been roughly the same as what I originally found—and as I report below, from that original story.

*   *   *

IT WAS a fairly normal day in most major cities in the world. No new wars. No governments toppled. No large, death-dealing disasters.

But not an altogether dull day either.

* The Carter administration said South Africa would be given a blunt warning to ease its racial policies or face American political and economic sanctions.
* The House of Representatives approved a bill providing hundreds of millions of dollars in federal aid to areas of high unemployment.

• Eleven major oil-producing nations, meeting in Cyprus, agreed
to cancel a scheduled 5 percent price increase.

Which of these events did American newspaper editors regard as the most significant of the day, May 14, 1977?

That depends on which newspaper you read the next morning.

The *Los Angeles Times* made the South Africa story its lead.
The *New York Times* led with the federal aid bill. The *Washington Post* chose the price of oil.

This disparity in news judgment is not an isolated example.
Far from it. A careful examination of the front pages of these
three newspapers every day for the first five months of 1977 revealed differences in judgment, interest, style, scope, and tone
of such immense proportions that when the highest ranking editors at the three papers were confronted with them, they pronounced themselves "stunned" and "astonished."

Only twenty-eight times in the 155-day study period did the
three papers agree on the most important story of the day—and
those were, invariably and unquestionably, the truly big stories
of early 1977 at home and abroad: arms talks with Russia; the
devastating winter in the East; the Canary Islands jet crash that
killed nearly 600 people; the Hanafi Muslims' takeover of three
buildings in Washington, D.C.; elections in Israel and India;
conflict in Uganda and Zaire; the inauguration, appointments, and
programs of President Carter. . . .

But on most days there were no stories of such overweening
significance, and on those days disagreement was pandemic. On
fifty-six days—one third of the time—each of the three papers
had a different lead story; that's twice as many days of complete
disagreement as there were of complete agreement.

More significantly, 20 percent of the time—thirty-three days—
there was not one single story that appeared on the front page
of all three papers, and on only thirty-two days did the three
front pages have more than two stories in common. Thus, 60

percent of the time the front pages of these three papers had only one or two of their eight or ten stories in common.

Most people tend to speak of the American press in monolithic terms—"The Press"—as if it were a single, mammoth, national newspaper with more than 1,700 slightly varying regional editions. But this is a glaring misconception—a misconception sometimes shared by the newspaper editors themselves.

Benjamin C. Bradlee, executive editor of the *Washington Post,* said, for example, that he was certain his paper and the *New York Times* had "four, five, six, seven front-page stories in common most everyday."

"In twelve years," he said, "I can't recall a single day on which we didn't have at least one story the same."

But in the first five months of 1977 alone, there were ten such days.

Sometimes differences among the *New York Times, Washington Post,* and *Los Angeles Times* will come within a fairly narrow range: On May 4 all three agreed that legislation proposed by the Carter administration was the major story of the day. But the *New York Times* selected one piece of legislation— a proposed ethics law—for its lead story; the *Post* selected another—military aid legislation; and the *Los Angeles Times* selected a third—energy legislation.

Moreover, the diversity of front-page news coverage evident in this study is by no means limited to these three newspapers. A survey of newspapers in more than a dozen other cities on fifty selected days shows an even greater divergence in page one selection.

More often than not, a reader looking at these front pages might think they were published on different days—if not in different weeks or months. In fact, only their common language negated the impression that they could sometimes have been published in different countries.

What makes this disparity especially remarkable is that most papers begin with a common base. Approximately 75 percent of the news most Americans read (and hear) is provided by the Associated Press and the United Press International.

In addition, both AP and UPI provide their client newspapers with daily "budgets" identifying the major stories of the day. Most newspapers also have easy access to information on exactly which stories the *New York Times* will publish on page one the next day. (The more than 300 clients of the *Los Angeles Times–Washington Post* News Service are given similar information about the front pages of those two papers.)

But the vast majority of those stories are national and international in scope, and most daily newspapers—even those in large, metropolitan, presumably cosmopolitan cities—are, in reality, local newspapers. Local stories dominate their front pages, generally leaving room for only one or two, if any, national or foreign stories. Editors at these papers will give front-page play to national stories of transcendent significance (President Carter's speech on the energy crisis) or to big disaster stories (the Canary Islands jet crash), but apart from such obvious stories they will generally fill their front pages with local news and features.

In 1977 these page-one stories included an account of how a zoo could use "the aphrodisiac qualities of Mississippi oysters" to mate two reluctant Peking pandas *(Baltimore Sun);* the tale of a sewer inspector who dreams of pink rats *(Cleveland Plain-Dealer),* and the theft of 9,000 milk crates over a two-year period from a local dairy *(Miami Herald).*

Crime is also big on most metropolitan daily front pages—much as it was thirty or forty years ago. In 1977 headlines told such stories as "Lovers Lane Stalker Kills 3, Wounds 3—Baffles Police" and "Ex-Con Found Slain Execution-Style in Auto Truck Is Linked to Syndicate."

Newspapers other than the *New York Times, Los Angeles Times,* and *Washington Post* seem especially indifferent to all but the most cosmic foreign news events. The *Baltimore Sun* and, to a lesser extent, the *Philadelphia Inquirer* are not as parochial as most, but even they did not match the big three in foreign coverage.

Of the major foreign stories published during the first five months of 1977, only the defeat of Indian Prime Minister Indira Gandhi was the lead story in virtually every American daily newspaper. Two months later, when Israel's ruling Labor party suffered a shocking and historic defeat at the polls in an election that would have a profound and far-reaching impact on the Mideast—and the world—the story didn't even make page one of the *Atlanta Constitution, Dallas Morning News,* or the *Portland Oregonian,* among others.

Similar examples abound, and even when some of these papers do publish a national or, less often, a foreign story on page one, it may not necessarily be a story the *New York Times, Los Angeles Times,* or *Washington Post* also displayed prominently. And there is no particular pattern when there is a similarity with one of those—no greater likelihood of agreement with any one than with any other (or with each other).

A classic example of the different perspective offered big-city newspaper readers in various cities came on March 24—a day of rare agreement among the *New York Times, Los Angeles Times,* and *Washington Post.* All three agreed that the major story was President Carter's acceptance of an invitation from Hanoi to resume negotiations in Paris on normalization of relations with Vietnam. The three papers also agreed on the day's other important stories: overwhelming congressional defeat of a labor picketing bill; drought relief; the kidnap and murder of the Roman Catholic primate in the Congo; and U.S. Supreme Court reaffirmation of its controversial Miranda ruling limiting police interrogation of suspects.

But most other metropolitan dailies used only two of these five stories on page one—and few agreed on which two. The *Boston Globe* used Vietnam and the Congo killing; the *Houston*

Post used the Supreme Court and picketing; the *Cleveland Plain-Dealer* used picketing and Vietnam.

The *Chicago Tribune* didn't put any of the five stories on page one. Instead, the *Tribune* had stories on a local fire (one person dead, one missing), several murders in Detroit, a state supreme court decision on blockbusting, a pool tournament in a retirement hotel, and a man who designed feather hats for Elizabeth Taylor, Marlene Dietrich, and Tallulah Bankhead.

"We have a strong interest in local news," says Maxwell McCrohon, then the *Tribune*'s managing editor, "and we don't have a totally page-one orientation. We don't feel a story has to be on page one to be important."

Says another editor, "If you don't have your own national and foreign staff, it's cheaper to fill the front page with national and foreign stories from the wire. Local stories require local reporters, and that costs money. But that's what we're here for. We figure most of our readers can get the national and foreign news they want from TV."

Not necessarily.

Television news does not generally provide detailed, thorough coverage of most issues, and what it does provide is largely influenced—often virtually dictated—by what the major newspapers play on page one. Thus, whether people get their news from television or from newspapers (or both), the residents of one city may have a considerably different perception of a given day's major events than the residents of almost any other city.

Bill Kovach, now Washington editor of the *New York Times,* thinks these differences are at least partially responsible for the polarization of contemporary society.

"When there's a big social movement—civil rights, anti-war, women's rights—New York and Los Angeles and Washington will write about it in detail, prominently, on page one, and their readers will see it and be able to discuss it," Kovach says. "But that won't happen in the other cities, and when the movement gets there—which it does, pretty quickly—with no real newspaper coverage beforehand, it's a big surprise to everyone; they have no context for understanding and intelligent discussion.''

If the movement represents a threat or challenge to the status quo, then fear, frustration, confusion, and anger may ensue.

"The *Boston Globe* did a good job covering the early antiwar movement,'' Kovach says. ''Just look at the difference in the way people there understood the issues and responded as compared with the people in, say, Kansas City, where there was no coverage until it was really too late.''

But for all the differences in front-page play among major newspapers around the country, the only truly valid comparisons of newspapers—and their front pages—must be limited to the *New York Times, Washington Post,* and *Los Angeles Times.* These are the papers with the largest staffs at home, the most reporters abroad, and the greatest commitment to comprehensive coverage of the day's events throughout the world.

Yet, despite their common purpose, these three papers provide their readers with widely varying views of the world.

During the first five months of 1977, almost 25 percent of the stories that led one of the three papers did not appear anywhere in either (or both) of the other papers. There were also many stories that one paper gave prominent page-one play and another put far inside the paper. There were, literally, several hundred stories that appeared on the front page of one (or two) of these papers and did not appear anywhere in either (or both) of the others.

On April 19, for example, the *New York Times* ran a lengthy story at the top of page one on Soviet Premier Leonid Brezhnev's warning that other countries should not ''meddle'' in Zaire. The *Los Angeles Times* published that story on page six—as the last paragraph in another story on Zaire. The *Post* ran the story on page seventeen.

Why did the three papers differ so frequently and so widely in 1977? And why do they continue to differ so frequently and so widely in 1984?

On some days—notably Sundays and Mondays—newspapers differ markedly in page-one play because little of substance generally happens over the weekend, and editors are free to use interpretive stories, analyses, light features, and other stories not directly related to the day's events. On other days, time differences between the East and West coasts may dictate news play—or front pages may differ simply because editors choose to present varying situation reports on developing events: a White House power struggle or a foreign election or congressional budget hearings.

Some page-one stories are of purely (or primarily) local or regional interest—the fiscal crisis and Concorde landing controversy in New York, school busing and automobile-oriented stories in Los Angeles, any number of political stories in Washington.

Other page-one stories reflect different, even conflicting, views of the same information. Still others are the product of individual initiative by one reporter or one newspaper. Or a newspaper may decide not to play a given story on page one because the competition already had it. Or because a reporter did so poor a job on it that his editors do not deem it worthy of page one. Or because a reporter, or the paper, did not have access to the story.

The patterns vary, however, especially in the coverage of foreign news, and the explanation for this may lie in the quality of the respective reporters, in the interests of their editors, in the personal or professional relationships between the journalists and the diplomats—or in simple logistics. For example, in 1977, the *Washington Post* gave the most page-one play to the closure of the American embassy in Ethiopia, in part because the *Post* reporter was the only one there the day the story broke. The *New York Times* gave more page-one play to India, in part because the paper's executive editor once lived there and retains a strong interest in the area. The *Los Angeles Times* gave more page-one play to African stories, in part because the paper's correspondent in Nairobi, Kenya, from 1967 to 1974 was a dedicated Africanist whose insightful stories awakened editors to the news potential of the continent.

Even when there are areas of agreement among the major papers, those areas are not always what one would expect.

One might think, for example, that the front pages of the *New York Times* and *Washington Post* would have more in common than either would have with the *Los Angeles Times*'s front page. They are, after all, only 200 miles apart, in the same social-political-economic corridor, and both are almost 3,000 miles from Los Angeles. The *Post* and the *Los Angeles Times* might also be expected to have much in common; they have access to each other's material via the *Los Angeles Times–Washington Post* News Service. But in 1977, the two front pages with the most in common—and that wasn't very much—were those of the *New York Times* and *Los Angeles Times*.

"That's not surprising," says one *Los Angeles Times* editor. "New York and L.A. are similar cities—both products of substantial migration. Washington is less heterogeneous; almost everyone there is a politician or a would-be politician."

An East Coast writer sees another difference:

"The *Post* goes more for style than substance on page one—hot stuff, trends, things people will talk about at a Georgetown cocktail party that night. They (usually) won't stay with a developing story very long, even if it's important. They're impatient, frivolous, erratic, not as solid in their judgments as either of the *Times*es."

Or, as iconoclastic journalist I. F. Stone once remarked, only half in jest: "The *Post* is the most exciting paper in town, you can never tell where you'll find a front-page story."

Early in 1977, for example, Larry Flynt, the publisher of *Hustler* magazine, was convicted in Cincinnati of engaging in organized crime and pandering obscenity; his conviction and sentence (a $10,000 fine and a seven–to–twenty-five–year prison sentence) and the use of an organized crime statute for such a case subsequently triggered a storm of protest over First Amendment rights and freedom of the press. The *New York Times* and *Los Angeles Times* put Flynt's conviction on page one; the *Post* ran just one paragraph in a news roundup on page seven of the third section.

There are many similar examples: stories on cancer-causing links between cigarette smoking and birth-control pills, the announcement that an American delegation would visit Vietnam for an accounting of soldiers missing in action, a speech by President Carter on NATO. . . . All appeared on page one of the two *Times*es, but not the *Post*.

The *Post* most differed from the two *Times*es, however, in foreign coverage. Sometimes the *Post* published on page one stories neither *Times* put there—as in the case of negotiations in Cyprus or press curbs in South Africa. More often the *Post* did not put on page one a foreign story the other papers believed should be there.

Between mid-March and mid-May the *Post* did not publish on page one any of four major stories that were published on page one of the two *Times*es on civil unrest in Pakistan. ("A major news story," says one *New York Times* editor. "Treating it like that was just plain stupid.")

Then, in late May, after publishing on page one the initial story about the Moluccan separatists taking school children hostage in the Netherlands, the *Post* did not publish on page one any of the five subsequent stories the two *Times*es published there on the plight of the hostages and the negotiations to free them. ("It was a new chapter in political terrorism—the use of kids," says one *L.A. Times* editor. "I can't understand the *Post*'s thinking.")

But Benjamin C. Bradlee, executive editor of the *Post*, insists, "I overwhelmingly approve of my judgment on those stories." The two *Times*es overreacted, Bradlee says, "In Pakistan, the unrest was finally quelled; in the Netherlands, nothing happened a lot of days; there was no progress.

"I saw no reason to front [page] the story just because TV spent a minute and a half looking at the train every night and all you could see was a goddamn bird whiz by," Bradlee says.

The *Post* ignored (or played off page one) several other foreign stories—often because its editors did not think them important, sometimes (as in the case of stories on 200 tons of missing uranium believed shipped surreptitiously to Israel) because Bradlee was "damned suspicious of the whole story."

By actual count the *Post* used significantly fewer foreign stories on page one than either of the two *Times*es.

"The *Post*," says one editor, "is really just a small-town paper, a company-town paper. But the town is Washington and the company is the United States government, so—especially after all they did on Watergate—the *Post* is now perceived as a national and international newspaper. But it's not. Bradlee just isn't that interested in foreign news."

Bradlee denies that foreign news gets short shrift in the *Post*. "I spent six years of my life living abroad," he says. "I'm fascinated by foreign news. But I'm in a city where government is big news and sometimes something has to give way."

Government—politics—is not just a national story but a local story for the *Post*. In fact, when political coverage is combined with the 25 percent of the front page generally devoted to suburban and District of Columbia news, the picture that emerges is that of a newspaper clearly more local than global in orientation.

But that is not necessarily a demeaning judgment: The *Post* probably makes a greater effort to relate directly to its readers on a daily basis, via the front page, than do either of the *Times*es. During the first five months of 1977, the *Post* published more page-one explanatory, interpretive, behind-the-scenes stories than either of the *Times*es. The *Post* also published more consumer stories on page one. In that sense the *Post* may have more in common with many other papers than with either of the *Times*es.

On April 8, for example, when the government banned the production and sale of a popular line of children's sleepwear treated with a flame-retardant feared to cause kidney cancer, the *Post* put the story on page one. So did the *Boston Globe, Philadelphia Inquirer,* and *San Francisco Chronicle,* among others. But the *New York Times* put the story on page fourteen, the *Los Angeles Times* on page twenty-three.

The *Post* also gave more front-page attention than the two *Times*es to the defeat of the Equal Rights Amendment in Florida, Indiana, and North Carolina. Some editors say this is because the *Post*'s publisher at the time was a woman. But one or more of the ERA elections also made page one of newspapers in Philadelphia, San Francisco, Portland, Dallas, and New Orleans—none of which has a woman publisher.

"The answer is simple," says one *Post* editor. "It's a major story, a major issue—the changing roles and relationships of the sexes. We were on top of it. New York and L.A. weren't. They screwed up. Period."

Bradlee agrees wholeheartedly, and there is no doubt that his interests, personality, and predilections influence page one of the *Post* as much as any other single factor.

Most editors tend to imbue their papers with a particular ethos, a personality, and even if that personality appears, at times, schizophrenic, reporters and other editors tend to absorb that personality, by osmosis as well as by direction. "I like a good people story," Bradlee says, "a good profile, a good adventure story, a good achievement story. They tell the reader more than some Ph.D. thesis." Thus, the *Post* runs more personality stories on page one than do either of the *Times*es. The *Post* also runs many light, offbeat stories—a product of what one editor calls "a built-in predisposition toward whimsy around here, a desire to balance Significance [with a capital *S*] with simple, readable pieces.''

There are many days, Bradlee says, ''when we look at our page-one dummy [layout] at the six o'clock news conference and say, 'Jesus, isn't that awfully serious?' We'd like to find at least one story that'll make people say, 'Well, I'll be. . . .' '' But because Bradlee also likes aggressive, enterprising reportage— especially that which results in stories exclusive to the *Post,* exposing wrongdoing and corruption—the *Post* also published more of these stories on page one in 1977 than did either of the *Times*es.

That is one area, in fact, in which the *Post* and the *New York Times* have a great deal in common. ''We've had a competitive thing going with each other since Watergate,'' says one *Post* editor. ''It's a joint legacy—a jousting of investigative gumshoe versus investigative gumshoe. Ben likes to go for the jugular.''

That competition sometimes distorts the journalistic process. A newspaper with an exclusive exposé has a tendency to continue publishing stories on the same subject on page one, even when subsequent developments do not warrant such displays. The editors develop an emotional investment—a psychic investment—in these stories. That's one reason the *Post* played the South Korean lobbying controversy on page one so frequently. ''Some of those stories wound up on page one by virtue of their exclusivity, not their intrinsic news value,'' says one *Post* editor. ''It's kind of an ongoing declaration of proprietary interest.''

But most newspapers fasten onto stories like that from time to time. Often, when a newspaper stakes out a particular story early, the opposition will, consciously or subconsciously, underplay it or ignore it altogether. But competitive pressures and lapses—or legitimate differences—in news judgment only partially explain the resultant differences in front pages.

The *New York Times* has, for example, a wider variety of subjects represented on its front page than does any other daily newspaper in the United States. Far more often than any other paper, the *Times* will publish front-page stories on science, the arts, sports, the economy, and religion. Some of these stories result from the personal, idiosyncratic preferences of individual editors. "We call it the 'whooping-crane' syndrome," says one editor. "There's always one editor whose juices start flowing at the mere mention of whooping cranes—or whatever—and he tries his damnedest to get those stories on page one."

In fact, a former assistant managing editor at the *New York Times* felt just that way about virtually every animal story that came along—and A. M. Rosenthal, executive editor of the *Times*, likes religion stories ("even though I'm not a religious person myself") because he thinks "few stories tell as much about a people as religion."

But there is more than personal whim involved in the decision to play such stories on the front page.

"The *New York Times* is a paper of constituencies," says one editor, "and we write for each of those constituencies individually. We don't homogenize our stories for the mass reader the way most papers do."

One of the *Times*'s constituencies is the intelligentsia; the paper is, in many respects, elitist. "New York," says *Times* managing editor Seymour Topping, "is the financial center of the United States, the cultural center of the United States, the communications center of the United States." Major stories involving any of those constituencies are published on page one of the *New York Times*. Thus, when NBC agreed to pay $80 million for exclusive rights to telecast the 1980 Olympic Games from Moscow, the *New York Times* ran the story on page one. The *Los Angeles Times* put the story in its sports section. The *Washington Post* published it in Style (an entertainment and people section).

That was not an atypical difference in news judgment.

Eighteen times during the first five months of 1977 the *New York Times* published page-one economic/financial stories that the *Post* and the *Los Angeles Times* published on their financial pages. These stories involved such matters as airline fares, steel and sugar prices, the wholesale price index, and international trade talks. "They're Wall Street stories, financial stories run for the New York financial community," says one *Los Angeles Times* editor.

Not altogether, reply *New York Times* editors.

"The economy may be the most important story in the world today," says one. "It's more subtle, but it's today's Vietnam or Watergate. Major corporate decisions are every bit as important and far-reaching as major government decisions. They belong on page one. That's one reason we've spent more money and hired more new people for our financial section than for any other part of the paper lately." (Today, seven years later, the economy remains a major story, and the judgment of the *New York Times* editors has been vindicated.)

The *New York Times* also published fourteen sports stories on page one during the first five months of 1977. The *Los Angeles Times* and *Washington Post,* almost without exception, put sports stories in the sports section (occasionally carrying a brief page-one note referring readers to the sports section). One explanation for this is that the *Post* and *Los Angeles Times* have separate, easy-to-find sports sections everyday. Until 1978, the *New York Times* sports section was, except for Sunday, part of either the main news, or financial sections. (Since 1978, the paper has also had a separate sports section on Monday.)

But *New York Times* editors have another reason for playing some sports stories on page one: It helps to offset the gray, serious, official tone of the rest of the page without trivializing the page. "All our page-one stories are 'The government did this,' 'Saudi Arabia did that,' 'This committee met here,' " says one editor. "Sports gives us relief and variety."

The *Post* uses personality stories to achieve this effect; the *Los Angeles Times* uses light pieces on such subjects as the world poker championship or a human cannonball.

New York Times editors, one senses, would feel uncomfortable with such stories on their front page. But a story on a strike at a racetrack or a legal battle over where the Jets will play football or a story disclosing that a nationally televised tennis match billed as "winner-take-all" actually provided substantial cash guarantees to both participants, well, those can be justified as news stories (a "labor story," a "court story," an "exposé"), not merely sports stories.

Moreover, sports stories are often local stories, and the *New York Times*—having lost 112,000 readers from 1970 to 1975—has been consciously trying to provide more local coverage in recent years, both on page one and throughout the paper.

Editors admit they didn't pay enough attention to local news for years. The metropolitan staff, traditionally, had the weakest reporters, the weakest editors, and the least space on the front page. No longer.

In fact, during the first five months of 1977 the *New York Times*, which has more national and foreign correspondents than the *Post* and *Los Angeles Times* combined, published 22 percent more local news on page one than either of those papers. Even more surprising, a number of those stories were pretty trivial— and many were crime stories. One simply does not expect to see, on page one of the *New York Times*, stories on robberies, murders, and narcotics arrests—or such headlines as "Four Linked to Cult Slain in Brooklyn."

New York Times editors defend such stories as "not just crime stories or local stories but economic stories; big corporations are moving out of New York because of crime."

True. But editors elsewhere say the *Times*'s use of crime stories, sports stories, and many other local stories on page one is—in the words of one—"an attempt to help them get readers among the garbage-collectors who live in Queens. They're in a dogfight for readers now, and they know it."

Evidence of that trend is abundant.

When a Nazi admirer killed five people (and himself) in suburban New York in 1977 the *Times* devoted almost 40 percent of its front page (and 75 percent of an inside page) to the story. When a mountain climber scaled the 110-story World Trade Center the *Times* again devoted almost 40 percent of its front page to the story.

Those are not the sort of cataclysmic international political struggles or subtle intellectual controversies for which the *New York Times* front page is generally known.

But most editors at the *Times*—and elsewhere—agree that the paper must continue to move in that direction. The *Times,* they all agree, still devotes too much of its front page to official statements, subtle nuances of political policy, incremental legislative progress—what one *Times* editor calls "the declamation and document mentality."

During one two-month period in 1977 the *New York Times* published on page one ten interviews with public figures, ten government/foundation studies of social/economic problems, and many other stories that editors admit were there more as matters of record than for their actual news value.

Being the newspaper of record has always been one of the *Times*'s unique strengths, of course. The complete texts, transcripts, and formal statements it publishes—the sense of tradition and historicity it embodies—provide a perspective, a continuity, a consistency not available in any other American newspaper. "The front page of the *New York Times* speaks a different language than any other paper," one editor says.

Sometimes that language is artificial.

"When I worked as a foreign correspondent for the *Times,*" says author and Pulitzer Prize–winning reporter David Halberstam, "the worst stories I did ran on page one, the automatic stories, announcements: 'The foreign office today reacted with'— fill in the blank—'anger,' 'joy,' 'regret.' . . . The best stories I did, the stories the *Times* does best, ran on inside pages—significant sociological pieces, stories on the periphery."

Says one of the paper's high-ranking editors: "When I went on my first foreign assignment, the publisher told me, 'Reputations at the *New York Times* aren't made on the front page.' "

Still, the front page is the prime showplace for any newspaper. As Leon Sigal notes in *Reporters and Officials*, the primacy of the front page is "rooted in the reading habits of the public as well as enshrined in the folklore of the Fourth Estate."

New York Times editors acknowledge this, and they acknowledge, too, that they must continue to move a bit away from the traditional formality of their front page. "Instead of running a page-one story every time the president belches or the Council of Churches issues its forty-umpteenth report," says one editor, "we need more stories out there [on page one] that directly involve and affect human beings in their everyday lives."

Such stories—"readers" in journalistic parlance—were rarely seen on the front page of the *New York Times* in previous generations. For the past several years they have been appearing, with increasing frequency, in the lower-left-hand corner of the page. Now there are some days when "readers" appear there and in the lower-right-hand corner as well.

"It's a good idea," says one editor. "It keeps us from taking ourselves too seriously.

Most editors around the country agree that the *New York Times* does indeed take itself too seriously at times—and that the *Los Angeles Times* often does not take itself seriously enough. They criticize the *Los Angeles Times*, for example, for not having published as many investigative pieces—exposés—on page one as either the *New York Times* or the *Washington Post*.

But William F. Thomas, editor of the *Los Angeles Times*, says that is deliberate. "We're considerably concerned about the tendency to publish exposés for their own sake, just to compete with the other guy, in the aftermath of Watergate. It can be dangerous and irresponsible."

In being "extremely careful" about such tendencies, he admits, "we probably miss some good stories for page one and underplay others."

More journalists are critical of the *Los Angeles Times* for what it does publish on page one, though, than for what it does not publish on page one.

During the first five months of 1977, the paper published significantly more outright feature stories on page one than the *New York Times* and *Washington Post* combined. That, too, is deliberate, Thomas says: "We're in an era . . . dominated by complicated events that tend to produce dull reading fare day after day. It seems only sensible to consciously seek out something different and interesting to add to that mix."

Toward that end the *Los Angeles Times* began publishing, in 1968, a non-news story in column one of the front page everyday. Sometimes these stories do interpret or analyze the day's events; often they are just light features, interesting explorations of the byways of life.

"It gives . . . [the *L.A. Times*] an interesting dimension," says one Midwestern editor, ". . . the seriousness and thoroughness of the *New York Times* combined with some of the leavening of the *Post.*"

But to many critics, inside the *Los Angeles Times* and out, these stories—and others on page one—are too frequently trivial. "We have too many silly page-one stories that just pander to the reader," says Jack Nelson, chief of the *L.A. Times* Washington bureau. "We waste too much page-one space on things that aren't really important. We need more hard-hitting, investigative stories."

The *Los Angeles Times* also publishes more front-page disaster stories—personal, natural, and mechanical—than either the *New York Times* or *Washington Post*. There were ten such stories in the first five months of 1977—poisoned water in Ohio, a train wreck in Chicago, trapped miners in Pennsylvania, a power blackout in Florida—none of which were played on page one of either the *Washington Post* or *New York Times*.

Los Angeles Times editors say they were unaware of this tendency and can ascribe it only to "the realization that ours is a transient population: A lot of people who came here from other parts of the country are still interested in what happens back in their hometowns.''

"Several years ago," said former managing editor Frank P. Haven, "I decided to throw [out-of-town baseball] box scores out of the paper. I got 5,000 letters from people who used to live in Chicago or New York or. . . . They related to their hometown teams and players, and they wanted to see those familiar names in the box scores." Haven put the box scores back in.

But that doesn't explain the *Los Angeles Times*'s page-one play of foreign disasters—an explosion in Moscow, a helicopter crash in Israel, a train wreck in Australia—all of which were left off page one of the *Post* and *New York Times*. "I guess it's just a subconscious reluctance to appear callous to the loss of human life," says one *Los Angeles Times* editor.

Editors elsewhere offer two other theories:

- An orientation toward the sensational and the spectacular that "has always been indigenous to the Southern California culture."
- "Journalistic immaturity," an unwitting carryover from the days when death and destruction sold extra editions of newspapers on the street.

"We call it the '13-Killed-in-Ecuadorian-Mudslide' syndrome," said one editor. "You always have to ask yourself, What's my choke-point on Ecuadorian mudslides? We had one editor here who actually had a formula for it: A plane crash abroad had to have eighty-two deaths to make page one, a local plane crash could make it with three dead."

The *Los Angeles Times*'s "choke-point" on such stories is apparently rather low; some disasters make page one with nary a death.

But the newspaper published far fewer crime stories on page one in 1977 than either the *Post* or the *New York Times*. "We decided long ago,'' one editor says, ''that routine crime coverage was a waste of our time and the reader's. Page one is too important for that.''

Moreover, despite the presence of so many disaster and light feature stories on page one, the *Los Angeles Times* runs more foreign news on page one than either the *New York Times* or the *Washington Post*. During the first five months of 1977 that predominance was especially pronounced in stories on the Mideast and Africa.

Part of this stems from a conscious commitment to a global orientation—the establishment by 1977 of seventeen foreign bureaus and the hiring of several excellent correspondents.

The *Los Angeles Times* gave page-one play to Egyptian food riots, for example—a story neither the *Post* nor the *New York Times* put on page one—because ''our correspondent there did such a good job,'' says one *Times* editor. ''The quality of his reporting made it a page-one story, not just the importance of the event.''

But logistics also helps dictate page-one play: In the *Los Angeles Times,* if a foreign story is not on page one, it will seldom get good display elsewhere in the paper. (In contrast, the *New York Times* uses the whole front portion of the newspaper, from page two well past the middle of the front section, for foreign news. Pages two and three, in particular, almost always have good display space for these stories.)

The *Los Angeles Times* published more foreign news on page one in 1977, but the *New York Times* published more in the total paper—in part because of its historical concern with foreign news, in part because most high-ranking editors at the *New York Times* are former foreign correspondents.

Just the opposite is true of local news. With the exception of the *Baltimore Sun,* the *Los Angeles Times* probably published less local news on page one than any other major newspaper in the country. Many people in the community—and many reporters at the paper—saw this as evidence that the paper, in its drive for national prestige, had abandoned the local community.

But editors scoff at that charge and point to the availability of two, wide-open, ad-free pages—page three of part one and page one of part two—that are used exclusively to get local news broader display, bigger headlines, and more illustration. Thus, the *New York Times* runs more local news on page one, but the *Los Angeles Times* runs more in the total paper. ("That's what we're here for," says one *Los Angeles Times* editor. "We're a California paper, a Western regional paper.")

Some differences between the two papers, and between either of them and the *Post,* are not so easy to analyze or categorize.

In March 1977, for example, an American diplomat, Brady Tyson, was called back to the United States from a U.N. conference in Geneva after publicly apologizing for America's role in the overthrow of Chile's President Salvador Allende—a role the U.S. has never publicly acknowledged.

Both the *New York Times* and the *Washington Post* played the resultant controversy on page one. So did the *Boston Globe, Houston Post, San Francisco Chronicle, San Diego Union, Portland Oregonian,* and *New Orleans Times-Picayune,* among others. But not the *L.A. Times*—despite the paper's generally heavy page-one play of foreign news.

The *Los Angeles Times*'s explanation: "It was clear that Tyson was speaking for himself, not officially for the State Department. Putting the story on page one would have given it a significance it didn't deserve."

The *New York Times*'s response: "The *L.A. Times* was dead wrong. A new president was being embarrassed in public. We knew Carter would have a hemorrhage the next day. That's worth page one."

Many editors would agree.

And yet: The *New York Times* published only half as many page-one stories as the *Los Angeles Times* during the first five months of 1977 on the various controversies surrounding U.N.

Ambassador Andrew Young even though the U.N. headquarters is in New York.

The *New York Times*'s explanation: "We don't feel compelled to put something on page one just because someone in an important position happens to say something outrageous. We're more interested in substance than texture."

The *Los Angeles Times*'s response: "Young doesn't just 'happen' to say these things. He's a high-ranking diplomat, a close friend of the president [who continues to have the president's public support], and he's saying things based on a black American's perspective on world events—something we've never had before in this country."

Many editors would agree.

But why, then, did the *Los Angeles Times*'s front page all but ignore the *Roots* phenomenon?

The *Washington Post* published three page-one stories on *Roots* during the week it was becoming the most widely watched television program in American history. The *Los Angeles Times* published none. Neither did the *New York Times*. Was that because the two *Times*es decided the story was more appropriate for its entertainment and/or local news pages (where each did publish *Roots* stories)? Or because Washington's population is 70 percent black? Or because the *Post*, with more black reporters and editors than either of the *Times*es, had arranged a special showing of *Roots* for anyone on the staff who wanted to see it?

Three months later, when some scholars and journalists began questioning the credibility of *Roots*, the *New York Times*—its interest in literary disputation aroused anew—published three page-one stories on the controversy and two other page-one stories that discussed the controversy in the context of author Alex Haley's return visit to Africa. The *Post* published a similar page-one story. The *Los Angeles Times*'s major news story on the controversy ran on page twenty-two.

"We blew it," says the editor of the *Los Angeles Times*. "We missed the boat."

Newspapers are often guilty of such errors and inconsistencies—many attributable to the vagaries and vicissitudes of everyday life . . . and of daily newspaper journalism.

How could the literature-conscious *New York Times* not put the death of novelist James Jones on page one? ("We made a mistake," says the executive editor of the *Times*. "I was out of town, in San Francisco, that day.")

How could the Watergate-conscious *Washington Post* not put on page one President Carter's post-press conference statement of May 12, 1977, that former President Richard M. Nixon was, indeed, guilty of breaking the law? ("We just plain goofed," says the *Post*'s executive editor. "Our reporter was a tiger; he left the press conference early that day.")

Sometimes editors simply differ in their judgments, even in retrospect: The *Los Angeles Times* gave substantially more page-one play than did either the *New York Times* or *Washington Post* to the 1977 story on federal trade commissioner Paul Rand Dixon calling Ralph Nader "a son of a bitch and a dirty Arab." The editors at all three papers still think their individual decisions on that story were right; a study of seventeen other papers indicates widespread disagreement. The same is true of many other stories.

What front-page decisions often come down to, editors say, is that there is no blueprint, no grand design, no formula or quota: just different editors—all human, all capable of error—viewing the world through the prisms of their different life experiences and making decisions on a daily basis for different readerships in different historical, cultural, and geographical contexts.

"The development of any paper's front page is a subtle, psychological matter," says Sidney Schanberg, a columnist and former metropolitan editor and foreign correspondent for the *New York Times*. "Watching it everyday is like watching a child grow. No. Slower. Like watching grass grow."

In such a format, with editors making deadline decisions on

stories that are often marginal or incomplete, perhaps it is not so surprising that competent, reasonable men frequently differ in their judgments.

Nevertheless, the *Post*'s Ben Bradlee says he can remember, early in his career, being "terrified" that he would make the wrong decisions on which stories should (and should not) appear on the paper's front page. "I'd heard about the editor somewhere who didn't put the first A-bomb on page one," Bradlee says, "and I was always afraid I might screw up like that some day."

Even now, Bradlee says, when he insists a particular story not run on page one—and other *Post* editors disagree—one of the other editors will shake his head and say, "You're going right into the history books, Benjie."

Bradlee is no longer "terrified" of history's judgment on these matters, he says, but he and his counterparts at other major newspapers around the country do weigh very carefully each day's page-one decisions.

At most papers these decisions are made during a daily news conference attended by most of the paper's ranking editors. But there are some differences.

At the *New York Times* and *Washington Post,* for example, the highest ranking editor at the paper, the executive editor, is in attendance. His subordinate, the managing editor, conducts the news conference, but the executive editor offers comments, suggestions, and questions—and his word (approval or veto) is final.

At the *Los Angeles Times* the highest ranking editor does not attend the daily news conference. "I get a copy of the news budget early in the afternoon," says editor William F. Thomas, "and I discuss page-one play with the other editors by phone . . . but there's a limit to how much I can impose myself on everybody's decisions. What the hell would the managing editor do if I were there?"

At the *Washington Post,* unlike the *Los Angeles Times* and *New York Times,* the Sports and Style sections are always routinely represented at the news conference.

That, says one *L.A. Times* editor, may help explain why the *Post* gave prominent page-one play to the widely watched *Roots* television programs and the *L.A. Times* did not, consigning the story, for the most part, to the View section (the paper's equivalent of the *Post*'s Style section). "It was a perfect example of how we get screwed up sometimes because we lack coordination between departments," the editor says. "My own feeling is that *Roots* belonged on page one, but we have different people making decisions about news stories for page one and entertainment-type stories for View."

At the *New York Times* and *Los Angeles Times* news conferences, the managing editor begins by conducting an informal inquiry of editors from the metropolitan, national, foreign, and financial departments. There are generally two such inquiries: an early one, involving primarily assistant editors, and a later one, involving just the top editors. The tone at both is generally quite casual, even lighthearted and bantering. From the two conferences, and from conversations before and between them, a consensus gradually emerges on the day's major stories, and an executive news editor sketches in the actual placement of the stories on a dummy (a layout form or design) during the second conference.

In Los Angeles that dummy is generally followed unless late-breaking stories force changes. In New York copies of the dummy are distributed to all major desks and to the Washington bureau, and editors are encouraged to challenge it ("appeal" is the word used).

At the early *Washington Post* news conference, the managing editor also questions various editors on their major stories of the day. But there is more time between the *Post*'s preliminary and final conferences—usually about four hours—than in Los Angeles (just a few minutes) or in New York (ninety minutes), and in that time the *Post*'s executive news editors dummy the front page themselves based on the first conference and subsequent conversations.

Then, at the final news conference, the managing editor goes over the dummy, asking the appropriate editor to comment on each story already tentatively sketched in. Either the managing editor or the executive editor—or any other editor—may suggest changes. As with other papers, late-developing events can force further changes through the night.

George Cotliar, the *Los Angeles Times*'s managing editor, has been known, for example, to disappear into his host's bedroom at a Saturday night party, telephone the news desk for word of any major new stories, pull a Xerox copy of the next day's front-page dummy out of one pocket and a blank dummy out of another pocket, and re-draw page one over the telephone, in consultation with the executive news editor on duty.

2

THE UNNAMED SOURCE

Barbara Walters was interviewing Alexander Haig, the former secretary of state. "A source high in the administration told me—" she began.

Haig interrupted her, "Another one of those . . ."

"Another one of those," Walters conceded, "but he exists. And he said that . . ."

"A source." One of the most common references in a reporter's vocabulary. Sometimes it's a "high source." Or a "well-informed source." Or a "knowledgeable source." Or two "knowledgeable sources." But just who are these sources? Readers want to know. They complain about unnamed sources all the time. So I decided to write a story about the subject.

I found some pretty interesting material, at my own paper and elsewhere. Angry memos. Policies that were being violated. Games that reporters and government officials played with each other, to the ultimate detriment of the general public. I also had some problems with my story—reporters at several papers who wouldn't talk to me about unnamed sources unless I promised not to name them, for example. And reporters at my own paper who for a variety of reasons were angry with what I wrote.

One reporter was upset because I said, at one point in my

story, that "everyone" I had interviewed had agreed that "the reliance on unidentified sources is excessive in the media today."

The reporter wrote to me, and to the editor of the paper, to complain: "In an interview you had with me in connection with the story, and in subsequent remarks to you, I took the clear position that this reliance is not excessive and, in fact, is necessary to convey adequate information to the public," he said. "This may be a minority view, but I am distressed that you did not note it, and in fact mistakenly reported that no such view was expressed to you. . . . I think it is unfair to describe a view as unanimous when in fact it was not unanimous. This may be customary procedure in a totalitarian state, but it should not gain hold here."

I wrote back to the reporter, pointing out that I had not interviewed him for my story. I reminded him that he had approached me a couple of times because he had heard I was working on the story and he wanted to register his opinion. But I had not formally interviewed him. I said I was "very careful . . . to make clear distinctions between 'interviews' and 'conversations,' especially here at the L.A. Times where I am available, accessible, and in contact with people all the time."

When I want to interview someone for a story, I tell them so specifically. I say that I'm working on a story and would like to ask them a few questions. I never did that with him. I didn't ask; he volunteered his views.

Another reporter was far angrier, for just the opposite reason. I had interviewed her, but after my story came out, she claimed I hadn't interviewed her—or, more precisely, that she hadn't realized I was interviewing her (or, as she put it to me and to several colleagues, she didn't think I'd told her I was interviewing her). I thought—and still think—she was wrong. I remember telephoning her and telling her I was working on a story about the overuse of unnamed sources and wanted to ask her a few questions about one of her stories. If she had called a politician and said she was working on a story about campaign contributions and wanted to ask him a few questions about one of his contributors, she certainly would have expected him to realize she was interviewing him.

Still, I realize—and this I told the first reporter I mentioned—that my position makes things awkward for my colleagues. They're accustomed to having other reporters call them with questions on a purely informal basis. That's why I don't use information I pick up in casual conversation unless I first go back to the person involved and say, "Look, I'd like to use what you said this morning. Is that okay?" But by the same token, when I do tell someone I'm working on a story on a particular subject and want to talk to them about it, I don't think I have to call them back later and say, "Are you sure you want me to quote you on that?" I wouldn't do that with a politician or a businessman or anyone else I interviewed. Neither would she. Why should I do it with another reporter?

In this particular instance, it probably wouldn't have created so many hard feelings had I not quoted the reporter as saying something truly foolish—and then quoted the editor of the paper as saying, "That's absolutely the goddamn dumbest thing I ever heard."

The reporter was embarrassed. Mortified. Enraged. I hadn't wanted to hurt or humiliate her, and I had thought about the matter a long time before deciding precisely how to handle it. I did not use her name, for example, because I generally believe that editors, not reporters, bear final responsibility for what appears in the newspaper. But I did not want anyone to think this reporter's mistake, and her remarks that tried to justify that mistake, were made by any other reporter. So I used just enough detail to protect the innocent and to make the identity of the guilty reporter evident to anyone who cared to check (or who had a good memory); but she was not readily identifiable to the general public, and I refused to divulge her name to anyone who asked. Many of our colleagues knew who she was, though. That's what so enraged her.

When I heard about her rage, I called to suggest that we meet over a drink or a cup of coffee to exchange explanations. She told me she had nothing to say to me. But a couple of weeks later I passed her in the hallway and said hello. She said hello back. I walked away thinking she had decided to forgive me. Wrong. When I passed her again a few minutes later, she said, "I didn't mean to say hello to you. I didn't realize it was you. I'm not talking to you."

This reporter has since become warm and friendly again, and I continue to think she is a good reporter. But like all of us, she isn't perfect. And like many in my profession, when she made a mistake and I pointed it out—in print—she resented it. No wonder my editor told me when I first took the job of media critic, "I hope you have a lot of friends outside the newspaper business. By the time you're through . . . you may not have many left inside it."

*   *   *

ONE DAY in late 1982 the *New York Times* published three front-page stories that included statements from, variously, "a Western ambassador," "a Western diplomat," "one American official," "a prominent local journalist," "police sources," "a State Department official," "one State Department official," "an administration official," "a senior administration official," "another administration official," and "administration officials."

That same week the *Los Angeles Times* published more than two dozen stories that included information and observations attributed, variously, to "one diplomat," "many critics," "Pentagon officials," "one official," "a senior official," "administration officials," "one White House source," "one union source," "sources," "another source," "one source," "various sources," and "informed sources."

A couple of weeks later the *Washington Post* published nine stories that included statements attributed to, variously, "U.S. officials," "Western diplomats," "diplomatic sources," "semiofficial sources," "a U.S. official," "knowledgeable officials," "a State Department official," "senior State Department officials," and "official sources."

These examples—from days chosen at random—are by no means unusual. Everyday, newspapers across the United States routinely publish stories quoting sources who are not identified by name. In fact, the *New York Times* is actually more careful—more restrictive—than any other newspaper in its use of unidentified sources. When the paper does rely on unnamed sources, as in the not uncommon examples cited above, its editors insist, somewhat more vigorously than most other editors, on the use of qualifying adjectives such as *"Western* officials" and *"senior administration* officials" to give the reader some hint, however vague, about the probable allegiance and possible biases of the sources involved.

But not even the *New York Times* is always as exacting as its editors would like in the identification of news sources: A page-one story on Lebanon last October contained three references to an "American official" and one reference to a "French official"—not exactly models of specificity.

When other less exacting newspapers attribute statements to "sources" and "informed sources," they give their readers no clues whatsoever as to the credibility of the statements or the vested interests of the sources. Neither are the readers of these statements attributed to unidentified sources alerted to the source's reasons for speaking to the press—or for wanting (and being granted) anonymity.

Just who is the "one intellectual" quoted in a November 7, 1982, *Chicago Tribune* story as saying of Mexico's ruling Institutional Revolutionary party: "They prefer to co opt you, to buy off opposition. And if that doesn't work, they will try to intimidate you." And who was the "one U.S. official" quoted in a November 2, 1982, Associated Press dispatch as saying, after a meeting with congressional leaders, "everyone seemed to support" President Reagan's decision to permit U.S. Marine to conduct limited street patrols in West Beirut?

Did the "intellectual" and the "official" really know what they were talking about? Did they have personal, or political, reasons for wanting their views promulgated? Even if both sources were knowledgeable and unbiased, how were readers to know that? It is a quandary that readers confront everyday. And despite some improvements in some areas, the problem is getting worse, not better.

The result: "Sources," under the protective cloak of anonymity, are permitted to use the press for personal and political purposes—to grind axes, advance ambitions, attack rivals and mislead the public.

" 'Sources' is my unfavorite word of all time," says William F. Thomas, editor of the *Los Angeles Times*. "I hate this . . . word. This is not the way to write a story."

When the *L.A. Times*'s frequent use of "sources" and "informed sources" was pointed.out to Thomas in the course of an interview for the story on which this chapter is based, he quickly tried to stop the practice by reminding other editors on the paper of his previously stated policy in opposition to that practice.

But since Thomas's policy was not written and was only communicated by him to the editors, many reporters on the paper's staff said they had no way of knowing such a policy even existed, before or after that reminder. So when the policy was violated ten times the very next week, Thomas issued a rare written memo to the entire staff reiterating the policy (which is similar to written policies at the *New York Times, Washington Post,* and most other major papers):

"Unnamed sources should not be used unless there is no other way to get needed information into the story. . . .

"When we do use them, we should give the reader all the information we can—short of indirectly identifying the source— that establishes his or her credibility. No more 'informed sources' when you can tell us it's 'a high army official' or whatever. . . ."

Why not just prohibit the publication of any statement from any unnamed source? Why not insist that anyone willing to speak to the public through the press must be willing to stand publicly behind what he or she says? A simple rule: no name, no story.

Not so simple.

It would be impractical and irresponsible to do that, Thomas says, and every other journalist interviewed for this story agreed. So did several government spokesmen, past and present. "There's no way to avoid it," says Jody Powell, former press secretary to President Carter and now a syndicated columnist. "You wouldn't get much if everybody . . . had to be identified as the source of every . . . statement."

Why not? Because people in power—in government and private enterprise alike—do not like to read stories critical of their programs, practices, policies, and personalities. If everyone who told a reporter about the flaws in a Defense Department plan or a power struggle in the White House were identified in print (or on the air), the certainty of immediate retribution by superiors (embarrassment, ostracism, demotion, dismissal) would surely discourage all but the most hardy (or foolhardy) from speaking to the press on controversial matters.

That means the press would publish and broadcast less speculation and less titillating gossip about internal government and corporate squabbles; that, in many instances, would be beneficial for all concerned. But it also means the press—and the public—would have less information about manipulation, malfeasance, corruption, inefficiency, hypocrisy, and a host of other improper (and sometimes illegal) forms of behavior for which those in power must be held publicly accountable in a democracy.

"To be an absolute purist, to say we will never permit anyone to say anything . . . without having his name attached to it would so restrict the flow of information that we would fail in our basic mission, which is to . . . keep people informed," says Gene Roberts, executive editor of the *Philadelphia Inquirer*.

"In Vietnam I knew one hell of a lot of people up and down the line who disagreed with the way the war was being waged," Roberts said, "but the army being what it is you just weren't going to get a story that said, 'Full Colonel John Jones, serial number such-and-such, today said that General [William] Westmoreland doesn't know what the hell he's doing here.'

"One very important role a newspaper performs is being a conduit for [internal] government political policy debates . . . like that one," Roberts says, "and we wouldn't be able to do that if we refused to print all anonymous quotes."

Nevertheless, Roberts—and everyone else interviewed for this story—agreed that the reliance on unidentified sources is excessive in the media today. Indeed it may be the most widely abused practice in contemporary journalism—to the growing chagrin of editors, newsmakers, and readers alike.

The protection of confidential sources from courtroom sub-poenas is not the question at issue here. Reporters have gone to jail rather than disclose sources to whom they have promised confidentiality, and virtually all journalists agree that such promises must be kept. But apart from any possible conflict be-tween the courts and the press, what angers and frustrates many critics inside and outside the press is the casual granting of an-onymity in routine stories everyday.

Reporters who write stories based on statements from sources they do not identify for their readers are, in effect, asking their readers to trust them, to assume that the reporters (and their ed-itors) have evaluated the source's credentials and credibility. Good reporters from good newspapers figure they have earned that trust. But recent public opinion polls show that the press is not widely trusted by the public, and many editors think a reduction in the use of unnamed sources might help "rebuild that valued trust," in the words of Eugene Patterson, president and editor of the *St. Petersburg* (Fla.) *Times*.

Both the American Society of Newspaper Editors and the National News Council have recently become sufficiently con-cerned with the problem of unnamed sources to conduct major studies. The news council study, released in the spring of 1983, says: "In these days of widespread public questioning about how well the press fulfills its mission, one question seems to exceed all others in both frequency and intensity: How do I know this news account is true when I don't even know where it comes from? . . .

"Increasing dissatisfaction is being expressed over the ob-scurity that too often surrounds the sources of journalistic infor-mation."

Some readers even wonder if the use of unidentified sources is just a journalistic ruse; is the reporter himself masquerading as an "informed source" or a "senate observer," either to pro-mulgate his personal view or to enable him to synthesize the views of several sources, no one of whom said precisely the words the reporter needs to make a particular point in his story?

"The real sloppiness I notice recently is . . . this business about . . . 'A number of people on the Hill believe . . . ,' " complains Tom Brokaw, anchorman on the "NBC Nightly News." "That becomes a kind of convenient coatrack on which they [reporters] can hang any number of judgments that the reporter may have put together on his own."

Brokaw is not alone in this concern.

"Everybody is sure you're talking to yourself [when you quote 'one informed source']," the *L.A. Times*'s Thomas said in his 1982 staff memo.

"Some reporters always seem to have just the right quote at just the right point [in their stories]," Jody Powell says. "The world just isn't that orderly. People don't always say just what you want."

Suppose the reporter quotes two or more unnamed "officials" on the same point, in keeping with many newspapers' policies that a reporter must have at least two sources for any controversial story?

"I often have a burning suspicion that it's just one source the reporter trusts a lot," says Frank Greve, a reporter in the Washington bureau of Knight-Ridder Newspapers.

The plural "officials," Greve suggests, is a ploy that enables a reporter to seemingly satisfy his paper's two-source policy and to impress his editors (and his readers) with the thoroughness and conscientiousness of his reporting. Most journalists say such subterfuge is not widespread. The attribution of many statements to unidentified sources is more a matter of individual laziness, journalistic necessity, and tradition than of reportorial dishonesty, they say.

Sometimes, in fact, a reporter may not identify his sources simply as a matter of convenience. A reporter may decide that a routine statement by the State Department can stand as such, without the specific identification of a third-level bureaucrat whose long title may take two or three lines of valuable space. Or a reporter may attribute a consensus opinion to "several administration officials" rather than identifying one official who may be no more responsible than any other for its formulation.

But most reporters rely on unidentified sources because the reporters think that is the only way to get a particular story. This is especially true for reporters working on investigative projects or covering organized crime. Sources of information for such stories are generally reluctant to talk to the press under any circumstance; the guarantee of anonymity is often the inevitable *quid pro quo* for information only they can provide.

Reporters covering Iron Curtain countries and other totalitarian regimes often have similar arrangements with their sources, for equally obvious reasons. Indeed, American reporters working in most foreign countries often find themselves routinely required to write stories without specifically identifying their sources, in part because tradition and diplomatic protocol make it inappropriate for a foreign diplomat to comment on the affairs of his or her host country (and in part because most other countries neither have nor understand the American tradition of a free press, poking around in sensitive matters, both before and after those matters are officially resolved).

But the most pervasive use of the unidentified source in the American media involves neither the niceties of diplomatic protocol nor the terrors of covering the Mafia or Moscow. On a daily basis, there are more statements attributed to unnamed sources in Washington, D.C., than anywhere else. In Washington, in fact, this practice sometimes reaches ridiculous extremes. William Umstead, a Democratic senator from North Carolina in the late 1940s, was certainly not the first (nor is he likely to be the last) man in Washington to reply to a reporter's question by pondering for several minutes and then saying, "Off the record, no comment." Some politicians even insist that their names not be used in a newspaper story, and then go on television and say the same things, with their names and smiling faces visible to all the world.

The request for—and granting of—anonymity is so routine in Washington that several Washington reporters interviewed for this story, while agreeing that the use of anonymous sources should be curbed, nonetheless asked for anonymity themselves.

One reporter, Steve Neal, then White House correspondent for the *Chicago Tribune,* provided several perceptive, on-the-record comments but also managed, in the course of a twenty-five-minute interview, to say on five separate occasions that he did not want to be identified by name as the source for what he was then saying.

For varying reasons, reporters covering the White House, the State Department, the Pentagon, and, above all, the intelligence agencies rely the most heavily on sources they do not name in print or on the air. Thus, a *Newsweek* cover story, charging that the United States was conducting a secret war to topple the leftist government in Nicaragua, relied heavily on intelligence sources and contained thirty-six statements attributed to unnamed sources (and only three to named sources—two of whom said, "No comment").

The next day the *New York Times* published a story in which Reagan administration officials and national security officials denied the charge (although they conceded that the United States is supporting "small-scale, clandestine military operations . . . intended to harass the Nicaraguan government"). But none of these officials was named either.

As Mel Elfin, a former air force intelligence officer and now the Washington bureau chief for *Newsweek* says: "In the . . . nether-nether world of 'spookdom' . . . the code of anonymity is part of the dress code."

But many Washington reporters who cover far less sensitive matters also routinely grant anonymity to their sources. Even Phyllis Richman, whose job as restaurant critic and executive food editor of the *Washington Post* isn't likely to produce stories that would compromise national security or topple foreign governments, says she often conducts interviews in which she agrees not to quote her sources by name. It's just a habit in Washington. Many reporters there grant anonymity to sources almost as reflexively as they offer cocktails to guests in their homes.

In most cities, says Ray Coffey, Washington bureau chief for the *Chicago Tribune,* someone meeting a reporter for lunch would generally begin the conversation by asking "How's your wife? How're your kids? Is your dog over the rabies?" But in Washington, Coffey says, "They come in [and the first thing they say] . . . is 'This is on background.' The whole thing is bizarre."

Other journalists agree.

"It's astonishing the number of stories out of Washington . . . without any names in them," said Paul Janensch, executive editor of the *Louisville Courier-Journal and Times.* "The Washington . . . press corps and the government sort of cooperate in this game . . . and the public is a loser."

Janensch says he spent a year in Washington and was "surprised at how acquiescent reporters were to requests . . . for anonymity." Reporters and government officials have devised "an elaborate set of rules . . . sort of a minuet," governing the attribution of published statements, Janensch complains, "and all it does is serve to hide important information from the public."

The "elaborate set of rules" Janensch speaks of dictates that government officials provide some information to reporters on a "not-for-attribution" or "background" basis (meaning the official cannot be identified by name in their stories), while other information will be provided on a "deep background" basis (meaning the reporter cannot even cite an unnamed official as his source; he must try to confirm the information elsewhere or write something like "It was learned that . . ."; or just state what he has learned as fact, without attribution: "President Reagan will announce . . . .").

The most restrictive category of nonattribution is the "off-the-record" statement. Such statements are not to be used at all, with or without names; they are intended to guide the reporter in evaluating information he gathers from other interviews and other sources.

To journalists outside Washington, as well as nonjournalists outside Washington, this list of subtle distinctions may seem like the monthly list of flavors at Baskin-Robbins ("Do you want chocolate chip or chocolate chocolate chip?"), but in Washington they are a code to live by for journalists and government officials alike.

Although journalists argue that government officials are to blame for the media's overreliance on unnamed sources, one could argue that it would be in the government's best interest, as well as that of the media and the public, for these officials to insist on more attribution. As Warren Christopher, former deputy secretary of state, says, "If a reporter is able to take casual corridor gossip and turn it into 'official sources,' the management of a bureaucracy becomes even more tenuous than usual."

The use of unidentified sources has been widespread in Washington and elsewhere for as long as journalists and politicians have been speaking to each other. Traditionally, in fact, presidents may have been the worst offenders. President Franklin Delano Roosevelt, for example, never permitted reporters at his press conferences to quote him directly. President Harry S. Truman operated under the same rule—except when he said something on which he specifically wanted to be quoted. Then he would give the reporters permission to do so. But the general problem of the overreliance on unnnamed sources has increased significantly in the last twenty years or so, and there seem to have been three specific stages in this evolution of what Charles

Bailey, former editor of the *Minneapolis Star and Tribune*, calls
"a practice that has . . . spread like cancer":

Camelot. President Kennedy enjoyed a good relationship with
the working press during his brief administration, in part because he and his key aides were very skillful at befriending (and
manipulating) individual reporters. Leaked stories attributed to
unidentified sources were common under Kennedy, and critics
of subsequent administrations sometimes forget that it was under Kennedy, not Lyndon Johnson or Richard Nixon, that the
term "managed news" first came into vogue.

Vietnam. Even more than most presidents, Johnson was a
man of secrecy and vanity—a man who reacted angrily when
his plans were criticized or leaked to the press. When criticism
of his Vietnam policies began to mount, his sensitivity became
even more acute.

Reporters eager for good stories, and administration officials
eager to have their dissenting viewpoints made public, quickly
learned that the safest way for both to get what they wanted was
to publish stories under the cloak of anonymity.

Watergate. Most journalists agree that the use of unidentified sources, in Washington and elsewhere, escalated geometri-
cally during and after Watergate. "Deep Throat" was the most
glamorous of the unnamed sources, but virtually every good reporter who spent any time on the Watergate story had at least a
"shallow throat" or two somewhere.

Political careers were in jeopardy then. There was talk of
impeachment and imprisonment. A government was being toppled. If every reporter had insisted that every source be quoted
by name, many key Watergate stories would never have been
written. In the competitive rush for Watergate disclosures, traditional standards for attribution often slipped badly. Getting into
print first, with a story from an unnamed source, was often
thought to be better than being second, with a story from a named
source.

Watergate spawned a whole generation of young, glamour-seeking "investigative reporters"—many of whom thought they could impress their editors (and their readers) with their contacts and savvy by writing of "informed sources" and "City Hall officials" even when those sources and officials were perfectly willing to be quoted by name.

James Squires, editor of the *Chicago Tribune*, is one of many editors who says he had to straighten out reporters dazzled by the image of the reporter-as-sleuth in the aftermath of Watergate; some of these reporters thought that quoting unidentified sources sounded sexier, more exciting than quoting people by name.

Bill Kovach, Washington editor of the *New York Times*, says he got sick and tired of hearing otherwise sophisticated reporters trying to impress him by saying they had a "Deep Throat" on various stories. Once, Kovach says, he overheard a *New York Times* reporter say to a source, at the end of a telephone interview, "I assume that's on background." Kovach gave the reporter a brief lecture and reminded other staff members that anonymity should never be volunteered and only reluctantly granted and that the *Times* was not impressed by information gathered "on background."

Reporters tend to blame the system—largely, the government—for the ubiquitousness of the unnamed source, but Kovach, Squires, and others agree that reporters themselves must share the blame for the phenomenon. It is often easier—quicker—to get a story from one person who does not have to stand publicly behind it than it is to burrow through the bureaucratic (or corporate) maze looking for knowledgeable sources who can be persuaded to be quoted by name.

Some reporters take the easy way out. They automatically offer to let a source speak anonymously for no discernible reason. I have been interviewed frequently, for example, by reporters writing stories on the *Los Angeles Times*, and almost invariably, the reporters will start by saying, "I'd like to talk to you off-the-record," or, "I won't quote you by name, of course."

I always say, "I'd prefer to talk on the record. I'm willing to stand behind what I say."

But misplaced priorities, laziness, naiveté, and glamour are not the only reasons reporters sometimes rely too heavily on sources they do not identify to their readers. Competition and television are also important factors in the anonymity equation.

There were 4,355 journalists accredited to the congressional press galleries alone in 1982—"a number that has about doubled over the past twenty years," according to the *National Journal,* a Washington, D.C.,–based magazine that covers politics and government. The *Journal* estimates that there are 10,000 "legitimate journalists and news writers" working in Washington for newspapers (daily and weekly, independent and chain), television (network, independent, and cable), magazines (general and special interest), radio (local, syndication, and network), and newsletters (of all kinds). With so much competition, there is great pressure on reporters to be first, even if they only have a piece—sometimes the wrong piece—of a good story.

Information from sources who do not want to be named can often be confirmed by other sources willing to be named. But a reporter must have the time to seek and probe and cultivate those sources. The rush to be first seldom leaves time for spadework, though, and reporters often rush into print—or on the air—with a story attributed to "White House sources" or "congressional sources," sources who may be ill-informed, manipulative, or self-aggrandizing. This is especially true of television, the fastest growing of all the media. In 1962 there were 242 accredited radio-TV members in the congressional press galleries in Washington; in 1982, there were about 1,500—all scrambling to be first.

Thus, when President Reagan was shot in 1981, Dan Rather of CBS News rushed to tell the nation—wrongly—that White House press secretary James Brady had been killed in the attack; Chris Wallace of NBC News rushed to report—wrongly—that President Reagan was undergoing open-heart surgery.

In earlier generations, when newspapers were the primary source of news for most people, newspaper reporters were often preoccupied with beating other newspaper reporters into print on even the most inconsequential of stories. Many newspaper reporters still feel that way. But television is indisputably the faster medium, and now it is the television reporter who can't wait to tell the public the first hint of a new break in a developing story, often without taking time to find on-the-record confirmation.

Some newspaper reporters, knowing how this system works, may opt to strike first themselves, also without on-the-record confirmation.

Television has exacerbated journalistic reliance on unidentified sources in yet another way.

With television increasingly being the first to report the bare, skeletal essence of a news story—the "who," "what," "when," and "where"—newspapers have increasingly, over the last fifteen or twenty years, tried to emphasize the "how" and "why" of a story.

The best newspaper reporters and editors—skeptical, probing, and iconoclastic by nature and eduction as the 1960s and 1970s unfolded—were already moving in that direction, but television hastened and made inevitable that development.

"When you do 'how' and 'why' reporting, you're bound to have fewer sources willing to be named," says the *New York Times*'s Kovach.

"How" and "why" questions are less easily answered than "who" and "what" questions. "How" and "why" involve speculation, interpretation, analysis, theory, opinion. Many people, in government and out, are unwilling to have their names attached to observations that may ultimately prove wrong or premature or unpopular with those in power (or with various special-interest groups).

But reporters, especially newspaper and newsmagazine reporters, need that kind of information, and news sources, knowing that, have become so demanding and so sophisticated in their requests for anonymity that the entire process has become self-perpetuating.

Some reporters do press their sources to permit themselves to be identified as specifically as possible—balancing the source's need for anonymity with the reporter's need for specificity. Negotiations over the exact phraseology of the attribution in a given story—"an administration source" or "a White House aide" or "a senior White House aide" or "a senior White House aide who attended the meeting"—may, on occasion, take almost as long as the interview itself.

But most news sources, especially in Washington, know reporters will often let them get away with minimal attribution, and the reporters know they know that. The reporter wants the story because that is his job and his instinct, because he thinks it is important to the public, or just because he wants to beat his competitors and to impress his peers and his editors. The source knows this, and he too wants the story out because he thinks it is important to the public, because he wants to promote (or damage) a program (or a rival), or because it will consolidate his power or improve his image.

It is a symbiotic relationship. Reporters and sources use each other for their own, often conflicting, ends. But as Hodding Carter III, former State Department spokesman and now chief correspondent for public television's "Inside Story," says, "When the source for the information is allowed to set the rules . . . who's getting used is the person who's taking the information."

Can that be changed?

In early 1981, Louis D. Boccardi, then executive editor and vice president of the Associated Press, sent a memo to his reporters and bureau chiefs complaining that AP had become "lax" in identifying the sources of many of its news stories. Too many sources were being quoted anonymously, "at the expense of *our* credibility," Boccardi said, and he urged AP reporters to make a greater effort to identify sources by name, whenever possible. "When someone asks not to be identified, ask them why" and put their refusal and their reason in the story, Boccardi told his staff.

Five weeks later Dennis Britton, then national editor of the *Los Angeles Times,* sent a similar memo to his staff. "Whenever possible, let's identify the source by name and title," Britton wrote, ". . . at the very least, please let's avoid, whenever possible, vague attributions such as 'sources said' or 'officials said.' "

Britton and Boccardi are not alone in their concern about the widespread publication of stories attributed to unidentified sources. Many major news organizations have formal, written policies discouraging the practice. CBS News, for example, has this longstanding policy: "Anonymous sources . . . should only be utilized when the source and information are highly reliable and when there is no other practicable way to report the information to the public." The *Washington Post*'s policy is published in a company stylebook given to all reporters and editors: "This newspaper is pledged to disclose the source of all information unless disclosure would endanger the source's security."

But policies are invariably much easier to enunciate than they are to enforce, so violations are not uncommon, and periodic reminders, like those issued by Britton and Boccardi, are valuable. A week after Britton's 1981 memo, virtually everyone in American journalism suddenly became convinced that more than "periodic reminders" were necessary on this particular policy, though.

On April 15, 1981, it was disclosed that Janet Cooke, a reporter for the *Washington Post,* had fabricated her Pulitzer Prize–winning story about an eight-year-old heroin addict she called "Jimmy." The journalistic world was scandalized. Reform was promised instantaneously. Henceforth, editors said, no story would be published in their newspapers unless they or their subordinates knew the name of every unnamed source. Indeed several editors said they had long had such policies.

Discussions about the Janet Cooke affair quickly came to involve more than the narrow issue of preventing reporters from lying to, or deliberately withholding information from, their editors. That, it was generally agreed, didn't happen very often. What did often happen was that reporters wrote stories based on interviews with, or background briefings by, sources whose names they might disclose to their editors but not to their readers and viewers. On this practice, too, editors promised immediate reform; their pledges and policies filled part of forty-six pages in a 1981 report entitled, "After 'Jimmy's World': Tightening Up in Editing," compiled by the National News Council. In fact, many editors are now pushing their reporters more than ever to identify their sources in print whenever possible.

But editors' admonitions aren't always heeded.

On the very day—shortly after the Janet Cooke affair—that Robert Phelps, then executive editor of the *Boston Globe*, circulated a memo that, among other things, asked the paper to "avoid such blind attributions as 'sources' or 'high officials' or 'well-placed officials,' " three of the *Globe*'s eight page-one stories relied exclusively on "well-placed sources," "ranking administration officials," and "an MBTA source."

Despite Britton's 1981 memo, research for the story on which this chapter is based showed that the practice was again pervasive in the *Los Angeles Times* in 1982. So Britton again spoke to his editors, and another memo was issued, this one written by Richard Cooper, the news editor in the paper's Washington bureau, urging reporters to "renew our efforts to combat the unnamed source syndrome."

Some news organizations try to explain their reliance on unnamed sources by making clear to readers that the source in a particular story "refused to be identified." Less often, a story will say specifically why a source refused to be identified. But many editors think even those explanations are inadequate.

The *New York Times* is probably more restrictive than any other newspaper on the use of unidentified sources. Policies discouraging the practice are delineated in two different sections of the paper's stylebook—under "sources of news" and "fairness and impartiality"—and memos criticizing violations of the policy are not uncommon:

"The use of an unidentified New York administration official yesterday as the source for a story on [the] possibilities of revenue decline was a mistake," A. M. Rosenthal, executive editor of the *New York Times,* wrote in one 1982 memo. "It was a violation of our policy of using unidentified officials as infrequently as possible."

Rosenthal realizes that it is impracticable for a newspaper to require that every news source be identified in print. But too many reporters grant anonymity to their sources when there is no compelling reason to do so. Thus, Rosenthal insists that his reporters try to persuade sources to permit themselves to be identified. When they cannot be identified by name, he wants his reporters to identify them as specifically as possible.

Virtually all editors demand the same thing of their reporters. But few editors enforce their policies as sternly as does Rosenthal. Indeed, when stories quoting unnamed "sources" and "knowledgeable sources" began to appear again in the *Los Angeles Times,* even after editor William F. Thomas' policy memo opposing them, the paper's science writer, Lee Dembart—a former *New York Times* reporter—was heard to mutter one day, "Bill's edicts don't seem to have the same force of Mosaic law as Abe's."

True enough—in part because the two newspapers are different, in part because the two men are different. Their standards are equally high, but Rosenthal tends to enforce his personally, while Thomas generally works through his subordinates. Moreover, Rosenthal becomes far angrier—visibly, sometimes loudly angrier than does Thomas—when his standards are violated. And Rosenthal becomes particularly enraged when he sees anonymous pejorative quotes in the paper. No one, he says, should be permitted to criticize another individual while wrapped in the protective cloak of anonymity. "It's unfair," he says.

Many editors agree with Rosenthal. News organizations ranging from the Associated Press to the *Boston Globe* to *Newsday* to the *Roanoke* (Va.) *Times & World News* also have policies prohibiting the publication of anonymous pejorative quotes. How successful are such policies?

"Not very," says Robert Phelps of the *Boston Globe*. Indeed an unidentified source was permitted to call a Massachusetts state official "a bitch" in a 1982 *Globe* story. And for all Rosenthal's eloquent fulminations on the subject, two anonymous pejorative quotes appeared in the *New York Times* in one four-day period in 1982. One of those stories quoted an unidentified source as, in effect, calling former Secretary of State Henry A. Kissinger a hypocrite. The other story quoted an unidentified source as calling a New York company "a cut-throat corporation."

After the latter story was published, Rosenthal says he wrote an unsolicited letter of apology to the chairman of the maligned company. He also wrote a memo to his subordinates, saying, "I was stunned and almost literally sickened to see the anonymous attack on [the company]."

He closed the memo by saying, ominously, "I would like a list of every person who read that story before it went into print. Obviously, there is a huge gap between my vision of journalism and theirs, and I want to see if it is at all possible to close it."

Several meetings ensued. But about two weeks later, a *New York Times* story on John DeLorean quoted an unnamed "prominent banker who keeps his eye on the entrepreneurial circuits" as calling DeLorean "flawed . . . always flirting with unreality." The same story quoted other unnamed sources (in the automobile industry) as saying, in effect, that DeLorean was a liar and that he had been fired from General Motors in 1973 and had not quit (as he has always claimed).

Sometimes the *New York Times* will publish an anonymous pejorative comment on someone by using a paraphrase—as in the DeLorean story—rather than a direct quotation. The theory behind that appears to be that a paraphrase is, somehow, less damaging.

But most editors interviewed for this story scoffed at the purported distinction between paraphrase and direct quotation in this context. "It's . . . all the same to the reader," said Jim Squires of the *Chicago Tribune*.

So what's the solution?

Rosenthal is convinced that on most stories a good reporter can find a knowledgeable, reliable source willing to speak critically of someone on the record. Failing that, he says, the reporter can find evidence that will enable him to "show by specific demonstration not just anonymous quotation" that the person he is writing about has certain flaws.

If this is not possible either, Rosenthal says, he would rather not publish the pejorative information than publish it anonymously. As he said in a memo last year, "A newspaper's ethic and judgment is based not only on what it prints but what it chooses not to print."

True. But one result of that philosophy is the publication of some stories—especially profiles of important people—that are all flattery, with no criticism. "If you'll look at most of our profiles," says Bill Kovach, "they're unsatisfactory for that very reason. The executive editor [Rosenthal] feels so strongly about the anonymous pejorative quote that he's willing to accept profiles that are not critical when they may need to be" (a policy Kovach agrees with).

But most people in a position to know a powerful person well just won't be willing to be quoted by name as speaking critically of that person, says William Thomas of the *L.A. Times,* and yet, any balanced, comprehensive profile should include such critical commentary.

Thus, the *Los Angeles Times* published several profiles in 1982 that included anonymous pejorative comments on powerful people. In each case Thomas feels the information conveyed in those comments was significant and would have been withheld from the *Times* (and from the public) had the paper insisted that the sources for that information permit the paper to use their names.

"It's up to you [the reporters and editors] to make damn sure the person giving you that kind of characterization is in a very good position to do so," Thomas says, "and it's up to you to also say that in the story, along with whatever qualifiers are necessary. . . . In a case like that the source has got to be identified in every way, except by name, that's feasible."

Thomas concedes, however, that in several *Times* profiles this detailed identification has not been provided.

A pre-election profile of then California State Attorney General (now Governor) George Deukmejian, for example, said, "His detractors say that beneath the 'nice guy' surface lies 'a real crackdown mentality . . . of a true believer, and that makes him dangerous.' "

Who were these detractors? Civil libertarians? Political opponents? Former colleagues? The story gave not the slightest clue. The reporter who wrote the story says she could have used the names of her sources for those comments but omitted them for most statements, positive and negative, because the names would have "broken up . . . the flow of the story." She added, "The content of the quotes was more important in that kind of profile . . . than who said it."

Apparently some of her editors agreed. Several of them saw the story, and none demanded she provide attribution. But when Thomas was told her comments—though not her name—he said; "That's absolutely the goddamn dumbest thing I ever heard."

Nevertheless, Thomas continues to believe that anonymous pejorative quotes should not be prohibited; he continues to feel there will always be some information he would rather publish without attribution than not publish at all.

Although most editors would agree with him in principle, there is some disagreement over just what kinds of information newspapers can justifiably ignore. Each editor has to decide for himself when the lack of specific attribution renders a story too suspect or too speculative or too irresponsible to publish. Similarly, each editor (and reporter) must decide for himself how to get that specific attribution—and how to avoid having his newspaper manipulated by sources hiding behind the veil of anonymity.

Individual interviews in which sources speak unkindly, but anonymously, of others is only one part of the problem, though. The formal but not-for-attribution government briefing presents a similar problem for the media. In many such briefings—conducted ostensibly to help reporters understand complex problems (budgets, diplomatic maneuvers, new weapons systems and the like)—a government official may actually be using the press to shape public opinion on a controversial issue. Or he may be testing a potentially controversial idea or program. Or he may be trying to mislead his opponents and the public. And he does it all anonymously; his briefing of the press is "not for attribution."

This is particularly true in Washington—and probably nowhere more visibly than in the quaint journalistic tradition of the airborne State Department briefing.

Reporters will fly with the secretary of state to some foreign capital. On the way the secretary may brief the reporters on what he expects from his meetings abroad. On the flight home he may brief them on the actual meetings. He may also comment on various world problems. All on one condition: Reporters cannot identify him by name as the source of their information.

So the reporters write stories quoting an unnamed "senior State Department official on the secretary's plane." The reporters know who that official is, of course. So does everyone in the State Department. And everyone in the foreign capital. And everyone who cares in every other foreign capital. Everyone knows, in fact, except the people the reporters are supposed to be informing—their readers and viewers.

The official explanation for this odd minuet is that, like so many other journalistic customs, the reporters and their news sources are helping each other. In this instance the secretary of state is helping the reporters by providing inside information and insights on high-level meetings, and the reporters are helping the secretary of state by serving as a conduit for information he wants made public and by withholding his name so that he can deny having made certain comments if any of his words upset foreign diplomats.

How can someone get away with denying something that everyone knows he said? Simple. Diplomats tend to speak in their own obscure code. Often it's not what they say but the forum in which they say it that gives a statement its significance. An official who makes a public pronouncement may mean, "We're definitely going to do this." But if that same official makes the same pronouncement in a briefing, where his name won't be used, he may really only mean, "We're considering this," or maybe even, "We're *not* going to do this."

That's a vast oversimplification, but it helps explain how the system works. And why.

"If the secretary [of state] isn't quoted by name, that tells the people [in the other country] something . . . and then they don't have to confront him or accuse him . . . or embarrass him," says Robert McCloskey, who spent twenty-six years with the State Department, nine of them as the department's press spokesman, before serving as the ombudsman for the *Washington Post* from 1981 to 1983.

Some reporters even seem to enjoy this little game. As Hodding Carter wrote in the *Wall Street Journal* early in 1983, ". . . it is satisfying to be within the temple [of mysteries], interpreting the oracles while knowing there is more to the story than their utterances. Being a keeper of the mysteries inflates the ego far more than being an observer from outside."

But all this seems elaborately silly to many journalists. Although they're grateful for the information they get in briefings, they object to being used to float trial balloons and to perpetuate an arcane code that may permit government officials to knowingly lie and sometimes force reporters to unknowingly mislead their readers.

This was particularly true during Henry Kissinger's tenure as secretary of state. He raised to the level of an art form the use of the press on a not-for-attribution basis, and many reporters and editors came to resent his machinations.

In 1971 the *Washington Post* did not have a reporter aboard a Kissinger flight home from a conference in the Azores, so the *Post* decided that the trip provided a long-awaited opportunity to scuttle the not-for-attribution briefing. The *Post* said it had learned independently what Kissinger had told reporters on the plane and it was not, therefore, bound to keep his identity secret. The *Post* identified Kissinger as the source of a story that then-President Richard M. Nixon might cancel a forthcoming trip to Moscow if Russia continued to support an Indian assault on Pakistan.

Much outrage ensued, but nothing changed.

Several years later the *Post* published a story on a similar briefing by then-Secretary of State Cyrus Vance. The story didn't name Vance, but it was accompanied by a photo of Vance and a caption using the same identifying phrase as the story: "a senior State Department official."

Much chuckling ensued, but nothing changed.

So, in 1982, when Secretary of State George Shultz flew to Canada, reporters briefed on the plane didn't identify Shultz by name as the source in their stories. Most attributed the briefing to a "senior State Department official" [or a "senior administration official"] "aboard the secretary's plane."

The *New York Times* didn't attribute the briefing to anyone. Its story said, "Reporters aboard Secretary of State George P. Shultz's plane . . . were told. . . ."

Should readers have been able to deduce from the construction that it was Shultz who did the telling?

"I hope so," Bernard Gwertzman, the reporter who wrote the story, told me in an interview.

But he couldn't come right out and say so in print?

"No."

The secretary of state is, of course, but one of many government officials of varying rank who give not-for-attribution briefings. But the press has been no more successful in changing the rules for briefings on the ground than in the air. Not that many journalists have tried all that hard to change those rules.

Hodding Carter says that when he was spokesman for the State Department in the last administration, only three of the "hard-core cadre" of twenty reporters he dealt with regularly would consistently press him to put briefings on the record. Often, Carter says, these three—from the *New York Times,* Associated Press, and United Press International—would argue with him, line by line, asking for full attribution. He respected them for that, he says. But most of their colleagues routinely accepted his ground rules, prohibiting attribution.

In 1971 the *Washington Post* denounced official briefings as "vehicles for the government to give its versions of the news, to use the press as a vehicle for its policy announcements and its political advantage without taking responsibility for what it is saying," in the words of executive editor Benjamin C. Bradlee.

Bradlee decreed that *Post* reporters would insist that all government briefings be "on the record and fully attributable." But that policy, Bradlee says, "didn't last three weeks."

Why not?

"No one [in the media] would go along with us. If the *New York Times,* the *Post,* and the wires [Associated Press and United Press International] agreed [to insist on full attribution at briefings], it would be over, over, over. . . . But we couldn't do it alone."

Why didn't other news organizations support the *Post?* In part because the press does not like to act in formal concert, in part because some editors didn't want the *Post* (and Bradlee) to get credit for any reform that might have resulted from the change, and in part because many reporters and editors worried that a demand for full attribution would eliminate many briefings, which provide reporters with information and insights that are often valuable if they are writing complex, sensitive stories on deadline. Many public officials "just wouldn't talk candidly to the press, even in formal briefings, if their names were going to be printed," says Joe Laitin, who spent seventeen years as a press spokesman for various government agencies in Washington.

Is Laitin right?

Most Washington journalists interviewed for this story agreed that many government officials would be more cautious if their names were always attached to their statements. But few journalists thought this would actually reduce the flow of news.

Jack Nelson, Washington bureau chief for the *Los Angeles Times,* said any changes would be in form, not substance. Officials might end formal briefings, he said, but they would then just call reporters in individually or in small groups, as many of them already do, to pass along the necessary information—on a not-for-attribution basis.

Bill Kovach of the *New York Times* disagrees. He thinks briefers need reporters as much as reporters need briefers. Without briefings, he says, the government couldn't transmit some of its messages to the public in the form the government desires. Kovach concedes that a demand for fully attributable briefings, or a press boycott of not-for-attribution briefings, would probably, in the short term, reduce the flow of information.

But he is convinced that the bureaucrats would soon realize that to accommodate all the reporters requesting information, they had no choice but to give fully attributable briefings.

Until that millennium is at hand, however, Kovach is taking his own steps to reduce the *New York Times*'s reliance on background briefings in which sources are traditionally not named. In January 1982, for example, the *New York Times* boycotted a briefing, on President Reagan's State of the Union address, by Treasury Secretary Donald Regan and David Stockman, director of the Office of Management and Budget. Reporters attending that briefing were required to identify Regan and Stockman only as "administration officials"—"a term we are trying to avoid at every turn," Kovach said in the memo to his staff.

The briefing was "clearly . . . an effort to shape the first important media presentation of the president's economic program," Kovach wrote to his staff, so the *New York Times* would boycott the briefing in order to emphasize that "we are serious in our effort to keep as much information as possible on the record for our readers and our insistence that we not casually put ourselves in a position where our presentation of material is open to manipulation."

Kovach has tried to extend this philosophy and policy to other briefings. He has urged the paper's Washington reporters to push all background briefers to permit their names to be used. This policy is quite similar to the short-lived 1971 *Washington Post* policy on briefings, but, unlike the *Post*'s policy, it was not announced publicly, just relayed to the *New York Times* staff in Washington by Kovach's memo (with the full support of the paper's executive editor).

A few *New York Times* reporters have invoked the policy and, on infrequent occasion, briefers have agreed to full attribution. But not all the paper's Washington reporters were even aware of the policy when I interviewed them, and most who were aware of it did not seem to have implemented it with any zeal. Of the two dozen or so reporters and bureau chiefs for other papers who were interviewed for this story, only one said he was even aware of the *New York Times* policy.

"If reporters at the [*New York*] *Times* were getting up and saying that at background briefings, I'm sure it would be all over . . . town," said Mel Elfin, Washington bureau chief for *Newsweek*. "I haven't heard a thing about it."

That may be, in part, because reporters from both major wire services and from a few other papers are also occasionally asking that briefings be fully attributed. The requests are sporadic.

So is success. As a result, no single news organization is widely perceived as trying to effect change. But most Washington journalists interviewed for this story said they support the *New York Times*'s (and other news organizations') efforts in this regard.

Washington journalists expressed even more support for another *New York Times* policy on unidentified sources—one more applicable to individual interviews than to mass briefings.

"Several times in recent months reporters in the bureau have been caught in the frustrating and embarrassing position of having a story denied by the same sources responsible [on a background or not-for-attribution basis] for the story," Kovach wrote in a September 28, 1982, memo to this staff. In one of these cases, Kovach said in an interview, a source who had given a *New York Times* reporter a story not only denied the story but publicly criticized the *Times* for having printed it.

This is not exactly unprecedented in Washington. Officials often use the press to float a trial balloon. If reaction is negative, the official denies the story. The *New York Times,* because of its influence, is a more likely recipient of such leaks than any other paper. Indeed, Hodding Carter enjoys saying, " 'The *New York Times* has learned . . .' is one of the great con jobs of America. What it means is someone slapped the document down on the *New York Times*'s desk."

There is, obviously, a certain amount of hyperbole in Carter's statement, but whatever the source of a newspaper story, Kovach thinks the use of the press to float trial balloons is pernicious, and he doesn't want the *New York Times* damaged by it.

"In order to guard against this sort of abuse," Kovach said in a memo, "we must adopt an inflexible rule that anytime a source who gives us information that we publish then publicly denies the story, we [will] publish the name of the source when we publish the denial."

As with Kovach's earlier memo on background briefings, though, most reporters and bureau chiefs at other newspapers in

Washington said they were not aware of this new *Times* policy. Nor did most Washington journalists think it would prove practical, largely because most sources who demand anonymity do so in part so that, if confronted, they can deny having made the unattributed statements.

Nevertheless, there is some feeling in Washington that the *New York Times,* being the *New York Times*—the nation's most influential and authoritative newspaper—just might be able to make some headway in this battle for public accountability of news sources. Not that everyone is ready to fight the battle.

Some reporters seem to like the whole idea of using unnamed sources; it makes them feel part of the decision-making process—a covert, "We're in this together" approach to governance and journalism, in Kovach's words. Newsmagazine reporters often seem most prone to this weakness. Their stories are often suffused with a breathless "insider's" prose, and it comes as no surprise that a 1982 study of national and international stories in a dozen issues of *Time* and *Newsweek* found unnamed sources used in 315 of 388 stories.

Many reporters worry, of course, that any attempt to demand more attribution from news sources will frighten those sources and severely restrict the flow of information—even though most of these same reporters readily concede that more attribution and fewer unidentified sources would make their stories more credible (and serve the public better). Thus, since some reporters are more reluctant than others to push for attribution, it's clear that editors must take the responsibility for bringing about any significant change.

"There's a tendency . . . to single out the reporter and make the reporter the only culprit in the whole drama," says Boccardi of the Associated Press.

But reporters don't have final decision-making authority on stories; editors do. "Editors are putting these stories on the wires," Boccardi says. "Editors are putting these stories in the papers."

Most editors share Boccardi's aversion to the unidentified source, but not all editors are themselves above reproach on this issue. Several years ago, when the American Society of Newspaper Editors polled its members on the problem of stories with unidentified sources, 81 percent said that unnamed sources are less believable than named sources.

But 28 percent of the editors in the survey requested that they not be quoted by name.

3

COVERING CRIME, NAMING NAMES

Alfred E. Lewis. For thirty-five years he covered the police beat for the *Washington Post*. In 1972 he covered the Watergate break-in.

Bob Woodward and Carl Bernstein talk about Lewis briefly in their book *All the President's Men*. Lewis was, they say, "something of a legend in Washington journalism—half-cop, half-reporter, a man who often dressed in a blue regulation Metropolitan Police sweater. . . ."

Half-cop, half-reporter.

For generations that was the role of the typical—the stereotypical—newspaper police reporter. Many—perhaps most—were even more than half-cop; their loyalties, their interests, and their instincts lay with the police, not with their newspapers. The police sweaters they occasionally wore, and the police badges they often carried, were but outer manifestations of their inner allegiances.

Not surprisingly, the police came to look on these reporters, and on the press in general, as part of the police department, as sort of a police auxiliary.

Then came the 1960s and 1970s. Cops were no longer arresting only robbers, rapists, and murderers, but antiwar protesters, campus activists, and civil rights demonstrators as well. Who were the good guys and who were the bad guys? And even when the cops arrested robbers, rapists, and murderers, there were now questions: Was the arrest legal? Was the suspect told his rights? Was the search constitutional?

Valid questions. Important questions. That's what the press said. But the police didn't think so.

Suddenly the police were no longer heroes making the streets safe for women and children. Often they were accused—justifiably—of bigotry, brutality, murder.

Newspapers began to change in the 1960s, too. The increasing complexity and contentiousness of society, and the increasing competition from television, required newspapers to be more probing and analytical, more comprehensive than ever before. Editors wanted more interpretive and investigative stories, and police often found themselves confronted by more liberal, more skeptical reporters than their police-beat predecessors. Newspapers no longer were satisfied with just the police—or the City Hall or the White House—side of a story. Police-press relations became polarized, embittered. Old-time police reporters were as confused—and as angry—at this turn of events as were old-time cops.

I used to work for a city editor, a former police reporter, who reminded many people of a cop. He was the sort of fellow who delighted in telling the young reporters on his staff about the various murders he'd covered and the various executions he'd witnessed. He seemed to have almost perfect recall of all the stories he'd written, and as he recited them to us, I noticed that they were almost invariably filled with such words as "grisly" and "grim" and "grotesque" and "bizarre" and "macabre" and "brutal." He said each word with relish—like the stereotypical, hard-boiled cop. One story, on a hanging, had been headlined "Jerked to Jesus," he proudly told us. Another story, on a murder investigation, began, he said, "Homicide detectives today labored in the twilight world of sexual perversion, looking for. . . ."

This editor was a bright, warm, generous man who quickly became my friend as well as my editor, and he told me that if he ever wrote a book about his journalistic career, it would be titled *Make Mine Murder*. Murder was his favorite subject and his favorite story, and cops were his favorite sources. But in the 1960s and 1970s, editors began to lose interest in murder stories, and reporters began to lose confidence in cops.

My friend didn't altogether understand this new breed of journalist at first. He didn't understand the reporter who wouldn't automatically believe a cop over a black militant or an accused killer; he didn't understand why any reporter would want to write a three-part series on the abuse of psychological testing in private industry when he could be covering a juicy murder. In time, my friend came to appreciate both kinds of journalism. But not everyone kept such an open mind. Journalism, like society, was changing, and a whole range of compromises had to be reached. Society is still changing. For the past several years, crime has again been a big story. But new reporters are covering it differently; reporters and readers alike are asking new questions, about invasion of privacy and sensationalism and racism. Just as police behavior was often questioned in the 1960s and 1970s, so the media's behavior is being questioned in the 1980s.

*   *   *

T EENAGE THUGS—juveniles—savagely beat and gang-rape a woman.
How prominently should newspapers display the story? How much detail should they give in describing the rape and the beating? Should they publish the names of the juvenile suspects when they are arrested? Should the name of the woman victim be published? Should newspapers identify the suspects or the victim by race?

As violent crime continues to increase throughout the United States, editors confront these questions with growing frequency, growing uneasiness, and, in some cases, growing disagreement.

Some editors—and some reporters (and some readers as well)—say newspapers have overplayed violent crime altogether in the last few years. In the 1960s and 1970s, these critics say, newspapers were blessed with the best of all possible journalistic worlds. The big stories of the day—race riots, social protests, Vietnam, Watergate, the hostages in Iran—were not only socially significant but dramatic as well. Newspapers could satisfy their readers' blood lust while simultaneously giving them serious news on important issues.

Thus, newspaper crime coverage remained relatively constant in those years—increasing from only 6 percent to 12 percent in each of nine major cities from 1948 to 1978, according to a study by the Center for Urban Affairs and Policy Research at Northwestern University.

But the big story of the early 1980s—the faltering economy—does not generally lend itself to dramatic treatment, and, especially in cities with competing newspapers (or failing newspapers), some editors think they see the beginning of a return to the sensationalism of the late nineteenth century and the first half of the twentieth century. The lurid tales of rape and robbery and murder and mayhem that were splashed across the front pages daily back then may be returning now in some cities.

As Reg Murphy, publisher of the Sunpapers in Baltimore, said in 1982, "Every study shows that papers increase their circulation when they begin to deal with crime stories."

The danger inherent in this approach, warns sociologist Marshall Clinard in his book *Sociology of Deviant Behavior*, is that newspapers can help create "a crime-centered culture [in which] . . . crime often seems more prevalent than it really is."

Studies going back as far as fifty years have shown that, as an analysis at Arizona State Univerity concluded in 1982, "A newspaper can start a crime wave independent of crime rates."

The result: People become frightened. They refuse to leave their homes at night. They move from the inner city. They vote for law-and-order demagogues. They buy guns. Violence, fear, and alienation become self-perpetuating.

Early in 1982 several reporters at the *Los Angeles Times* were sufficiently concerned about their paper's increased crime coverage to bring it up during a regular meeting with the paper's top editors. As an example of what they saw as the *Times*'s recent overemphasis on crime, one reporter cited a day when every story but one on the front page of the paper's local news section involved crime.

"There seems to have been an increase in the amount of crime and violence coverage and the intensity with which it is covered [in the *Times*]," another reporter told the editors. "Is this just happening [haphazardly] or is it a [conscious] decision made by the editors to focus attention on crime in the community?"

The editors' answer: There had, indeed, been "a conscious decision . . . to focus attention on crime in the community." For many years, the editors said, the *Times* had underplayed crime. In fact, a study I conducted in 1977 showed that the *Times* published fewer crime stories on page one than did any other major paper in the country.

But crime, especially violent crime, is now pervasive in American society, despite a small decrease in the past year or so. U.S. Justice Department statistics show that violent crime increased 60 percent in the decade of the 1970s; in Los Angeles alone, violent crime increased almost 70 percent from 1975 to 1980. *Times* editors concede that the paper may overplay it occasionally now, but they insist that violent crime is a legitimate story, one that both interests readers and illuminates an important, contemporary social problem.

Most editors elsewhere agree.

Although violent crime is sometimes sensationalized by "desperate editors . . . reaching for anything they can . . . on newspapers with decreasing circulations," *Boston Globe* editor Thomas Winship said he thinks violent crime has become "such an overpowering, tragic fact of life today that I'm not sure you. can overplay it."

In December 1981 the *New York Times* conducted a poll on the most serious problems facing New York. More people cited crime than anything else—more than inflation, unemployment, housing, transportation, taxes, schools, and the environment *combined.*

After that poll, said Allan M. Siegal, news editor of the *New York Times,* "A bunch of us [editors] went to lunch . . . and asked ourselves and each other, 'Are we treating this [crime] the way we treated the civil rights revolution when we realized that was a historic period in the American experience? Are we treating crime the way we treated inflation when we realized it was a serious . . . factor in people's lives?'

"The answer was 'No.'

"We're not going to sensationalize crime . . . now," Siegal says, "but we are . . . trying to conceive and execute in some depth stories on how crime influences people's lives."

Adolph S. Ochs, former publisher of the *New York Times,* was once quoted as saying, "When a tabloid prints it [crime and scandal], that's smut. When the *Times* prints it, that's sociology." But at the *New York Times,* as at other papers, editors are not always so certain of those distinctions on the crime beat.

Once the decision is made to cover crime more thoroughly, a whole range of questions present themselves, not the least of which involve matters of taste.

Although violent crime accounts for only about 10 percent of the crime in this country, a Northwestern University study shows that newspapers have traditionally devoted about 70 percent of their crime coverage to it; that means editors frequently have to make decisions about how much detail to publish on blood and gore and sexual abuse.

In recent years some newspapers have reported violent crimes in considerable detail, even publishing such gamy details on sex crimes as "a semen-stained napkin" (*New York Times*); ". . . She grabbed his genitals with both hands," (*Arizona Daily Star*); "Parks then inserted a bar of soap into her vagina" (*Nashville Banner*); "[They] . . . sodomized her and forced her to commit oral copulation [and he] . . . urinated on her" (*Los Angeles Times*); and "They leaned me against the outside of the car, and . . . raped me vaginally and rectally . . . I was bleeding a lot from my rectum and both of them were rubbing their penises over my face, spreading the blood on it" (*Sacramento* [Calif.] *Bee*).

In contrast, a *Trenton* (N.J.) *Times* story reporting on a brutal rape used such general phrases as "the severity of the crime," "grotesque," "repugnant," "animals," and "nightmare of terror" without ever specifying just what made this rape more "repugnant" or "grotesque" than any other.

Charles Bailey, former editor of the *Minneapolis Star and Tribune,* echoed many of his colleagues when he said he favors "a strong general principle" in reporting the details of violent crimes in general and of sex crimes in particular: "When in doubt, leave it out."

When reporting sex crimes, many editors feel that providing too much detail can not only offend readers but can also embarrass victims, prolong their psychological trauma, and perhaps even encourage attacks by sex offenders eager to acquire what one sociologist terms "a reputation for aggression and 'masculine' virility."

But reporting that is devoid of detail may not be good reporting, and it may do the victim (and society) a disservice.

In 1977 an Australian sociologist wrote of a rape trial in which a professional courtroom observer, whom he interviewed, said she was "startled at the discrepancy between what of importance she thought was happening and what she read the following day in the newspapers.

"That the victim had been menstruating at the time of the charged assault and that her tampon had been pushed deep into the vaginal channel was taken by the viewer as not unpersuasive evidence . . . that she [the victim] had not consented," the sociologist wrote. But the media "made no mention of this fact," thus presenting a story that was "more favorable to the defendant than the court proceedings justified."

So how much potentially offensive detail should a newspaper furnish? Sometimes the answer depends on how essential the detail is to the specific story. Sometimes there are broader questions to be considered.

"I don't want to give so much detail that we turn readers off or turn the lip-smackers on," said Norman Cherniss, executive editor of the *Riverside* (Calif.) *Press-Enterprise,* "but I want to find a balance between that . . . and leaving readers with . . . no awareness of what goes on in the jungle . . . out there today."

Indeed some editors argue that only by providing specific, graphic detail in covering violent sex crimes can readers be made to face the brutal realities of these crimes and, thus, be alerted to protect themselves against them. That was publisher David Seaton's thinking in 1981 when he permitted his *Winfield* (Kan.) *Courier* to publish a detailed account of court testimony in a rape case. The *Courier* story included such testimony as "[the man] entered her rectum" and "I . . . kept moving my pelvis so he couldn't penetrate."

Seaton might have been able to get away with that in a large, more cosmopolitan city, but in Winfield, Kansas (population 11,000), he was immediately bombarded with calls and letters of outrage.

The National News Council looked into complaints against the *Courier* and rejected as "unwarranted" the charge that the paper's reporting had been "sensationalized." But the News Council did say the paper's story "raises issues of needlessly explicit reporting and its impact on the victims, their families, and the community."

Seaton said he had run the detailed story because he thought the people of Winfield should "know how severe rape cases are. I felt the town was very reluctant to face the danger . . . I took the view we ought not to cover up."

Now Seaton is not so sure that's the paper's role. "As a result of everything that took place, the protest and the soul-searching . . . [I realize] there's a limit to the amount a daily newspaper can do to expose the detailed truth of what takes place in a rape," he said.

But sexually explicit details were not all that caused Seaton problems in that story; neither are they the only problems other editors face when trying to decide how specific violent-crime stories should be. Racial identification is also a sensitive—and potentially explosive—issue.

In the *Winfield Courier* case, the newspaper identified the man accused of committing the rape as being black. One of his victims had told her children about the rape but had only done so in general terms, omitting [among other things] her assailant's race.

Although the paper did not identify either victim by name, in a small town like Winfield, many townspeople easily figured out who they were. That forced at least one of the victims to go into more detail on the rape than she had wanted to with her children—especially since one, an adopted son, was black.

Blacks are involved in crime—as perpetrators *and* as victims—in numbers disproportionate to their population. To examine the underlying causes of that phenomenon is a valid and valuable journalistic function, and a few major papers have been doing just that of late. But most editors say that to identify individual criminals (or victims) by race in a routine crime story is not only gratuitous but likely to contribute to the perpetuation of harmful and unjustifiable racial stereotypes.

There are, however, some cases in which racial identification is appropriate—as, for example, in the identification of a suspect by race as part of a complete physical description provided by police while the suspect is still at large. That description could alert citizens to possible personal danger and also, perhaps, help police capture the suspect.

But such descriptions should only be used if they are truly complete, if they would actually help identify a specific individual rather than a whole racial group. Racial identifications that are so vague and sketchy as to be useless should not be published.

"In the old days we'd say the cops were looking for 'a 5-foot-7-inch black,' " said Benjamin C. Bradlee, executive editor of the *Washington Post.* "No more. Now we want more detail or we won't use the racial identification."

Editors also agree that racial identification is legitimate when a crime has racial implications. If a gang of white men beat up a black man and shout racial epithets at him because he came into their neighborhood, race obviously must be mentioned in the story.

Sometimes, in fact, race must be mentioned because a crime, or some incident, takes place under circumstances that would generally indicate racial implications but in which, this time, there are no such implications. If, for example, white and black gangs have been feuding violently for several months in a particular neighborhood known for racial animosities, stories on a fight between two black gangs in that neighborhood with no racial overtones whatever should make clear that race was not· involved. The only way to do that might be to identify the combatants by race.

Perhaps the most difficult problem for all editors—and reporters—in covering crime stories is the identification of victims by name.

"Putting a . . . victim's name in the paper is one of the least pleasant aspects of an editor's job," one editor said, and indeed a small but growing number of journalists are beginning to ask if victims should ever be identified in crime stories except in the most sensational or celebrated cases.

What social purpose is served, those journalists ask, by reporting that John Green was the victim of an armed robbery? It embarrasses Green, lets other would-be robbers know that he is vulnerable, and may open him to reprisals by the original robber. A crime victim whose name is in the paper may also be subjected to harassment and threats and to unwanted solicitations by security service companies.

If editors want to alert the community to the dangers of crime, isn't it sufficient, critics ask, to report that a robbery took place in a particular neighborhood at a particular time? What does the specific name of the victim add to the story other than an element of danger to someone who has already been victimized?

In 1982, for example, the *Lexington* (Ky.) *Leader* published a short story on a man stabbing a woman. The story included the woman's name, address, and place of employment. Since the assailant was still at large, might not such information have made it easy for him to attack her again, to try to silence her as a witness should he ever be arrested?

"It's something to think about," conceded Steve Wilson, then editor of the *Leader*. "If she's assaulted a second time by the same guy in her home . . . or where she works . . . we'll really have to think about it."

Won't it be a little late then?

Wilson admitted that it might be and, on reflection, he said, "In the future, when we have an assault victim like this . . . we probably won't use the name and address."

Most major papers already avoid publishing specific addresses of crime victims—and witnesses, too. But sometimes those policies are inadvertently violated.

In the fall of 1980 the *Los Angeles Times* published not only the name and address but also the photograph of a woman who had helped police identify two suspects in the slaying of one California Highway Patrol officer and the wounding of another. One reader wrote a letter to the editor of the paper accusing the paper of "sheer, unmitigated stupidity and irresponsible journalism" in that story. The *Times*'s top editors, at a loss to explain why the reporter put the sensitive information in her story and why her editors left it in (and added the photo), said they were inclined to agree with the letter-writer (and had, in fact, made the same criticism themselves as soon as they had seen that day's paper).

(The editor in charge of this story subsequently tried to defend her decision on the grounds that the woman's name and address had previously been disclosed in a press conference and in other media. But that seems insufficient justification for exposing her to potential reprisals and harassment. Fleeting mention of a name or an address on television isn't the same as a permanent record in the newspaper. Moreover, just because the woman chose to expose herself is no reason for an otherwise responsible newspaper to compound that error.)

This problem is not limited to crime-ridden big cities, though. Traditionally, newspapers in small towns have been much more likely than their big-city brethren to print specific addresses in all kinds of stories, crime stories included. Last year a group of citizens in Racine, Wisconsin, complained to the National News Council about the publication of crime victims' addresses in the newspaper stories, and at about the same time, a White House task force recommended that the addresses (and telephone numbers) of crime victims and witnesses be kept secret unless a court decides otherwise. That kind of secrecy can be abused by those in power, of course, but the task force's reasoning was that this might alleviate the fear some victims and witnesses have of reprisal after their testimony in court.

In an effort to minimize this problem many papers, in cities large and small, now publish instead only block numbers—"in the 4800 block of Elm Street," for example. But this practice seems to render a victim only slightly less vulnerable than would publication of the specific address.

Editors whose papers publish block numbers defend the practice as essential to making people aware of crime problems in their immediate neighborhoods. But block numbers (like names, ages, and occupations) are primarily published to give readers a point of reference and personal identification—a reason to read a given story: "Oh, Cousin Bob lives on that street." Or, "Gee, a sixty-one-year-old woman was mugged coming out of the grocery store. I'm a sixty-one-year-old woman, too; I'd better be careful when I go shopping." Or, best of all; "I know him."

Thus, the vast majority of editors, even those who think that printing either specific addresses or block numbers in crime stories is irresponsible, flatly reject any suggestion that they not publish the names of most crime victims. Newspapers, they say, are in the business of printing news, not withholding it. Sometimes, in cases involving a clear and present danger to personal safety or national security, information should be withheld. But that should be the exception, not the rule. In an open society, most editors say, newspapers would create more problems than they would solve by withholding the names of crime victims simply because of what someone might do.

Names make news. It's the oldest maxim in the reporter's notebook. Specifics are what make a story believable and readable. And publishing names can also prevent—or help dispel—rumors about innocent, uninvolved people. Withholding names may trigger such rumors and, in some cases, invite charges of a cover-up (to protect an editor's friend, a big advertiser, a powerful politician). The result: A society that is even more cynical and disillusioned than it is now.

But, as with all rules, there are exceptions to the rule of using names, cases in which newspapers routinely withhold the names of individuals involved in crimes. The most common such instance involves juveniles. Almost without exception, newspapers do not publish the names of juvenile crime victims or offenders unless they are prosecuted as adults (and/or unless the heinous or public nature of the crime, or some other circumstance, makes identification advisable or unavoidable). $\partial\partial 3$/oη

It can be argued, of course, that many juvenile offenders should be identified by name, both to enable their neighbors to take precautionary measures and to embarrass and thus, perhaps, deter both the juvenile involved and other potential juvenile offenders from committing future crimes.

But editors generally feel, and in many states the courts have ruled, that publication of a juvenile's name unjustly exposes him to a lifelong social stigma. This desire to avoid social stigma is what has prompted most newspapers and, in past years, a few state legislatures as well to take a similar attitude toward the publication of the names of rape victims.

Early laws prohibiting the publication of the names of rape victims were limited to Southern states where they were probably racist in origin, according to sociologist Gilbert Geis of the University of California, Irvine. "Miscegenous rape always has played a powerful role in defining the ingredients and parameters of the law of rape," Geis has written.

A Northern state—Wisconsin—passed a similar law in 1925, but in 1975 the U.S. Supreme Court ruled, by an 8–1 margin, that the First Amendment entitles the news media to identify rape victims whose names are available in "official court records open to public inspection."

In 1980 the Kentucky General Assembly tried to make it impossible to print the names of rape victims anyway; a bill was introduced in the assembly to make it illegal for law enforcement agencies to disclose the identities of rape victims. The bill was designed to protect victims of rape and other sex crimes from public humiliation, but Kentucky newspaper editors argued that it would also undermine the average citizen's right to find out about these crimes (and to knowledgeably question police tactics and practices in the investigation of the crimes). ". . . [T]he officer who treats rape victims callously—or even illegally—is home free [under this bill]," the *Lexington Herald* editorialized at the time. "Such an officer is free to operate in secrecy—a secrecy guaranteed by law. He can never be held accountable by the public he supposedly serves."

The bill was killed in committee.

But that doesn't mean that Kentucky newspapers routinely identify rape victims by name. Both the Kentucky Press Association and most of the state's individual news organizations, like the vast majority of news organizations throughout the United States, have formal policies against identifying rape victims by name in most cases.

Several editors disagree with this position, though, and arguments over the issue are often heated.

Interestingly, this disagreement does not divide along expected lines. One might expect that big-city newspapers, often regarded as being callous and insulated from the feelings of their readers by the very size of their circulation areas, would be the least sensitive to the problems of individual rape victims. But according to a 1982 study by Carol Oukrop, associate professor of journalism at Kansas State University, that's not necessarily true. This study showed that only 30 percent of 128 small newspapers (under 10,000 circulation) strongly agreed that adult rape victims' names should be withheld from publication, but 51 percent of 106 large papers (more than 50,000 circulation) strongly agreed with the proposition.

A hypothetical story: A man comes home and finds his wife has been raped. The rapist is still in the house. The husband, in a blind rage, beats the rapist to death with a baseball bat, then runs off. When police catch the husband, they arrest him, pending further investigation.

Question: Although most newspapers do not publish the names of rape victims, how does a newspaper cover that story without either implicitly or explicitly identifying the rape victim?

Naming the husband would seem unavoidable since he has been arrested in a homicide case. But if the husband is named in the story, anyone who knows the family will know the wife's identity. And if the rape were left out of the story, the husband looks as if, unprovoked, he savagely murdered someone.

Another hypothetical case: A man is arrested for raping the police chief's daughter, and while he's being booked, police officers beat him up.

Question: How does a newspaper cover that story without either implicitly or explicitly identifying the rape victim?

If the chief's name isn't used in the story, there's no explanation for the police brutality. If the chief's name *is* used, his daughter's identity becomes obvious.

These are hypothetical but not altogether unlikely situations in a country where rape is increasing at an alarming rate—and where, as elsewhere in the world, rape victims are still stigmatized, still unfairly regarded in some quarters as having somehow contributed to their own plight.

That long-standing stigma is the main reason most American newspapers prohibit the identification of rape victims by name unless there is what John McMullan, former executive editor of the *Miami Herald,* calls "compelling justification" for doing so.

Most newspapers will identify a rape victim, for example, if she is killed in the assault; editors reason that murder must be reported in full and that a dead victim obviously cannot suffer the stigma or harassment that prevents papers from identifying living rape victims.

Many newspapers also identify a rape victim if she's a celebrity (as in the rape of singer Connie Francis) or if there is something so notorious about the rape that identifying the victim is the only way to satisfy legitimate public curiosity or to dispel widespread rumors. Some papers also identify rape victims if a case comes to trial and the victim testifies in open court. Editors of these papers say there's no reason to withhold a victim's name if anyone can walk into court and listen to her testimony.

But most editors say there's no comparison between the few dozen people who might crowd into a courtroom and the hundreds of thousands who read the next day's paper. Publishing a rape victim's name just because she testifies in court serves only to satisfy the morbid curiosity of some of these readers.

"Rape is a crime that stigmatizes the victim far more than any other," says Paul Janensch, executive editor of the *Louisville Courier-Journal and Times.* "It's archaic and unfair for the woman . . . so we don't identify them . . . not even if the case comes to court."

A few editors insist, however, that rape victims should be routinely identified—and at least one of these editors is a woman.

"As long as we do not report the names of [rape] victims, we are perpetuating the mythology that the rape victim is somehow to blame for what happened to her, which is just dead wrong," says Eileen Shanahan, senior assistant managing editor of the *Pittsburgh Post-Gazette.* "The only way to get rid of this wrongheaded . . . concept . . . ," she says, "is to treat it [rape] like any other crime."

Although Shanahan's own paper has a policy against identifying rape victims, Gilbert Geis, a California sociologist who has studied rape reporting in the media, thinks her position is valid. "I believe that anonymity plays directly into the sniggering innuendos that surround rape," he says. "The anonymity provision suggests that the public will in some subtle or not so subtle manner conclude that the victim in a way contributed to her own fate . . . and that her reputation will be compromised."

Until fifteen or twenty years ago, most newspapers contributed heavily to the stigma rape victims suffered, in part by not even using the word "rape." They used the term "criminal assault" or some other euphemism, as if the very word "rape" carried some shameful connotation for the victim.

Even today, newspaper stories on rape often omit the word "rape," especially from their headlines: "$50,000 bail set in kidnap case in Fall River" (*Providence Journal*), "Man Accused of Assaulting 'Most Eligible' " *(Omaha World-Herald)*, "Abduction suspect charged with burglary" *(Dallas Times Herald)*. The *Los Angeles Times* published a brief story on a rape in 1981 that not only omitted "rape" from the headline ("Kidnapped Woman, 18, Freed in Sierra After Car Is Snowbound"), but also said the victim of the rape "was not seriously wounded."

Although the reporter says he meant the woman had not suffered "great bodily injury" of the sort that indicates a severe physical beating, angry letter-writers saw his phrasing in the story—and his editor's failure to change it—as typical of the media's traditionally "insensitive . . . ridiculous . . . very destructive and unsympathetic" attitude toward rape victims.

Other critics raised another point. The *L.A. Times* has a policy against identifying rape victims by name, but this victim was named. Why?

The reporter says he remembers discussing the issue with an editor, but he can't remember why they decided she should be identified. The editor says he does not remember either the discussion or the story. Two other editors who generally edit such stories say they did not edit this one. No one knows why the paper's policy was violated.

Newspaper policies are far from infallible, of course. Despite the best intentions, names may slip through. Sometimes the name of a rape victim's mother or husband or daughter will be printed, making identification of the victim herself inevitable. Other times a paper will print a rape victim's name because the other media in town have already done so.

But some editors think the whole question of trying to protect rape victims with a shield of anonymity is reminiscent of the way society used to regard victims of cancer. Until relatively recently, having cancer was regarded in many quarters as, somehow, shameful—a disease in which "the patient . . . is made [to feel] culpable," as Susan Sontag writes in *Illness as Metaphor*.

Bringing the fight against cancer out into the open has greatly alleviated, if not eliminated, this stigma. Many rape counselors feel the same should happen with rape victims. Some counselors even encourage rape victims to let newspapers use their names. But these counselors insist that, ultimately, that decision should be left up to the individual woman involved. As Hannah Evans, a Denver psychologist who has counseled rape victims for ten years and was herself raped in 1982, says, "There is no reason we should feel ashamed. But I don't want to have the newspaper making that decision for each woman. If a woman is able to take the heat . . . Okay. . . . But if she doesn't want that . . . she should have that option."

Increasingly, some women—especially younger women, who are less intimidated by the old taboos on the subject—are telling their rape stories to the press under their own names.

In 1981 a Washington woman wrote a story for the *Washington Post* under the headline, "The Night I Was Raped." Four days later the *Boston Globe* published a front-page interview with a nurse who had been raped by three doctors a year earlier. In San Francisco a television reporter told the press about having been raped and knifed in her Berkeley home. In Los Angeles actress Diane McBain disclosed that she had been raped on Christmas Day 1982; she said she had been "greatly helped by having heard horrible stories of women going through things like this before," and she thought that by going public with the story of her own rape, she might be able to help other rape victims deal with their own trauma.

Some editors think it is wrong to permit rape victims to decide when and if their names should be published, though; no one else the press writes about has that opportunity. In fact, Claude Sitton, editorial director of the *Raleigh* (N.C.) *News and Observer* and the *Raleigh Times,* says the entire approach most papers take toward rape smacks of a double standard.

In reporting virtually all other crimes, Sitton says, newspapers publish the names of both the accuser and the accused. But in rape cases, most papers print only the name of the accused, and Sitton says that implicitly suggests to the readers that the paper believes the accuser (the victim) even before the trial has begun. "We feel it is wrong and unethical—and I emphasize the word *unethical* —to pass judgment on a person charged with rape until he . . . is found to be guilty by the judicial process," Sitton says.

Why not solve this dilemma by omitting the names of suspect and victim alike—at least until guilt or innocence is established in a court of law?

A few papers do that, but most editors think that's a mistake. It mythologizes rape, they say, creating even more stigma for the victim and more satisfaction for some rapists and would-be rapists.

Sitton says his papers have tried to balance the conflicting demands of fairness and privacy by not naming a rape victim until a specific suspect has been arrested and formally charged. At that point, Sitton says, the rape victim becomes "a complaining witness . . . and we use the names of complaining witnesses . . . in crimes . . . unless they're juveniles."

Only a few editors around the country support this position—and most of them have been berated, boycotted, and denounced. Don Marsh, editor of the *Charleston* (W. Va.) *Gazette,* says there was "almost universal external condemnation" when he ordered the identification of rape victims in his paper. Reluctantly, he yielded to pressure and reinstated the old policy of not naming rape victims. But he continues to think "it is ridiculous to have trials and not to name the accuser."

The more common view among editors, however, is that naming a rape suspect but not his victim does not imply the suspect is guilty. They say readers recognize the withholding of a rape victim's name as a sensitive, humanitarian gesture designed to protect the victim's privacy—not as a legal judgment.

Moreover, despite recent improvements in society's treatment of rape victims, rape counselors say it is still the victim, not the suspect, who is most often prejudged—the victim, not the suspect, who must prove innocence. Newspapers should not contribute to this continuing traumatization by publishing rape victims' names.

"When a woman gets raped, one of her very first reactions is to feel a total lack of control over her life," says Margaret Gordon, a former journalist who is now chairman of the national advisory committee to the U.S. Secretary of Health and Human Services on the prevention and control of rape. "One important way for her to feel she's regaining control . . . is to have control over who knows she was raped. If a newspaper prints her name, she loses that control."

Many rape victims whose rapes became widely known say they subsequently received obscene and harassing telephone calls, threats, obscene letters, taunts, leers, and vulgar sexual propositions. Worse, they worry that the man who raped them will return to try to silence them—or that some other rapist will decide they're fair (and easy) game.

Because of these fears, most experts who work with rape victims are convinced that if newspapers routinely printed victims' names, far fewer victims would report their rapes to police. It is generally agreed that only a small percentage of rape victims actually report their rapes to police anyway. In recent years, as the stigma of having been raped has diminished somewhat, that percentage has been increasing. This growing willingness to report rape, along with an increase in the actual incidence of rape, explains why U.S. Justice Department statistics show the number of rapes quadrupling, from about 21,000 in 1964 to more than 82,000 in 1980.

"There's no doubt in my mind this [progress in persuading rape victims to go to the police] would be reversed and that many victims wouldn't report their rapes if their names were going to be published," says William Heiman, chief of the rape prosecution unit in the Philadelphia district attorney's office.

In 1982, Andrew Rutherford, a senior lecturer in law at the University of Southampton, England, told an international conference on criminal justice that he thought increases in rape statistics in England in recent years could be directly attributed to a 1975 law that made it illegal for newspapers there to publish the names of rape victims.

In 1975, Rutherford said, there were 1,040 rapes reported in England. In 1980 there were 1,225—an increase of 17.8 percent.

"I think the increase . . . is due more to . . . increased reporting of rape than to an actual increase in the crime . . . of rape," Rutherford told me.

But when pressed for further statistics, Rutherford said there were 884 rapes reported in 1970—which means the increase from 1970 to 1975 (*before* the enactment of the law prohibiting publication of rape victims' names) was 17.6 percent, almost identical to the percentage increase in reporting *after* the law was passed.

Doesn't this indicate that the legal guarantee of anonymity for rape victims has actually had no measurable effect on the willingness of rape victims to go to the police?

"I admit it's a little ambiguous," Rutherford conceded. "I share your skepticism."

So does Michael Rouse, managing editor of the *Durham* (N.C.) *Herald*.

That's why his paper has a policy, drafted after a series of meetings with three women and two men on the staff, requiring that an adult (but not a juvenile) rape victim be identified when the state issues a warrant against a specific suspect.

Rape is a difficult crime to prove oneself innocent of, Rouse said, and he worries about a man who's accused of rape, identified by name in the paper, and then acquitted—but stigmatized for life because he was identified as a rape suspect.

If a suspect pleads guilty, there is no reason to identify the victim, says Herbert J. Obermayer, editor and publisher of the *Northern Virginia Sun*. But in what Obermayer calls a "credibility contest"—"He says 'No,' she says 'Yes' "—Obermayer thinks the identities of both victim and suspect should be published.

The American judicial system guarantees anyone accused of a crime the right to confront his accuser, and Obermayer, Rouse, and several other editors believe the newspaper is an integral part of the public arena in which that confrontation should take place. Rouse cites a case in which a young man was charged with raping the daughter of the mayor of a town near Durham. The charge didn't hold up, and the young man and his family then sued the mayor and the police department for false arrest.

"The issues in the case involved serious questions of the abuse of police power—questions that are certainly in the realm of the public interest," Rouse's paper editorialized in one of a sixteen-part series of editorials on the naming of rape victims.

"How would a newspaper report that case without identifying [at least implicitly] the complainant who made the rape allegation?" the editorial asked.

Sometimes the publication of a rape victim's name can actually save a man from going to jail.

In July 1980, Raymond Randle, Jr., a Berkeley police officer, was accused of having forced Susan Bird to perform oral copulation on him in the men's room of a San Francisco disco. Randle, who was off-duty at the time, testified that Bird had performed that act willingly—for $6. The jury didn't believe him. He was convicted and sentenced to three years in prison.

The *San Francisco Chronicle* has a general policy of not using the names of rape victims, but because this was a court case and involved a police officer, the paper decided to use Bird's name when it reported the verdict in the trial. When the *Chronicle* story appeared, a real estate man from a San Francisco suburb recognized Bird's name and called authorities. Subsequent investigation turned up seventeen men willing to sign affidavits saying Bird had a well-established reputation for dishonesty and for soliciting sex for money.

Women who solicit sex for money can be raped, too, of course—they often are—but in this case, the state Court of Appeals ruled unanimously in 1982 that the new evidence on Bird "tends to destroy her testimony by raising grave doubts about her veracity and credibility."

The appellate court reversed Randle's conviction and said the trial judge should have granted a new trial. The San Francisco district attorney's office then dismissed the case "in the interest of justice."

Does that mean newspapers should routinely publish the names of rape victims to avoid such a miscarriage of justice?

Most editors think not.

"Maybe one out of 500 rape cases falls in that category," says Beverly Kees, executive editor of the *Grand Forks* (N.D.) *Herald*. "You can't print the names of 499 victims just to save that one innocent guy."

And what of a newspaper's own credibility?

Many years ago, one Florida editor told of having reported a robbery and beating in his newspaper. The victims were identified by name. Subsequent investigation showed that the woman had also been raped.

As Marc A. Franklin wrote in the *Stanford Law Review:* "Since the newspaper had already given the name of the woman it felt obliged to discontinue its coverage of the case [to avoid identifying her publicly as a rape victim]." But the woman involved was "the mistress of a prominent local businessman, and rumor spread that in fact he had gotten drunk and beaten her and that the paper had dropped the story because of his influence.''

In that case, the woman, her lover, and the newspaper all suffered because the newspaper adhered rigidly to its policy.

Every editor I interviewed for this study says the editor of that paper just made a bad decision. Several editors said they have acted differently under similar circumstances.

One editor said that when a rape was disclosed after a woman had already been identified in his paper as having been the victim of a related crime, he published her name in connection with the rape, too: "It was unavoidable then unless you wanted to look silly.''

But another editor, faced with an almost identical case, said he just dropped the woman's name from all ensuing stories once he learned she had been raped. "It [his decision] was academic by then,'' he admits. "People probably remembered her name from our first story and put two and two together. But I thought it was the only decent thing to do anyway.''

What these complicated cases and differences of opinion really prove, many editors say, is that newspaper polices on the identification of rape victims, like newspaper policies on virtually everything else, must be more flexible. Too often, newspapers blindly apply rigid policies without considering individual cases independently.

"These are matters of editorial judgment, not matters of statutory law,'' says Charles Bailey, former editor of the *Minneapolis Star and Tribune*.

Or, as William German, executive editor of the *San Francisco Chronicle*, puts it; "I hate to say 'never' on anything. It's only 'never' until proven otherwise.''

4

COVERING THE COURTS

"Special writers." That's what they are called at the *Los Angeles Times,* and the nomenclature is similar at other newspapers. It's not necessarily that their writing is so "special"— although sometimes it is. They're given their title because they're specialists. Most reporters—known in the trade as "general assignment reporters"—cover different stories all the time. A fire. A murder. A press conference. A neighborhood feud. But "special writers" have special beats. They write only about medicine or education or politics or religion or the environment, day after day and story after story.

Some of these writers have special training. Lawrence Altman, medical writer for the *New York Times,* has a medical degree, for example. Russell Chandler, a religion writer for the *Los Angeles Times,* is an ordained minister. Other "special writers" at these and other papers have studied, formally or informally, the subjects they cover. The best special writers read voraciously in the technical literature of the field, meet regularly with qualified experts, and attend conferences, seminars, and symposia.

This trend toward specialization has been growing over the past two decades, but it is not universally acclaimed. Some journalists think the concept of the reporter-as-generalist would serve the reader better. The generalist, they argue, is more likely to ask the kind of simple but important question the average reader wants answered. The specialist may be too deeply involved—and too sophisticated—in his subject to realize that he must supply his readers with basic, fundamental information in each story. The medical writer may forget that his typical reader isn't exactly certain what DNA is. The environmental writer may forget that her typical reader hasn't memorized the current list of endangered species. The religion writer may forget that not everyone is as familiar with the Bible as he has come to be.

For some special writers, the danger is just the opposite. They know they are dealing with complex material, and in trying to simplify that material for their general readership, they often inadvertently oversimplify or sensationalize or distort what they report. This can be particularly dangerous in the fields of science and medicine, in part because the typical newspaper reader has few, if any, alternative sources of information for most stories in those fields. What he or she reads in the newspaper (or sees on television or hears on the radio) is often his or her only exposure to the story. When I wrote a story on science and medical writers several years ago, I was appalled by the irresponsible treatment the press gave such important subjects as birth-control pills, breast X-rays, cancer "cures," vitamin "C" as a "cure" for the common cold, earthquake predictions, the dangers of caffeine, megavitamins as a treatment for schizophrenia, new "breakthroughs" in genetics . . . the list went on and on, and one prominent scientist I interviewed told me, "When there's a science story in the newspaper that I know something about, it almost invariably will lack perspective and be a very distorted account."

Although some journalists argue that newspaper reporters should all be generalists—covering a political rally one day, a scientific discovery the next, a baseball game the next—most agree that in this age of specialization, the world has become too complex for that approach. If newspapers are to avoid distortion, and provide perspective, on important, complicated stories, they must assign many of those stories to specialists. Sure, a good reporter ought to be able to cover almost any story, but too many subjects are now too complex to permit even the best reporters to drift in and out on a daily basis and still be able to understand and to report intelligently all the issues involved in many areas.

The courtroom is a good example. It used to be regarded as an easy place for a young reporter to break in. A young reporter can still cover the courts, of course. But the legal process itself has become convoluted beyond even what Dickens envisioned in *Bleak House*. The law is now in a constant state of flux and confusion. New judges issue new rulings and establish new precedents in new fields, and it's a full-time journalistic job to keep track of them, comprehend them, and explain them to readers.

About 150 years ago Alexis de Tocqueville said, "Scarcely any question arises in the United States which does not become, sooner or later, a subject of judicial debate."

That is more true today than ever before.

*   *   *

ALMOST twenty years ago, Fred Graham was a lawyer in Washington working for the secretary of labor. Then—"out of the blue," as Graham recalls it—he was offered one of the most prestigious jobs in American journalism: covering the U.S. Supreme Court for the *New York Times*.

The last man to have had that job won a Pulitzer Prize, and, as Graham says now, "I was amazed they offered me the job. I hadn't done any reporting since I worked my way through law school as a reporter for the *Nashville Tennessean*."

But Graham had a couple of powerful sponsors at the *New York Times*—Washington bureau chief Tom Wicker and reporter David Halberstam, both of whom had also worked at the *Nashville Tennessean*.

Moreover, in 1965, attorneys with journalistic experience—or journalists with law degrees—were a very rare breed.

"If that same job opened up today," Graham said, "there would be 300 qualified applicants." Though this is an exaggeration—there would probably be no more than two dozen qualified reporters for the job—it is still a lot more than there were in 1965.

All three television networks now have reporters who are also lawyers covering the legal beat—Graham himself has worked at CBS since 1972—and the *New York Times* now has two lawyers with journalistic experience to write about legal affairs.

Even reporters with no formal legal training—and they are still the vast majority—are becoming increasingly sophisticated about the law. As their sophistication grows, once-common complaints from the legal profession about inaccuracies, irresponsibility, and sensationalism in media coverage of the courts are diminishing. "The media is doing a much better job than it used to," says Miami attorney Paul Levine.

District Attorney Cecil Hicks of Orange County, California, calls this improvement "remarkable." Twenty years ago, Hicks says, "There was often very little similarity between what actually happened in court and what I read in the papers. That seldom happens now."

Despite this improvement, however, media coverage of the nation's legal system is still largely inadequate, according to interviews with almost a hundred attorneys, judges, legal scholars, reporters, editors, and journalism professors in more than a dozen American cities.

Only five newspapers have full-time reporters covering the U.S. Supreme Court. Only one newspaper—the *Newark* (N.J.) *Star-Ledger*—has a reporter assigned to cover its state supreme court full time. Even at the trial court level, many newspapers provide only part-time, hit-and-miss coverage.

Too often, critics say, reporters still make serious mistakes, miss good stories, overlook important legal issues, misinterpret major court decisions, and fail to follow up their stories. The latter charge was the most oft-voiced complaint in this study— "my most serious criticism, the most troublesome thing the press does," in the words of Robert Morgenthau, district attorney for the borough of Manhattan in New York City.

There are countless examples in virtually every city of the many ways in which the press fails to follow up stories on the law.

- A newspaper will publish a story on an arrest or an indictment but, through oversight or lack of space or interest, will never publish the result of the case, especially if there is a dismissal or acquittal.
- In civil suits, the press often publishes a story about a multimillion-dollar lawsuit, then fails to publish the final judgment or out-of-court settlement, especially if it involves little or no money.
- Controversial court decisions often trigger angry forecasts of doom and disruption, which are duly reported by the press. But there is little subsequent effort to reexamine the situa-

tion and see if, in fact, the "landmark decision" actually changed anything.

But the most significant criticism of press coverage of the legal system today is not so much neglect (or inaccuracy) *inside* the courtroom as it is neglect and superficiality *outside* the courtroom—an overemphasis on day-to-day, case-by-case coverage and a concomitant laxity in the coverage of the larger issues confronting the legal system (and, ultimately, society at large).

This is especially true of television because of limitations on time and format.

When an official of a Midwestern bar association called a television news director in 1980 to suggest that one of his reporters might find it "educational" to attend a background press briefing on the association's evaluation of judges, the news director snapped, "I don't have time to educate my reporters."

But newspapers also devote too little attention to the inner workings and ultimate impact of the legal system—to what one lawyer calls "the 99 percent of lawyering that never gets to court."

"Press coverage of the really important issues is somewhere between lousy and abysmal," says George Edwards, chief judge of the Sixth U.S. Circuit Court of Appeals in Michigan, Ohio, Kentucky, and Tennessee until last November.

Many journalists agree.

"I've been in the business since 1948," said Lyle Denniston, who covers the U.S. Supreme Court for the *Baltimore Sun* and is the author of the book *The Reporter and the Law,* "and I know of no beat where reporters are lazier and do less to penetrate the process they're supposed to cover than legal reporting."

Although a few papers generally do a better job than most in covering legal affairs, critics say the press too often:

- Fails to write about incompetent (or unethical) lawyers or abusive, tyrannical, incompetent judges, unless a formal, investigative proceeding is already under way.
- Ignores or covers only superficially and sporadically many important subjects, issues, problems, and developments in the law.

Among these are legal clinics, increased prosecution of white-collar crimes, lawyers' fees and billing procedures, the quality of legal representation given the poor, unaccredited law schools, lawyers' trial strategies, experiments in nonjudicial forums for dispute resolution, the burgeoning cost of litigation, procedural complexities that delay cases, regulatory agency law, and multimillion-dollar awards in personal injury cases.

- Misunderstands the role of the judge and the function of the courts as a co-equal, independent branch of government.

("Judges are generally bound by legal precedents," says one judge, "but the press sometimes gives the impression that our rulings are personal preferences, and they criticize us for 'thwarting the will' of the people or the legislature.")

- Virtually ignores the intermediate appellate courts (all the courts above the trial level and below the U.S. Supreme Court), where many interesting cases are resolved and many important principles of law are enunciated.

Four reporters who cover the U.S. Supreme Court all told me they come across significant stories virtually every day that should have been covered—but were not—before they reached Washington.

Says one appellate judge, "We make a lot of controversial decisions, but we're almost completely invisible."

The *Baltimore Sun* has long had a reporter assigned full time to the Maryland state appellate courts, and the *Philadelphia Inquirer* created a similar beat three years ago after Gene Roberts, executive editor of the *Inquirer,* said, "It's become glaringly clear that we're blowing it at the appellate level. We are convinced that we'll never have a responsible court unless we cover them responsibly."

Preble Stolz, a law professor at the University of California at Berkeley, says he wishes newspapers in California would also cover the intermediate appellate courts, especially the California Supreme Court, full time. "A reporter who just shows up [at the supreme court] on decision day can't read the briefs and the lower-court opinions and get the necessary background to cover the court intelligently," Stolz said.

Not surprisingly, coverage of the legal system is generally poorest at smaller papers with fewer resources. Neither is it surprising that the best big-city papers generally do the best job. The *Wall Street Journal,* the *New York Times,* and the *Los Angeles Times* were the most widely praised in interviews for this study. But most papers of any size, including these three and other generally respected metropolitan dailies, do not consistently provide the kind of legal coverage that even many editors say they should offer their readers.

"We just don't do very well on either day-to-day court coverage or looking at the larger legal issues," Bill Burleigh said of his own paper's coverage when he was editor of the *Cincinnati Post* a few years ago. I'm often let down personally by all the press on this, though. I want to know a lot that the press just neglects to cover."

The press can never, of course, cover the legal system as comprehensively as those involved in the system would like—anymore than it can cover any other area (medicine, business, literature) as well as people involved in those areas would like. There simply is not enough time, space, or manpower to cover every subject exhaustively in a daily newspaper. And there is no indication that the average reader wants his paper to become a legal (or medical or business or literary) journal.

"It is somewhat unreasonable . . . to blame the press for

not printing a daily civics textbook or law book,'' said Joseph Mandel, former president of the Los Angeles County Bar Association. "That really isn't their function.''

Moreover, some attorneys and judges contribute to superficial and inaccurate coverage of the legal system by refusing to talk to the press. But this occasional inaccessibility—and the limitations imposed by the media's own resources and general-interest audience—notwithstanding, critics say there is a great deal more the press could be doing (and should be doing) to cover the legal system. Especially now.

The courts have become the ultimate forum for resolving not only personal, commerical, and criminal matters but also for a whole range of public policy decisions on the air we breathe, the food we eat, the books we read, the people we marry. There are now five million lawsuits filed every year in this country. Civil suits alone tripled from 1940 to 1974 and then doubled again from 1974 to 1982. Federal appeals increased seven-fold from 1960 to 1982. No wonder the number of lawyers has doubled since 1960, with 35,000 new law school graduates coming into the profession every year.

"Hair-trigger suing" is the term used by Maurice Rosenberg, a law professor at Columbia University, to describe this litigation explosion, and it is unique to America.

"I don't think there is any other society in the world that relies as we do on its formal legal system to substitute for a whole range of traditional, personal, and societal mechanisms,'' said Howard Miller, editor of the *Daily Journal,* a newspaper published for the Los Angeles legal community.

In California alone, Superior Court filings increased more than 50 percent in the decade of the 1970s, creating a whole series of interrelated problems—massive court backlogs, an increasingly complex body of procedures and case law, litigation so expensive that many Americans can no longer afford a legal redress of their grievances.

Critics say that despite the increased staff, time, and space devoted to legal matters in the press—especially in the best newspapers—the press just has not kept pace with the growing phenomenon (and the accompanying problems) of the law as a social, political, and governmental institution.

"The only two questions really worth asking about the courts are 'Is there justice?' and 'How do they [the courts] operate as a political institution?' " said Bob Woodward of the *Washington Post*. "The press doesn't do a very good job of trying to answer either [of those questions].

"The courts are a political institution, and we don't cover them as such," Woodward says. "Anyone who thinks differently has his head in the sand."

Woodward—co-author of *The Brethren*, a best-selling book on the Supreme Court—is particularly interested in the personal and political relationships among judges on appellate courts and other collegial courts and also in the politics of judicial promotions and case assignments.

"My father was an appellate judge in Illinois," he said, "and the courthouse politics he used to tell me about, which you just never see in the press, is highly relevant to how judges are elevated . . . and [how] cases are assigned and decided and whether there really is justice in America."

Many in Washington and elsewhere are critical of the *Post*'s own coverage of the legal system—especially its erratic Supreme Court coverage. In fact, most newspapers fail to cover the Supreme Court properly, if only because of their tendency to overstate the scope of Supreme Court decisions.

Supreme Court decisions on affirmative action, closed pretrial hearings, product liability, and the patentability of new life forms were almost universally perceived by the press as establishing far broader precedents than was actually intended by the Court, these critics say.

"There is sometimes a tendency for the press to paint these things with too broad a brush," said Laurence Tribe, a law professor at Harvard.

The press too often ignores, or is unaware of, the gradual evolution of case law, and by using such terms as "sweeping" or "landmark" or "precedent-shattering" it misleads the American public on the scope and impact of an important decision. Worse, the press may mislead other judges—lower court judges who may be influenced more in their own subsequent decisions by what the press says the high courts have ruled than by what the high courts actually ruled.

"Unfortunately, press coverage of Supreme Court decisions is characteristic of the way the press covers many things," said Yale Kamisar, a law professor at the University of Michigan. "It's the 'last-night's-tennis-match-was-the-greatest-of-all-time' syndrome."

Columnist Anthony Lewis of the *New York Times,* who won a Pulitzer Prize for his coverage of the Supreme Court, offers a similar analysis: "Any newspaper person—and I include myself—has that urge to make things seem more important rather than less."

But the press is not solely at fault in this tendency toward overstatement-cum-sensationalism.

The press often relies on legal scholars to help analyze and interpret Supreme Court decisions, and some of these scholars also overstate the potential impact of court rulings—in part because the very act of specialization that has made them experts has also given them certain prejudices and predispositions.

Attorneys in a given case, caught up in the euphoria of victory or the bitterness of defeat, also overstate the impact of Supreme Court rulings at times. So do judges, including Supreme Court justices themselves, eager to point out the folly of their brethren. This is particularly true of the current Supreme Court, which has been known to render opinions so fragmented and contradictory that, collectively, their only message is ambiguity. "When the Supreme Court makes a hash of a case, the press does, too," says one reporter who covers the Court.

Sometimes even lawyers and other judges do not understand

the muddled decisions of this Court. "No wonder it's hard for anyone with a daily deadline to make sense out of some of the judgments from the Court these days," said Phillip Kurland, a law professor at the University of Chicago. "The judgments are so full of irrelevancies."

Other legal scholars agree.

"To a certain extent, the Court itself has to share the blame for any overstatement of the intent of its ruling," said Dennis Hutchinson, a professor at Georgetown Law Center when I interviewed him. "The Court may have all kinds of qualifiers in its decision, limiting its scope, but if you read the dissents or follow the logic of some of the justices, it's easy to see it as a landmark case."

One 1979 Supreme Court case—*Gannett v. DePasquale*—provides a classic example of the tendency of the press to overstate the precedent established by the Court, and also of the Court's own contribution to that overstatement. Interestingly, the case also provides a good example of another shortcoming in press coverage of the legal system: a preoccupation with (and an overreaction to) any court decision that appears to diminish freedom of the press.

The press often gives more prominent front-page play (and more editorial-page outrage) to such decisions than to other, more important decisions on other issues. Anytime a First Amendment case goes against the press, newspapers immediately invoke the specter of star chamber proceedings, the death of freedom of the press, and the impending arrival of fascism on American shores.

The media's "plaintive . . . self-regarding tone . . . gets pretty sickening at times," Anthony Lewis says.

Thus, although the Supreme Courts 1979 decision in *Gannett v. DePasquale* said only the public (and the press) has no constitutional right to attend pre-trial hearings, many in the press angrily interpreted the decision as closing actual criminal trials, too.

Chief Justice Warren Burger was so disturbed by what he saw as a gross misinterpretation of the Court's decision that he spoke out publicly to correct this misimpression. But the Supreme Court decision itself helped spread the seeds of confusion and outrage.

It was a 5–4 decision with five separate opinions, and while Burger emphasized in his concurring opinion that the ruling was limited to pre-trial proceedings, Justice Harry Blackmun said publicly that the opinion "allows the closing of full trials as well." Justice William Rehnquist wrote, in his concurring opinion, "The Court today holds, without qualification, that 'members of the public have no constitutional right . . . to attend criminal trials.' "

A year later, in July 1980, when the Supreme Court ruled that the public and press do, indeed, have a constitutional right of access to criminal trials unless an overriding interest to the contrary is demonstrated in a specific case, Blackmun wrote, in his concurring opinion, "It is gratifying . . . to see the Court wash away at least some of the graffiti that marred the prevailing opinions in *Gannett.* No less than twelve times in the primary opinion in that case, the Court . . . observed that its Sixth Amendment closure ruling applied to the *trial* itself. . . . The resulting confusion among commentators and journalists was not surprising."

Yes, the press overreacted to the *Gannett* v. *DePasquale* decision. But Rehnquist and Justice Potter Stewart, the author of the primary opinion in that case, contributed to that overreaction—and to the subsequent closing of several actual trials by lower court judges.

As attorney Spencer Toll, former editor of the Philadelphia Bar Association quarterly magazine, said, the justices committed "the ultimate judicial sin: It wasn't clear just what the decision decided."

There are other flaws in most newspapers' coverage of the legal system that involve the system itself—the legal establishment, the network of high-priced, well-connected lawyers who often dominate the upper echelons of government and private enterprise.

"Every time I see a big Washington law firm, I realize that's a whole area of American power we don't cover at all," said Jim Mann, who reports on the U.S. Supreme Court for the *Los Angeles Times*.

The *Los Angeles Times* has more reporters covering the legal system than any other newspaper in the country—six who cover various courts full time and several others who routinely cover suburban courts as part of other beats. But critics say there are still too few stories in the *Times* (and other papers) like the insightful series published in the *Times* in 1980 on the changing power and responsibility of the judiciary.

"The *Times* rarely has the kind of think piece . . . on the courts that we see there on other institutions of government," said Robert Thompson, a former federal judge now teaching law at the University of Southern California. "Some stories nibble around the edges of that, but very little is really in depth."

Roderic Duncan, a reporter for two years before he went to law school, now a municipal court judge in Oakland, has another complaint. He said he is continually astounded by the number of "people stories, human interest stories, that come through the court and are never covered by any newspaper. I keep wondering, Jesus Christ, where are the reporters?"

More important, the press rarely writes about the principal players in the courtroom—the judges and lawyers.

Several years ago, Chief Justice Warren Burger made a speech about the incompetence of a great many lawyers. But except for reporting the resultant attempts by some in the American Bar Association to rebuke Burger, the press did little to pursue or evaluate Burger's charges.

Similarly, although journalists and lawyers in virtually every big city know of judges who abuse lawyers, fall asleep on the bench, drink heavily, make racist remarks in court, or act incompetently, stories are rarely written about them unless formal disciplinary proceedings are invoked.

Carol Benfell, a reporter for the *Oakland Tribune* said she once had firsthand evidence of a judge's incompetence but failed to write the story, for reasons that "even now, I'm not sure I know. I was inexperienced, I guess. And chicken. I was afraid I'd lose the other judges as potential news sources. And I really didn't have the time to do the job right."

No time. That's the biggest complaint of most reporters who cover the courts—especially those who cover the courts for the wire services.

Dick Carelli, who covers the U.S. Supreme Court for the Associated Press, often has to write about twenty to thirty different cases in one day. Not only does that leave virtually no time to probe the deeper issues involved in significant decisions, but, inevitably, Carelli concedes, he makes mistakes.

"There have only been a few cases . . . where I figured, 'Hey, Carelli, you better get it right the first time.' Most often my initial screw-up isn't going to change the course of history. I can fix it [when I file subsequent stories that same day]."

But five years ago, when Carelli was covering the court's controversial decision in the Alan Bakke affirmative action case, he realized, "It could affect race relations in this country for years to come if the press gives the wrong initial impression [of the court ruling]."

So how much time did Carelli spend studying the decision before he filed his "initial impression"—what the wire services call a "bulletin lead"?

"Three minutes," he says.

Within thirty minutes he had filed his entire story.

Television moves even more quickly. NBC went live with the Bakke decision ninety seconds after it was handed down.

Since most people learn about Supreme Court decisions either from network television or from wire service reports on the radio or in their local papers, it is obvious that the vast majority of Americans receive only the most superficial, and sometimes distorted, accounts of these decisions.

But the pace is hectic for reporters covering local courthouses in big cities, too. Reporter Dave Racher says he turned in 1,800 local court stories to the *Philadelphia Daily News* one year. *L.A. Times* reporter Myrna Oliver says she spends so much time—three or four hours a day—just checking the daily court calendar and daily filings and keeping track of potentially newsworthy cases in her card file that her job covering the downtown civil courts for the *Times* is little more than a "bookkeeping nightmare."

Robert E. Drechsel, a former court reporter who is now a journalism professor at Colorado State University, says, in his 1983 book, *News Making in the Trial Courts,* "Huge caseloads covered by few reporters means coverage that is relatively chancy." Too many reporters rely too heavily on prosecution sources because these sources are often the most readily available, Drechsel says, and that leads to one-sided court reporting. Reporters burdened with daily court coverage just don't have the time to cultivate sources elsewhere or to study the issues carefully themselves.

That is why some newspapers are increasingly hiring reporters to cover the legal system from outside the courthouse, with no responsibility for daily case coverage.

The *New York Times* in 1980 hired Stuart Taylor, Jr., to travel around the country, writing about the law under the broad rubric of "Justice in America."

Taylor, who graduated first in his law school at Harvard and was working for a prestigious Washington, D.C., law firm when he was hired, had been a reporter for the *Baltimore Sun* for three years before he went to law school. When he decided he preferred journalism to law, he gave *New York Times* editors a nine-page memo on what he would like to do for the paper.

"The *Times* and other daily newspapers do not cover the law as insightfully or as comprehensively as they could . . ." Taylor said, and he listed almost thirty possible stories in a variety of subject areas that now "receive only occasional and sporadic attention and little in the way of informed analysis." Taylor said he wanted to probe "beneath the surface of events to identify underlying issues, problems, and trends and explain their significance, and to provide insights into some of the more fundamental issues and problems that characterize our system of justice."

To a certain extent, Taylor is now doing just that, but his stories often seem more tied to the day's news than to broad, underlying problems.

Must a reporter be a lawyer to even attempt to do that job?

In the early years, the courthouse beat, like the police beat, was routinely given on most newspapers to young, inexperienced reporters. On many smaller papers, that is still true. But as editors have come to realize the growing significance of the legal beat, they have increasingly assigned better, more experienced reporters—especially to write about legal affairs beyond day-to-day case coverage.

Although few would insist that a reporter must be a lawyer to write intelligently about the law, there are many who say some formal legal training is advisable, perhaps essential.

"You just can't cover the legal system in depth, the way it has to be covered today, if you don't have legal training," says Bernard Witkin, the author of several books on the California legal system. Witkin thinks a six-to-twelve-month law course designed specifically for journalists would contribute immeasurably toward more enlightened press coverage of the legal system.

There are other alternatives as well. Since 1976 the Ford Foundation has sponsored a program for five journalists a year to attend the first year of Yale Law School—not a special course, just the regular first-year law school curriculum. But many editors are reluctant to send reporters to law school for fear that they will be tempted to abandon journalism for the more lucrative field of the law—as several participants in the Yale/Ford program have done.

There are also some editors and reporters who think formal legal training may be more damaging than beneficial for reporters.

"Every reporter I know who went through law school wound up thinking like a lawyer, not a journalist," said Lyle Denniston of the *Baltimore Sun*.

"I think it was Dean Acheson who once said, 'The law sharpens the mind by narrowing it,' " Denniston says, "and that's true. A reporter with a law degree starts looking on the law as theory. . . . He loses some of his skepticism, too. He becomes part of the system . . . too respectful of lawyers and judges, too obligated to courtroom procedures . . . too likely to write for other lawyers, not the general audience."

The *New York Times* is particularly guilty of that in its Supreme Court coverage, Denniston says.

Linda Greenhouse, who attended the Yale/Ford program and now covers the Supreme Court for the *New York Times* does, indeed, occasionally become too enmeshed in legalese as she did in one long story she wrote that involved little more than a legal dispute over "the meaning of the word 'accrues' in the Federal Tort Claims Act."

But Greenhouse, who generally does a good job covering the Court, says of her legal training, "The more you know about anything, the better reporter you are, no matter what you cover."

Most journalists and attorneys concur. They say some legal training is helpful; it enables a reporter to speak the same, often arcane language as the people he covers and it also enables him to invite confidences not easily given to nonlawyers, and to provide historical perspective for his daily reportage.

Steven Brill, editor of *The American Lawyer* magazine and a graduate of the Yale Law School, says legal training simply enables a journalist to "avoid being buffaloed . . . intimidated.

When a lawyer says he's going to file a motion to blah-blah-blah, you don't draw a blank or have to ask a question . . . or maybe make a mistake.''

Intimidation seems to be a major problem for many reporters covering legal affairs. The formal panoply of the courtroom and the stilted language of the lawyers and judges cow some reporters into silence and acquiescence.

Several lawyers told me they were astounded by the number of reporters who accepted what they said—or did not say—without either question or challenge, either out of laziness, ignorance, or a fear of being perceived as ignorant.

"If you ask some prolix, wordy guy like me a few questions, you might learn something,'' said attorney John Martzell of New Orleans, "but most reporters never bother to ask. . . . They don't even bother to ask to look at the actual physical evidence in a trial most of the time, and I can think of a couple of trials when I've put some of the damnedest things in evidence.''

Presumably, a reporter with legal training would be less likely to overlook such potentially newsworthy material or to refrain from asking a pointed question or two.

But Brill thinks that debates over legal training for reporters miss the main point, the main shortcoming, of the coverage of legal affairs.

"You don't have to be a lawyer to cover the law any more than you have to be a . . . cop to cover the police beat,'' Brill said. "What you have to be is a good reporter, and there are too few of them covering the law. The law is the only beat I know of where the attention is focused almost exclusively on the result—who won or lost the case—not on the system, the process.''

When reporters do write about the process, Brill says, they too often accept and perpetuate inaccurate myths and stereotypes. "Look at the stories over the years about plea-bargaining—so-called revolving-door justice—with maniacal murderers

let loose after they're permitted to plead guilty to lesser charges
. . . by lenient judges and bleeding heart [lawyers] who give
the courthouse away.

"Well, I was involved in a study of more than a thousand
cases a few years ago, and we found it was a lot more complicated than that," Brill says. "We found out that a lot of defendants who plea-bargain actually wind up with more jail time
than the average defendant who goes to trial. But I didn't see
any real follow-up media coverage of that." So the "myth" en-
dures.

The press bears a special burden—and responsibility—where
myths involving the judiciary are concerned because of what one
judge terms the "unique . . . constitutional predicament" of the
judiciary.

People in the executive and legislative branches of government may—indeed must—explain their actions to the public; but
the courts must rely almost exclusively on the press to do that
job for them. "The force of judicial decisions depends . . . on
a fragile constitutional chemistry, and it flows directly from
popular knowledge and acceptance of their decisions," said Irving R. Kaufman, chief judge of the Second U.S. Circuit Court
of Appeals in New York.

"Courts cannot publicize; they cannot broadcast," Kaufman
said. "They must set forth their reasoning in accessible language and logic and then look to the press to spread the word."

Too often, critics say, the word that is spread is inaccurate.
Or oversimplified. Or distorted. Or sensationalized. Or, worse,
the right word, the important word, is not spread at all.

For all the criticism of the press, some good stories are occasionally published on various aspects of the legal system. In
fact, says attorney Robert Meserve of Boston, a former president of the American Bar Association, "some stories explaining
complex, emotional legal issues have been helpful not only in
enlightening the public but in defusing unfair criticism of the
courts."

Even some less well-known newspapers have published insightful stories on the law from time to time.

The *Pittsburgh Post-Gazette* ran a story on proposals to regulate specialization among lawyers. The *Cincinnati Enquirer* ran a series on juvenile court problems. The *San Francisco Examiner* published several articles on life in the courtroom of Municipal Judge Perker Meeks, Jr.

But such articles are the exception to what should be the rule, and sometimes even these good articles do not get the display they deserve. For example, one *San Francisco Examiner* article on Meeks's courtroom was published on the fifth page of the third section—next to the classified ads for massage parlors and lost and found.

5

THE REPORTER AS IMPOSTER

When I speak to groups of professional journalists and to classes of college journalism students, one of the questions I'm most frequently asked is: "Do your stories have any effect on your paper? Do things improve, do policies and practices change, after you've written about something?"

I usually answer: "I have a sister who's in politics in Denver. She was elected state senator the same year I became the media critic for my newspaper. The most valuable lesson she told me she learned after a frustrating first year in the senate was, 'It's amazing how much you can accomplish if you don't care who gets the credit for it.' "

She's right. So I don't go around looking for, or bragging about, specific changes that may have been made at my newspaper, or elsewhere, because of stories I've written. There may have been a few such changes—not many—but the most interesting changes (and those I feel most comfortable talking about) have been changes in me personally. I say "most interesting" only because of the precise nature of the changes. I have always thought of myself as a very careful, very ethical reporter. I have always tried my best to quote people accurately, to be sensitive to the privacy of others, to avoid conflicts of interest or even the appearance of a conflict of interest, to avoid doing anything that could compromise my objectivity as a journalist.

But as ethical as I thought I was before I took this job, I'm even more so now. Just as this job has helped make me a better reporter, a more careful reporter, so it has made me a more ethical reporter. When you spend a good portion of your workday thinking about and looking for and writing about the mistakes that others make, you try to make damn sure you aren't guilty of the same mistakes yourself. I can remember interviewing a reporter in his late fifties a couple of years ago, for example, and when we were all through, he said, "Now, I don't want you to use my name in your story." Well, he had made several very provocative remarks—remarks that directly contradicted what his editor had already told me. I told him I'd have to use his name.

"Look," I said, "you've been a reporter longer than I have. You know the rules. If you want to go off-the-record or speak not for attribution, you have to get that understood up front, before the interview, not after."

He asked me, repeatedly, not to use his name. He said he'd be fired.

Earlier in my career, I think I would have extended my sympathies, asked him how many people he had put out of work by quoting them on controversial matters, and written my story—with his name included. But I didn't do that. I thought about the situation. The man, I realized, was from another generation, someone not accustomed to this newfangled idea of reporters interviewing and writing critically about their peers. If he had been a younger, more sophisticated reporter—or if he had worked for my own paper, so he would have been familiar with what I was doing—it would have been different.

Did the story really require his name? Was it worth jeopardizing his job? No and no. I wrote it without his name.

Another example: I was writing a story about various mistakes reporters make. Several reporters, at my own newspaper and elsewhere, volunteered examples of their own errors. But one reporter in particular, who sat near me at work, kept coming back to me, day after day, with more examples of his errors. The temptation was to use them all, quoting him. But he wasn't telling me about so many of his mistakes because he made more than anyone else; I was just more accessible to him than I was to reporters at other papers. So I used one of his mistakes with his name and used several others without his name, as general examples of the kinds of mistakes that newspapers make.

Too often reporters are eager to practice "Gotcha/Getcha" journalism: "Gotcha to say something you shouldn't have said, and now I'm gonna getcha in trouble." It's a tempting game and sometimes, on some stories, a valid and valuable one. But all reporters—myself included—occasionally play the game when it isn't necessary. We are gratuitously cruel. My job writing about the press, and thinking about these issues, has made me better able to resist this temptation.

Writing about the press has also made me more sensitive to the question of unnamed sources, the subject of chapter two. In that chapter, and in the original story on which it is based, I did not rely on any unnamed sources. Not one. But in rereading the other chapters in this book, including this one, during the final editing process, I was stunned—and embarrassed—to see that I had not always been so circumspect. In far too many instances, I did not name my sources; too often I didn't even provide readers with a general idea of their allegiances and possible biases. I suspect many of my colleagues and friends have learned similar lessons, on this and on other journalistic subjects, since we now talk about these issues much more frequently.

In fact, I sometimes feel like the journalistic equivalent of a born-again Christian; so I try to avoid a holier-than-thou attitude. I remember all too well my own occasional transgressions early in my career.

I can remember carrying a concealed wire recorder with a wristwatch microphone during interviews for an exposé on a candidate for the U.S. Senate. I can remember "borrowing" a confidential government document on the same story. Or take the ethical question of reporters who misrepresent themselves, who pretend not to be reporters, who pose as someone else in the pursuit of a story. In most instances, most journalists would now say, that's wrong. I agree. But I've done it myself. I can remember, in particular, working for a newspaper in a navy town and receiving reports that attractive young women were luring sailors into an ocean-front store in order to sell them vastly overpriced sets of encyclopedias.

I borrowed a navy uniform from a friend of mine, strolled in front of the store, and was invited inside. All the while, my photographer was stationed across the street, tucked behind the open door of a car, with his telephoto lens aimed right at the young ladies and me.

My story ran the next day. Page one. Quicker than you can say "Britannica," the encyclopedia business was evicted, the store was closed, and the state attorney general announced plans for as investigation. I was twenty-four at the time, and I felt pretty damn proud of myself.

Now, sixteen years later, I realize two things: (1) It wasn't such a big story after all; and (2) more important, I behaved unethically and illegally in getting the story.

I knew at the time that I was breaking the law by wearing the navy uniform, but I decided to take the chance anyway, for the ''greater social good'' of the story. But I put myself above the law. I broke the law to catch a lawbreaker. Even if what I did hadn't been illegal, it was unethical. And unnecessary. I could have gotten that story by watching the young ladies approach the sailors and by talking to the sailors and the women myself—in short, by observing and interviewing. That's what a reporter is supposed to do. He's not supposed to misrepresent himself.

*   *   *

A REPORTER for the *Detroit News* poses as a Michigan congressman to prove how lax security is at a treaty-signing ceremony on the White House lawn.

A reporter for the *Los Angeles Times* poses as a graduate student in psychology working in a state mental hospital to expose conditions there.

A reporter for the *Wall Street Journal* works three weeks on an assembly line in a large plant to investigate charges that the company routinely violates fair labor practices.

Are these unethical activities? Are these journalists compromising their professional integrity—and, ultimately and cumulatively, their profession's credibility? Do the special rights granted to the press under the First Amendment also impose upon the press special responsibilities that preclude deception and misrepresentation?

Or is the public benefit to be derived from the disclosure of certain conditions sometimes so great, and the obstacles to such disclosure sometimes so difficult, that reporters are justified in pretending to be what they are not?

In short, does the worthwhile end sometimes justify the deceptive means?

Because journalists are so determined these days to expose the deceptions and misrepresentations of others—in government, big business, and elsewhere—there is now widespread disagreement among reporters and editors over just when (and if) they can indulge in such activities themselves.

In past generations such ethical concerns were far less prevalent. Many reporters routinely posed as police, doctors, government officials—anything that was necessary to get a story.

It was long considered normal practice for, say, a police reporter named Sam Flanagan working in the pressroom at the Los Angeles Police Department to call police in another city and try to obtain information by saying, "Hey, this is Flanagan over at LAPD"—knowing full well that the man at the other end would assume he was an LAPD officer. Some reporters would even identify themselves as "Lieutenant Flanagan over at LAPD."

As recently as the mid-1970s, says Thomas Winship, editor of the *Boston Globe,* "we got an excellent story by having a reporter pose as a guard at a youth detention center and report on the maltreatment he saw. We wouldn't do that now."

The new ethical standards born of Watergate have "heightened our consciousness on these matters," another editor says.

"We in the press are arguing for an open, honest society, demanding certain behavior from our public officials," says William Hornby, former president of the American Society of Newspaper Editors. "We ought to be just as open and as frank and straightforward in getting information as we claim other people ought to be in giving it to us."

But some editors see such proclamations as both unrealistic and self-righteous.

"Sure, being the champions of truth and all that, you always have to be concerned about doing anything that appears to be misrepresentation," says Michael J. O'Neill, former editor of the *New York Daily News.* "On the other hand, there are some situations where it's the only way to get the story."

That's the decision editors at the *Los Angeles Herald Examiner* made in 1981 when they assigned reporter Merle Linda Wollin to work undercover in the garment factories of Los Angeles in an effort to document the poor working conditions and the exploitation of illegal aliens in that industry. Wollin posed as an illegal alien to pursue that story, and her findings won many awards. But not a Pulitzer Prize. The jury that makes nominations in that category made Wollin's series a unanimous first choice for the 1982 Pulitzer gold medal for public service. But the Pulitzer Prize Board, which has final say on the awards, overruled the jury—as is its prerogative. The board's reasoning, in part, was that reporters shouldn't deliberately misrepresent themselves in the pursuit of a story.

This was the second time in recent years that the board made such a judgment. The Pulitzer Prize–loser the first time was the *Chicago Sun-Times,* which had assigned a team of reporters to operate the Mirage Bar incognito for four months in 1977 to expose graft and corruption in the city.

The results: City inspectors volunteered to overlook health and safety violations at the bar in exchange for money. Jukebox and pinball operators offered kickbacks. Accountants offered counsel on the fine art of tax fraud. Contractors served as bagmen for payoffs to public officials.

The *Sun-Times* ran stories on its discoveries for four weeks— and almost won a Pulitzer Prize for it in 1979. The *Sun-Times* series was one of four entries in local reporting recommended to the board by the Pulitzer nominating committee.

In earlier years, enterprising efforts like that of the *Sun-Times* had often won Pulitzers. The *Chicago Tribune* won in 1971, for example, when one of its reporters worked as an ambulance driver to expose collusion between the police and private ambulance companies.

But in 1979 the *Sun-Times* did not win, largely because several editors on the Pulitzer advisory board objected to their journalistic methods. "In a day in which we are spending thousands of man-hours uncovering deception, we simply cannot deceive," says Benjamin C. Bradlee, executive editor of the *Washington Post* and then a member of the Pulitzer advisory board.

"How can newspapers fight for honesty and integrity when they themselves are less than honest in getting a story?" Bradlee asks. "When cops pose as newspapermen, we get goddamn sore. Quite properly so. So how can we pose as something we're not?"

Joseph Shoquist, managing editor of the *Milwaukee Journal,* argued, however, that the widespread corruption uncovered by the *Sun-Times* ". . . was a worthy subject that needed a dramatic presentation to capture the public's attention." Moreover. insists James Hoge then editor-in-chief of the *Chicago Sun-Times,* "We couldn't have gotten that information and presented it as effectively any other way. We had reported for a number of years on bribery in Chicago . . . with no effect."

Even Hoge agrees, though, that the kind of journalism practiced on the Mirage Bar story "should be used only with extreme caution and selectivity and only when certain standards are applied."

Most editors seem to agree, in principle, on those "standards":

* The story involved should be of significant public benefit.
* Past experience, common sense, and hard work should first

demonstrate that there is no other way to get the story, that conventional reportorial techniques just will not yield the necessary information.

The problem with these general standards is that in any given situation, virtually every editor seems to have his own definitions for such terms as "significant" and "conventional" and "no other way" and "necessary."

Take the following hypothetical situation I posed to more than two dozen editors around the country:

"Someone tells one of your reporters there is a report by three doctors that a prospective gubernatorial candidate has a very serious drinking problem. That report is on a doctor's desk in the hospital, and all your reporter has to do is put on a doctor's white coat, walk into the office, and copy or photograph it. Would you let him do that?"

Almost all of the editors agree that to thus impersonate a doctor would be improper. Most also agreed that if the candidate's drinking problem were that serious, there would be other ways to learn about it. They generally agreed, with varying degrees of certainty, that they would not let their reporters copy the medical reports.

But when these same editors were then asked:

"Suppose the medical reports are from three psychiatrists who agree unanimously that the president of the United States is mentally unstable. Then do you tell your reporter to get the reports?"

Most editors agree with William F. Thomas, editor of the *Los Angeles Times,* who said:

"I think you have to be very careful about doing that kind of thing in most circumstances . . . but in these particular circumstances, absolutely; you do it. You tell your reporter to do anything he has to do to get those reports—even if they're locked in a safe and he has to dynamite the safe. Christ, you're talking about an unstable president with his finger on the . . . button."

Any journalist who actually broke the law to get a story—
any story—would, of course, have to pay the penalty, Thomas
says, "and the editor should make the call."

Other editors agree.

But some editors who agreed with Thomas on the tactics they
would permit their reporters to employ in the hypothetical "unstable president" story did so reluctantly, in much more doubt-
ful and qualified terms. A few editors tried to dodge the question
altogether.

A. M. Rosenthal, executive editor of the *New York Times,*
said he was vigorously opposed to the practice and once had to
have a new reporter reprimanded for donning overalls and trying
to pose as an airline mechanic to get close to the plane where
the wife of defecting Soviet ballet star Alexander Godunov was
being detained.

"Reporters should not masquerade," Rosenthal says. "We
claim First Amendment rights and privileges, and it's duplici-
tous for us to then pass ourselves off as something other than
reporters. Saying you'll get a better story or perform a valuable
public service doesn't change anything. It's still wrong."

But even Rosenthal, when pressed, concedes that if "the only
way to save someone's life would be to masquerade, I might
change my mind."

In discussing precisely when they would or would not permit reporters to misrepresent themselves, several editors invoked an old joke:

A man asks a woman if she'll go to bed with him for $1
million. She agrees to. Then the man says, "Will you do it for
$5?" She refuses and asks, quite indignantly, "What do you think
I am?"

The man replies, "We have already established what you are,
madam. Now we are merely discussing price."

That, some editors say, is the real issue in the misrepresentation question: Misrepresentation is misrepresentation, no matter how exalted the objective.

"Our general policy and our general philosophy is that it's wrong," says David Lipman, managing editor of the *St. Louis Post-Dispatch*. "We don't pose as doctors or anything else.

"But what's the price? When do I bend? I'd like to be moral and say, 'No, we wouldn't do it, not even in your example about the president.' But because of the overwhelming significance of the situation . . . there comes a time in our lives when, no matter how much we respect the law, we think civil disobedience is the only way to change immoral laws. This might be the same thing. I'd have to see."

Although most editors see this as an ethical issue, a few interpret it in almost strictly legal terms.

"Our responsibility is to get information, and if we can do it legally, I'll do it," says Neil Shine, senior managing editor of the *Detroit Free Press*. "I wouldn't let a reporter says he's a policeman. That's illegal. But I don't draw many lines. When our young medical writer heard about some guy selling phony arthritis medicine, she didn't go up to him and say, 'Hi, I'm the medical writer from the *Free Press*. Are you a charlatan?'

"She went to him and pretended to be someone with arthritis. He sold her $200 worth of his medicine. We exposed him."

On another occasion, Shine says, the same reporter visited several abortion clinics, pretended to think she might be pregnant, submitted urine samples from male colleagues, and exposed the clinics when they said she was, indeed, pregnant and offered her an abortion.

The *Free Press* has also used masquerading reporters to expose marriage counselors, a surgery mill, and real estate agents who practice racial discrimination. Reporters who indulge in such masquerades almost invariably do so because they have reason to believe they will uncover wrongdoing. Rarely are they on a fishing expedition.

"You can do that [real estate] story one of two ways," Shine says. "You can have your reporters call the realtors and ask if they're doing this illegal thing and they'll say, 'No,' or you can send a white couple over there—two reporters—and the real estate people will tell them about a charming, lovely home in . . . a mostly white suburb.

"Then you send a black couple—two other reporters—who have the same needs, income, and wants to the same office, and when they point to a picture of the same house, the real estate people say . . . 'No, I wouldn't have my cat live there,' and they steer them to a black area.

"That way you get the story and you get it with the impact of firsthand experience."

But editors at Shine's competitor, the *Detroit News,* disagree.

Lionel Linder, then managing editor of the *News,* called this type of reporting "stunt journalism." Other, equally critical editors call it "gimmick journalism" or "romantic journalism."

"We wouldn't have done it that way," Linder said. "It isn't right. It looks like you're deliberately trying to drag the worst possible information out of a situation. Legitimate homebuyers might act differently than reporters pretending. It makes the situation artificial.

"You should just do it [the story] by interviewing some people who've had the experience."

And yet, for all Linder's dismay, one of his own reporters posed as a Michigan congressman several years ago so he could expose lax security conditions during the signing of the Israel-Egypt peace treaty in Washington.

The reporter, Gary Shuster, found out that one of his state's congressmen was not planning to attend the ceremony, so he simply appropriated the man's name, got on a special bus with other congressmen, and wound up, as he wrote in a front-page story the next day, ". . . fifty feet from the table where Mideast peace documents were signed [on the White House lawn]."

Both Shuster and Linder still think this ruse was justified. But some of Shuster's colleagues were so upset that the Standing Committee of Correspondents, the governing body of reporters who cover Congress, voted unanimously to reprove him. Posing as a congressman is a serious matter—perhaps even illegal—and this particular story did not warrant such behavior.

The major criticism of Shuster was that he practiced active deception: He specifically said he was someone else.

Many journalists are willing, often eager, to permit others to assume they are not reporters, but they say they would not actually lie or give another name or identity. Most agree that it is not unethical for, say, a consumer reporter to take a television set to a variety of repair shops without identifying himself as a reporter. Similarly, they say, restaurant critics need not—in fact should not—identify themselves to restaurateurs when they dine out.

"There are certainly times," says Frank McCulloch of the *Bee* newspapers in California, "when you don't rush forward . . . wave your press card, and say, 'Be advised: I am a reporter.' "

But deliberate deception?

David Roman, a reporter for the *Potomac* (Va.) *News*, was fined $500 and given a six-month suspended jail term in 1983 when he was convicted of impersonating a law enforcement officer to gain entry to a maximum security prison to interview an inmate on Death Row.

Most newspaper editors frown on even lesser deceptions.

The *Chicago Tribune* "severely reprimanded" a reporter for getting a phony driver's license during an investigation of handgun sales, former *Tribune* president Clayton Kirkpatrick told me a few years ago.

"It's acceptable to play a role so long as there is no . . . fraud involved," Kirkpatrick says. "But this was a constructive effort to deceive somebody. That was a very serious error.

"It's perfectly proper to take a job under your own name to observe the operations of a public office or company and just not say you're a reporter," Kirkpatrick says. "But you shouldn't assume a false identity. You shouldn't wear false identification

. . . or call the scene of an air crash and pretend to be an official with the FAA or go under forged credentials or positively identify yourself as someone else.''

There is often, however, a very thin line between permitting someone else to assume you are something other than a reporter and carefully nudging someone toward that conclusion.

One Midwest editor said that when he was a reporter he "had the great good fortune" to strongly resemble a local FBI agent. He never actually said he was with the FBI, but he certainly exploited the situation by showing up at banks right after robberies, officiously rapping on the door with a key or coin, and, invariably, gaining access to interview witnesses while other reporters were kept outside.

Tammy Jones, a reporter for the Associated Press in San Diego, crashed a Richard Nixon party in San Clemente in 1979 by donning a long dress, a string of pearls, and driving right up to the security gate. She gave her right name but not her occupation. When guards said her name was not on the list, she spotted the names of two Angels baseball players on the list and asked if they had arrived yet.

When the guard said none of the Angels had arrived yet, Miss Jones said, "Oh, I must be ahead of the caravan."

The guard waved her through.

Gene Roberts, executive editor of the *Philadelphia Inquirer*, can remember using a variety of misleading tactics when he covered civil rights in the South for the *New York Times* in the late 1950s and 1960s.

Often he deliberately stuffed a thick notebook in the inside breast pocket of his jacket, knowing that the resultant bulge clearly resembled those made by the shoulder holsters worn by FBI agents. "FBI agents were the only people who walked around those Southern towns in the summer with coats and ties and bulges like that," Roberts says. "People thought I was an FBI agent, too, and I was able to move around some pretty hostile crowds more easily than I could have as a reporter."

Sometimes, Roberts says, his deceptions were not so subtle.

"Reporters were systematically excluded from the first desegregated schools," he says, "and we thought that finding out how the black kids were treated once they got in was important." So Roberts, who has a Southern accent and could look quite young back then, always kept a sweater and a school notebook handy. On occasion he would throw his coat and tie under a nearby bush and stroll onto a high school campus, wearing a sweater, carrying a notebook, and looking, for all anyone knew, like a typical white student.

But Roberts's most blatant deception came in no such noble cause. He was covering a murder once when he learned that police had shot the suspect and were interrogating him in a hospital emergency room that was off-limits to reporters.

Roberts scouted around and found a stethoscope near a soft drink machine. He put it around his neck, strolled into the emergency room, listened to the suspect's confession, and wrote his story.

"I never said I was a doctor, but the stethoscope would certainly have given that impression," Roberts concedes.

Would he have put on a doctor's white coat, too, if it had been available?

"It's quite possible."

But the confession of a murder suspect is hardly a story of transcendent social value. Doesn't that misrepresentation bother him now?

"No. If in all circumstances, you're going to require reporters to just walk up to people and state their name, rank, and serial number and say, 'Tell me the truth,' you're flat not going to get the truth. The public will be ill-served."

Some reporters have made a virtual career out of masquerading as others in the pursuit of stories.

Mike Goodman of the *Los Angeles Times,* for example, has posed as an animal keeper in a zoo, an employee in a juvenile detention facility, an oil pipeline worker in Alaska, a hippie in

Hollywood, and, like Roberts, he once carried a stethoscope into a hospital emergency room to get a story.

"I'm a great believer in the reporter as observer," Goodman says. "Firsthand observation is the ultimate documentation.

"A reporter doesn't have a badge or subpoena power or . . . wiretap authority. He has to use his . . . wits. That's what I try to do. . . . Almost every big story I've done I've had to impersonate someone. . . . And I usually get results."

After Goodman wrote his story on conditions at Los Angeles County Juvenile Hall, there was a major shake-up among top-level personnel.

"I was told that we'd been trying to do that story for thirty years without that kind of impact," he says.

Perhaps the most daring of the journalist-as-impersonator breed is Gunter Wallraff of West Germany, who has posed as an assembly-line mechanic, a Fascist, and a government official. Once he chained himself to a lamppost in Athens, was arrested and beaten, and then wrote a story on torture under the Greek military regime.

Wallraff, who was tried (and acquitted) on charges of "false impersonation and unauthorized use of title" after one of his stories, justified his behavior by saying: "The method I adopted was only slightly illegal by comparison with the illegal deceptions and maneuvers which I unmasked."

Wallraff believes that his job is "to deceive in order not to be deceived—to break the rules of the game in order to disclose the secret rules of power."

But many American editors worry that such expediency and self-justification can lead reporters into clearly unethical, even illegal, tactics. "It's not just posing as someone else that bothers me," says one editor. "It's what the reporter does while he's posing."

Many editors were critical of the *Chicago Sun-Times*'s work at the Mirage Bar, for example, because they feared it involved entrapment—actually encouraging bribes and other illegal activity.

But *Sun-Times* editors say the paper carefully instructed its reporters in the laws against entrapment and made clear to them that they could "never offer anybody anything, nor hint, imply, or in any other way suggest we were prone to making a payoff. We would only respond once an overture was made," one editor said.

Such distinctions are not always so easily drawn.

When reporter Beth Nissen of the *Wall Street Journal* worked on the electronics assembly line at the Texas Instruments plant in Austin, Texas, a few years ago to investigate charges of illegal antiunion activity by the company, she openly engaged employees in talk about a union.

Some editors think such behavior may help create—or, at least, contribute to—the very sort of behavior the reporter is trying to expose. "You can make your story a self-fulfilling prophecy," says one editor. "It's deception, pure and simple. I don't like it."

Moreover, if Miss Nissen's sources were right, she could have jeopardized the jobs of the legitimate employees seen talking to her.

Laurence O'Donnell, then managing editor of the *Wall Street Journal,* says he is aware of the problems inherent in such a story and he is usually "quite cautious" about permitting reporters to do them. But he thought this one was justified because ". . . there was no other way to get the story [and] . . . the information was worth getting."

That is pretty much what reporter Michael Cordts of the *Rochester* (N.Y.) *Democrat and Chronicle* says about once having worked for two weeks as a stock clerk at the Strand bookstore in New York. Based on what he learned at the Strand, Cordts wrote a story disclosing that book critics for several of the nation's major newspapers were selling their complimentary review copies to the store and "pocketing thousands of dollars."

In the immediate aftermath of Cordts's story, one book editor was fired, another was asked to resign, a third was reassigned, and a fourth killed himself (although no one is willing to say he did so because of the story).

Cordts says he could not have written his story had he not worked at the Strand. While there, he says, he saw crates of books from the various book editors with their names and business or home addresses on the return address labels. Thus, when he began calling book editors and they denied selling their review copies, he was able to force their confessions by telling them what he had seen at the Strand.

Cordts and his editors deny charges by the owner of the Strand that Cordts went into areas of the store that were off-limits to him and that he violated the store's right to private dealings with its customers. But Cordts does admit falsifying his job application—falsely listing previous employment at another bookstore among other things.

Lois Timnick, a reporter for the *Los Angeles Times,* went a couple of steps further in 1979. Under circumstances that cannot be fully disclosed because of promises of confidentiality, she used a phony name and posed as a graduate student in psychology so she could work for two weeks at Metropolitan State Hospital and expose conditions for mental patients there.

Although Timnick signed her phony name to an "oath of confidentiality," promising "not to divulge any information or records concerning any client/patient without proper authorization," she did look at—and write about—patients' confidential medical records.

Did that violate her oath?

"No, I don't think so," she says now. "When I wrote about the patients . . . I changed their names and some of the details about them so other people couldn't recognize them."

But Timnick took the job precisely because it would give her access to confidential medical records—something she felt was essential to her story, but something many editors see as an invasion of the patients' privacy despite her subsequent precautions in writing the story. (Even Timnick admits she would not want a reporter looking at her own medical records, whether he wrote about them or not.)

Timnick's editors support what she did. The only thing the paper should have done differently, says one editor, was to make it clearer to the readers that what she did was most unusual and not a practice lightly or frequently engaged in by *Times* reporters.

Although Timnick says she does not think she could have gotten as good a story by conventional interviews with patients, doctors, and other hospital employees, Eugene Patterson, president and editor of the *St. Petersburg* (Fla.) *Times*, says, "She'd have a hard time convincing me of that."

The deception, misrepresentation, falsification, and possible invasion of privacy all bother Patterson and other editors.

Twenty years ago, Patterson says, a reporter who worked for him in Atlanta won a Pulitzer Prize for exposing conditions in a mental hospital, "and he did it with routine, aboveboard reporting, without posing as anyone he wasn't." Patterson concedes that there might be some circumstances in which he would authorize a reporter to pose as someone else "as a last resort . . . in the critical public interest," but he insists that such tactics are generally unnecessary and unethical.

"Most of those kinds of stories can be done by conventional means if the reporter is willing to work hard," he says. "It's often much easier to get a job some place and pretend you're not a reporter than it is to do all the interviewing and investigating you have to do by traditional techniques."

A reporter for another paper says that when she assumed another identity to do an investigative story, all the questions of professional ethics did not bother her as much as those involving her own personal ethics.

"When I did my story," she says, "I had to make friends with the people I was working with . . . I shopped with them and babysat for them . . . trying to get them to talk to me. I'd never made a friendship before that was blatantly [a] fraud. That bothered me personally a great deal.''

But she did it anyway. And her editors supported her.

"It's a judgment," says one editor, "that we all have to make on a case-by-case basis. But we'd better be damn sure we make the right decisions.''

6

"WE BLEW IT"

Newspapers, it has been said, provide the first rough draft of history. But like all first rough drafts, newspapers make mistakes—errors of omission and commission, occasioned by the pressures of time and competition and by individual and institutional interests, idiosyncrasies, habits, personalities, and shortcomings.

In recent years many newspapers have begun to acknowledge their errors of commission more freely. They regularly publish corrections of misstatements, misquotations, and misrepresentations that have appeared in the paper. But how does a newspaper acknowledge more important errors—especially when it is an entire story or an entire issue that is neglected? More important, why—and how—do newspapers sometimes miss important stories altogether? "Blow" them, in the vernacular of the trade. Or cover them so briefly and inadequately that they might just as well have missed them entirely.

Instances of this phenomenon are abundant. My Lai, for example. Reporter Seymour Hersh won a Pulitzer Prize for disclosing that American troops had murdered more than a hundred men, women, and children in that small South Vietnamese village. But the My Lai massacre took place in March 1968; Hersh's stories did not begin running until November

152

1969. In the intervening twenty months, no newspaper examined the murders—not even after the U.S. Army issued a press release that disclosed the army's own investigation of the murder of "an unspecified number of civilians" by an American officer in Vietnam.

Watergate was similarly ignored by most papers for months after the initial break-in. Only the *Washington Post* covered the story aggressively in the early stages. Other papers dismissed the Watergate break-in as an inconsequential incident.

In both cases—My Lai and Watergate—the stories may have been largely ignored because they were what sociologist Herbert Gans calls "unbelievable news."

American soldiers massacring innocent children? Unbelievable. Members of the White House staff involved in the burglary of Democratic headquarters? Unbelievable.

Such stories suffer from "a taboo on unbelievable news," Gans writes in his book-length study, *Deciding What's News*. These stories ". . . transcend the journalists' expectations of what people are capable of doing. . . . Journalists are trained by experience to develop a cynical attitude toward the incredible. . . . Stories are self-censored when journalists doubt their veracity."

One former *New York Times* reporter says precisely this phenomenon came into play in that paper's weak early coverage of the New York City financial crisis.

"Some reporters covering City Hall were cynics," he says. "They assumed all politicians are crooks and liars, so when all the talk about financial trouble started, they didn't believe there really was a crisis. They kept looking to see what political angle was being played."

The idea that the most important and vibrant city in the United States could go bankrupt was inconceivable to people—journalists included. Thus, as late as April 11, 1975, a *New York Times* "News Analysis" said:

"Can New York City default on its debt and go bankrupt? The answer is no, and it can be given without qualification, according to city and private financial experts. . . ."

But five weeks later the paper was forced to concede in another "News Analysis":

"New York could quite soon become a city with no available cash, with poor credit, needing to borrow money from a financial market that is resisting. . . . In short, if the money is not found soon, it could become a city in default."

One reason newspapers sometimes miss major stories in their early, developmental stages is that they, and their editors and publishers, are themselves part of the stories. The *New York Times* is part of New York and, in some ways, part of the very New York establishment whose leaders (former Governor Nelson Rockefeller and former Mayor John Lindsay among them) helped foster the conditions that made the fiscal crisis inevitable.

It was not so much a matter of the newspaper consciously trying to protect its friends by suppressing bad news; it was more a matter of the men running the newspaper and the men running the city often sharing the same perceptions—and misperceptions. They just didn't see the story early enough.

That may help explain why the two daily newspapers in San Francisco—the *Chronicle* and the *Examiner*—were so late covering the Reverend Jim Jones and the Peoples Temple.

More than eighteen months before the mass suicides and

murders in Guyana, *Chronicle* reporter Marshall Kilduff began looking into the strange hold Jones had on his San Francisco congregation and on many members of the San Francisco establishment as well.

But the *Chronicle* told Kilduff they'd done a routine personality profile on Jones several months earlier and saw no need for further stories on him—not even when Kilduff told his editors about Jones's surprising political influence in the city . . . and about the curious and vigorous resistance he had encountered to his inquiries.

Kilduff wasn't surprised by his editors' disdain—not after he went to Jones's church for the first time and saw his city editor sitting behind him.

"I felt I was being put on notice very quietly that Jones was a friend of my superiors," Kilduff says now.

Although a magazine ultimately published Kilduff's story, neither the *Chronicle* nor the *Examiner* or any other big-city daily paper rushed to assign reporters to investigate his charges of "exploitation" and "physical discipline" in the church. Despite Kilduff's detailed account of Jones's political clout and his attempts (through powerful intermediaries) to have the story killed, the press still did not appear to be in any hurry to answer the question Kilduff and co-author Phil Tracy posed in the article: ". . . what is going on behind the locked and guarded doors of Peoples Temple?"

This question was coupled with a warning: "The story of Jim Jones and his Peoples Temple is not over."

Steve Gavin, Kilduff's city editor at the *Chronicle* at the time, denies that his own relationship with Jones prompted his coolness toward Kilduff's story. He does concede, however,

that he went to Jones's church services "once or twice . . .
liked him and thought he was doing good things."

Kilduff thinks Gavin just "may have blinded himself to the
. . . more weird aspects of Jones"—only partly because the
two had come to know each other personally. Kilduff also
blames the pressure exerted by Jones's influential followers
and friends (the lieutenant governor, the mayor, the district attorney) and Gavin's own genuine acceptance of the message
Jones was putting out through these people: "If you write
about him and he becomes a media celebrity, the poor blacks
who need him the most will turn skeptically away from his efforts to rescue them."

Peoples Temple is a dramatic example of a "missed"
newspaper story, but many press critics are more concerned
about the media missing (or being very late to cover) whole
movements (civil rights, feminism, environmentalism) than individual stories.

Many editors resent that criticism.

"You simply can't repeat, for the purpose of social benefit,
the same information over and over," says William F.
Thomas, editor of the *Los Angeles Times*. "If there is new information or a new incident, then you owe it to your readers to
print it, whether they want to read it or not.

"[But] you can only write so much about Watts or smog,
and if there's nothing new and the readers aren't interested
. . . you can't shove it down their throats."

Says Benjamin C. Bradlee, executive editor of the *Washington Post:*

"There's a kind of story you write and get a very discouraging reaction on. You write stories and it's like dropping a stone in a well and never hearing it.

"We had that with all the energy stories we wrote (in the mid-1970s). There was no appetite for them so we didn't serve them up again. I felt I had discharged my obligation."

The result: Many critics now charge that the press didn't provide the public with ample warning of the 1979 gasoline shortage.

Unfortunately, newspapers tend to be crisis-oriented. "The best newspapers do remarkably well in crisis situations," Bradlee says. "The uniqueness of the event [the crisis] is easily spotted. But the ability to do as well when the truth is less obvious, when you're at . . . cruising speed, is another matter."

Thus, several papers provided good coverage of the nuclear accident at Three Mile Island in Harrisburg, Pennsylvania, in 1979. But prior press coverage of the potential dangers of nuclear power was so inadequate that a panel of twelve journalists and educators named it "the most censored story of 1978.

. . . Lack of coverage . . . comprises a form of media censorship . . ." the jurors said.

Some newspaper executives are equally critical.

"Why did it take a Three Mile Island to focus national press attention on this issue?" asks David Kraslow, publisher of the *Miami News*. "There is enough evidence to suggest that the press should have covered the story long before Three Mile Island."

In all these "missed" stories—Three Mile Island, Peoples Temple, My Lai, Watergate, the New York City financial crisis—hindsight tells us that alert, aggressive journalism could have performed a valuable public service.

Business writer Martin Mayer, for example, insists that the "public ignorance" born of inadequate press coverage compounded New York's fiscal problems. Surely, other critics say, the agonies of Vietnam and Watergate would not have dragged on so long—and the deaths in Guyana and near-disaster in Harrisburg might have been averted altogether—had the press eagerly pursued the appropriate stories early enough.

But virtually every newspaper reporter, editor, and publisher in the country can remember a story or two that he and his colleagues missed badly.

Luke Feck, former publisher of the *Cincinnati Enquirer,* is still embarrassed by (perhaps even ashamed of) his paper's failure to write about the dangerously crowded conditions at the Beverly Hills Supper Club in nearby Southgate, Kentucky, before 165 persons were killed there in a 1977 fire.

"All of us at the paper had been there before," Feck says, "and I can remember all of us saying, 'What would you do if you ever got jammed in here in a fire?'

"But we didn't think journalistically about that question. We didn't write anything until it was too late."

Sometimes newspapers miss stories because of such neglect. Or because their reporters are lazy. Or because their sources lie to them. More often they miss because "missing stories is endemic to the business" in the words of Stuart Loory, former managing editor of the *Chicago Sun-Times.*

Eugene Patterson, editor and president of the *St. Petersburg* (Fla.) *Times,* says editors often "handle such a huge volume of stories everyday that you just don't see the red lights blinking on certain stories.

"When you're in a blizzard of events everyday, you're going to miss one once in a while, and people are going to second-guess you. Unfortunately, our critics always think the worst when that happens. They accuse you of deliberately covering up.

"They don't leave us any room for common stupidity, of which we sometimes have a very high level."

That's why editors at the *Los Angeles Times* were, ultimately, mortified when their newspaper failed to cover adequately or promptly two of the most controversial stories of the late 1970s in Los Angeles. Other newspapers have blown stories, too, of course, but these two cases are particularly enlightening.

* * *

ON OCTOBER 3, 1977, Columbia Pictures Industries, Inc., issued a press release announcing that the audit committee of its board of directors had "commenced an inquiry into certain unauthorized financial transactions between David Begelman and the company."

Begelman had resigned as director and senior vice president of Columbia, the release said, and he was "taking a leave of absence from his operating responsibilities [as president of the motion picture and television division of] . . . the company."

Begelman was a big man in Hollywood—a flamboyant agent-turned-producer who had taken charge of production at Columbia when the studio was more than $220 million in debt and who had been largely credited with putting the studio back on its financial feet with such smash hits as *Shampoo, Tommy, The Front, Funny Lady,* and *The Deep.*

Now, suddenly, Begelman was out. Why?

Begelman was, it would seem, an ideal story for the press—especially for a newspaper like the *Los Angeles Times.* Here was a tale of power, scandal, and intrigue in the most glamorous business in the world, right in the *Times*'s own backyard. Ultimately, the story would become a best-selling book (*Indecent Exposure* by David McClintock). But the morning after the Columbia announcement, the *Times* carried only a one-paragraph story in the financial briefs column on page eight of the paper's Business section. The next day the *Times* published another short item, essentially restating the original story . . . in the "Film Clips" column on page eight of the paper's View section.

Those were the only stories on the Begelman affair to appear in the *Times* for more than two months. Even when Columbia reinstated Begelman as president of its motion picture and television division ten weeks later—and announced that he had returned, "with interest," $61,008 in corporate funds obtained by "improper means"—the *Times* published only one paragraph . . . this time on page nine of the Business section.

No other newspaper had published much on the Begelman case before this announcement either. Personnel changes, contract disputes, and charges of wrongdoing often seem as common as popcorn in the movie business. But this latest announcement spurred most papers to action.

On the same day, the *Wall Street Journal* published a twenty-three-paragraph story, pointing out that Begelman had "obtained much of the money by forging checks . . . using the names of Cliff Robertson, the actor, and Martin Ritt, the film director." Five days later, the *Washington Post* published an even longer and more provocative story on the Begelman affair. But not until five days after that did the *Los Angeles Times* run anything of consequence on Begelman—an edited-down version of the *Post* story, about one-third the length of the original.

In the ensuing weeks and months, the *Times* began to show somewhat more interest in the Begelman story. But at no time did the *Times* produce a single story as revelatory as the original *Journal* and *Post* stories. It was not until July 12, 1979—nineteen months after the story first broke—that the *Times* finally published a lengthy, on-the-record interview with Begelman.

Why was the *Times* so passive and inadequate in its coverage of the Begelman affair?

"It was bad judgment," says *Times* managing editor George Cotliar. "A lot of us didn't even see the original story . . . [and] once we blew it . . . the hardest thing for anyone to do is admit making a mistake. Subconsciously we tried to wish it away. The editors made a terrible mistake. We screwed up on Begelman and we continually compounded our error."

Some editors at the *Times* insist that the *Wall Street Journal* was first on Begelman because Begelman was essentially a financial story and the *Journal* is a financial newspaper based in New York, as is the headquarters of Columbia Pictures, with the best possible Wall Street sources.

But the *Los Angeles Times* had three reporters in New York—one of whom wrote about business full time. And Begelman himself, and most of his colleagues and victims, lived in Los Angeles.

Other *Times* editors say the *Post* got the story because Cliff Robertson and his wife, Dina Merrill, are old friends of then *Post* publisher Katherine Graham. But Robertson says they called Mrs. Graham primarily because ". . . the whole thing had been dragging on for months, and the *Los Angeles Times* had been so conspicuously mute on it that they didn't seem to be interested at all."

That seeming lack of interest at the *Times* came largely from the paper's longtime structural and attitude problems, which the Begelman error exposed.

"I've just never had the feeling that the top editors at the *Times* take the people in my business very seriously," says one veteran Hollywood producer, echoing many in his industry.

Editors at the *L.A. Times* concede the essential accuracy of this charge.

The writers in the paper's entertainment section had traditionally been "critics and feature writers, not news reporters," says Irv Letofsky, editor of the paper's Sunday Calendar section. "We cover the artistic element in Hollywood," he said in the immediate aftermath of the Begelman affair. "We're not equipped to do hard-news investigation."

Moreover, because of the entertainment section's deadlines—the section is printed a day ahead of time—coverage of breaking news stories is necessarily limited.

"That creates an atmosphere in which the hard-news kind of story is not encouraged," one reporter said.

Thus, most entertainment reporters routinely referred to the paper's financial and/or news sections any entertainment story that seemed to have a hard-news angle. Or, more often, they just assumed someone in those departments would handle the story.

But reporters and editors in the news and financial departments generally made just the opposite assumption: If it was an entertainment story—be it a change in studio personnel, a controversy in a network news operation, or a rumor of rock music payola—it was a story for the entertainment department to handle.

So, in the absence of strong, head-to-head competition from another large metropolitan daily paper, it was easy for some stories to fall between the cracks in the editorial hierarchy.

That kind of jurisdictional confusion is not altogether uncommon on large newspapers, and when the Begelman story broke, it was the *Times*'s undoing: John Lawrence, assistant managing editor for financial coverage, assumed the entertainment staff would handle it; his counterparts in the entertainment department assumed the financial staff would handle it. No one handled it.

"Everyone was sitting around waiting for someone else to do something," Letofsky said.

When the *Washington Post* story on Begelman came to the *Times* over the wire service the *Post* and the *Times* share, it went first to Lawrence, then to Letofsky, then back to Lawrence again, sitting on and/or in various desks for several days. Finally, William F. Thomas, editor of the *L.A. Times*, directed the editors to use the *Post* story. It ran the next day.

But didn't people in the *Times* news and entertainment departments ever speak to each other? Shouldn't someone in one of those departments have asked someone in the other department early on, "Hey, are you guys looking into Begelman or do you want us to do it?"

"Of course," said Jean Sharley Taylor, associate editor of the *Times*, whose responsibilities include supervision of the View and entertainment staffs. But Taylor and her people had traditionally had little contact with the daily news operation at the paper, and therein lay the real problem.

At many large newspapers, editors in the entertainment department ultimately report to editors in the news department. These editors then represent the entertainment department at the daily news conference where each day's major stories are discussed. So there is some daily give and take between the departments.

But at the *Los Angeles Times*, neither Taylor nor anyone on her two staffs reports to, or is represented by, anyone who attends the daily news conference. Unlike their counterparts at the *New York Times*, they have their own, virtually autonomous sections each day.

This (along with some individual differences in interests and attitudes among the various editors at the two papers) may help explain why there are, according to an eighteen-month study I conducted especially to examine this problem, about twice as many entertainment-oriented stories on the front page of the *New York Times* as there are on the front page of the *Los Angeles Times*.

There are other reasons for this disparity—among them the varying judgments of the individual editors on each story and the existence every day of more ad-free pages in the *Los Angeles Times* than in the *New York Times*, pages on which major stories that don't make page one can still be given prominent display.

It may also be significant that the *New York Times* office is located (and many top-ranking *New York Times* editors live) in midtown Manhattan, the hub of the city's cultural life, whereas the *Los Angeles Times* office is in downtown Los Angeles and most *Los Angeles Times* editors live in the suburbs, far away from the west side movie community.

Had top *Los Angeles Times* editors lived in Beverly Hills or Brentwood or Bel Air or Malibu, they might have recognized the significance of the Begelman story earlier simply by hearing their friends and neighbors talking about it.

But the top editors at the *Los Angeles Times* lived in Sherman Oaks, Newport Beach, Pasadena, La Canada, and Arcadia, and they heard little there about Begelman. Taylor herself says she doesn't even recall being aware of the Begelman affair until perhaps three months after he was relieved of his duties.

Times editors did not even hear much about Begelman in their offices, for the division between the news and entertainment departments was virtually total.

Reform may have been particularly difficult at the *Los Angeles Times* for several reasons, among them:

• Because the paper's news and editorial pages were so bad in earlier generations (and because those pages are a newspaper's primary function and showcase), the improvements that began at the paper in the 1960s focused first on those areas rather than on entertainment.

• In this effort to improve the paper and to be perceived as a truly serious paper, comprehensive coverage of entertainment ("Hollywood") may have been subconsciously (even defensively) passed over as not quite worthy of the same journalistic examination as Sacramento, Washington, London, or Moscow.

Many entertainment writers and editors at the *Times* say they have always felt that their news-side counterparts looked down on them.

"I often passed things on to financial and city-side and they just disappeared," said Wayne Warga, then the paper's assistant arts editor. "I stopped [doing it]. I figured they didn't respect us. They didn't think what we were doing really mattered."

News editors say, however, that the poor performance of some entertainment writers on news stories prompted their disdain. Moreover, they say, they just never had enough reporters to pursue all the stories suggested. Neither did they have a financial writer who specialized in covering entertainment. Editors in the entertainment department cite the same deficiencies.

But newspapers never have enough people to do all the stories that should be done. They must establish priorities—and Hollywood *is* Hollywood: visible, productive, interesting, watched by millions the world over. At the *Los Angeles Times,* editors later conceded, a higher priority should long ago have been given to assigning someone to cover the business side of the entertainment industry.

Because this was not done, and because there was so little contact between the entertainment and news departments, such stories as the Begelman affair sometimes went uncovered.

Not that the Begelman story was unique. In general, the *Times* did not cover the entertainment industry the same way it covered, say, the aircraft or automobile industries.

"Had Begelman been the president of Lockheed we would have been on it right away," one *Times* financial reporter said.

Not until perhaps three months after Columbia issued its first press release on it did *Times* editors—prodded by Thomas and worried that *New West* (now *California* magazine) was about to break a major Begelman story—decide they had to get on the Begelman story right away.

On January 13, 1978, Taylor told her staffs she wanted an interview with Begelman or "at least . . . a strong summation or backgrounder" as quickly as possible.

Arts editor Charles Champlin got a telephone interview with Begelman and wrote a story for the January 16 paper—a story that tried to explain Begelman's side of the entire affair.

"I couldn't pretend it was a piece of reporting," Champlin said later, and, sure enough, Champlin's story was sympathetic to Begelman, referring to his forgeries as a "crimeless crime" and to him as "a culprit who doubles as a victim . . . both liked and admired . . . dapper, affable, suave, articulate, and energetically imaginative."

Had that story followed investigative stories by the *Times*, it may have been seen by most readers as a humane and fully justified exercise in fairness. But because it was the *Time*'s very first effort at enterprise on Begelman—more than three months after the fact—critics justifiably assailed it as an "apologia."

Champlin's story embarrassed the *Times* and only further contributed to an already widely held public perception that the *Times* had deliberately ignored the Begelman affair because the paper was "protective" of Hollywood, ". . . like a company paper in a company town . . . [defending] the film industry from . . . outsiders" in the words of one national journalism review.

But there was (and is) no stated (or unstated) policy at the *Times* about being supportive of Hollywood, though Champlin himself is certainly an especially kind, decent person, a man more inclined to praise than to pillory. Even he admits that this aspect of his personality may have subconsciously affected his evaluation of Begelman.

But there are many other editors and reporters at the paper

whose personalities are far harsher—more aggressive and more cynical—than Champlin's, and they did not rush to investigate Begelman either.

"I wish we had," one editor said. "We'd love to expose a big Hollywood scandal anytime. On Begelman we just dropped the ball."

In fact, the reporter most directly responsible for covering the Begelman story said he just missed stumbling onto it himself on two separate occasions.

Gregg Kilday, then the writer of the *Times*'s "Film Clips" column, said that shortly after his first "Film Clips" item on Begelman appeared, he received a message that Sid Luft, whose ex-wife, Judy Garland, had once been a client of Begelman's, wanted to talk to him.

Kilday twice tried unsuccessfully to return the call, then went on to other matters.

What Kilday did not know was that Luft had another story on Begelman: charges that Begelman had swindled Miss Garland out of several hundred thousand dollars more than ten years earlier.

Luft ultimately took the story to *New West* (now *California*) magazine.

At a party one night two months later, Kilday heard someone mentioned that a well-known agent was saying bad checks were involved in the Begelman affair. But this was the first mention of that angle; the report seemed vague, and Kilday did not realize that this agent represented Cliff Robertson—whose name had not yet surfaced in the case.

Thus, when the agent sat down next to Kilday a few moments later, Kilday, dismissing what he had just heard as "mere gossip," did not bother to ask him anything about it.

"I guess I blew it," Kilday said—a phrase many at the *Times* now use to describe their roles in the story.

But Champlin, Taylor, and Thomas also feel that others in the media ultimately overplayed the Begelman story.

Many newspapers and magazines quickly seized on the Begelman affair as proof of pervasive corruption in Hollywood. *Newsweek* ran a seven-page cover story—"Inside Hollywood: High Stakes! Fast Bucks! Shady Deals!" *Esquire* likened the Begelman affair to Watergate. The *New York Times* Sunday magazine ran a story about "the Godfather of the New Hollywood." Even the *Milwaukee Journal* made it its lead page-one story one day, "Bribe, Kickback Charges Plague U.S. Film Industry."

Amid all these charges, reporters and editors at the *Los Angeles Times* finally began to scurry in a desperate attempt to catch up.

"We were absolutely in a state of panic," Champlin said.

But neither the *Los Angeles Times* nor any other newspaper or magazine ever really advanced the Begelman/Hollywood scandal story substantially beyond what was revealed in those first *Wall Street Journal* and *Washington Post* stories.

Reporters for many papers—including the *Times*—uncovered intriguing rumors, fascinating gossip, and explosive charges, but very little they could prove.

At the *Times,* this problem was compounded by the feeling among some editors that since the paper had been beaten so badly in early coverage, it could only recoup by publishing a major, comprehensive exclusive.

"We picked up little bits and pieces and a couple of pretty good things," said one reporter who worked on the story, "and, in retrospect, I guess we should have run them as we got them. But we wanted to do the definitive story, and by the time we got involved, most of the good stuff was already out, the key people weren't talking anymore, and most of what we did find, we couldn't prove."

Since Begelman, the *Times* has tried to rectify the conditions responsible for its poor performance on that story.

Reporters with experience in covering the business side of entertainment have been hired for the paper's entertainment and financial sections. Editors and reporters in both these departments, and those on the paper's metropolitan staff, now communicate with each other regularly and even help each other out on some stories. The paper has published several very good stories on the business side of Hollywood in the past couple of years.

But old habits die hard. The paper still misses some good entertainment stories—not nearly as many as it used to but more than it should.

EULIA LOVE. She was shot to death by two police officers who had gone to her home after a dispute about an overdue $69 gas bill. They opened fire, it turned out, because she was about to throw an eleven-inch boning knife at them and because they knew that she had assaulted a gas company serviceman with a shovel earlier in the day.

Almost immediately the Eulia Love shooting became a *cause célèbre* in the black community, rekindling old charges of racism and police brutality. But the *Los Angeles Times* was slow to recognize the significance of the story—even after it was disclosed that Mrs. Love had been shot eight times and that she had in her purse at the time a money order for $22.09, the minimum amount necessary to keep her gas service connected.

The morning after the shooting, the *Times* carried only one paragraph on page two. No further stories appeared in the paper until a brief story a week later—on page thirteen of the third section. No mention of the shooting appeared on the front page of the paper until more than three months after it happened.

Meanwhile, the *Los Angeles Herald Examiner*, which had also published just a short item the day after the shooting, followed up with a twenty-two-paragraph story on page three the next day, a long front-page story six days after that, and an even longer front-page story twelve days later.

Some editors at both papers say the papers' respective competitive positions help explain these differences in news play.

The *Times* has long been the dominant leader in both circulation and advertising in Los Angeles. "We don't have much daily competition, so we don't always move as quickly on some things as we should," one *Times* editor said.

Sometimes, of course, the absence of daily competitive pressures is beneficial; it enables a newspaper to move more cautiously and responsibly, carefully examining complex and potentially volatile issues rather than rushing into print.

Day in and day out, even most *Herald Examiner* editors admit, the *Times* covers far more stories far more comprehensively with far fewer "misses" than the *Herald* does.

"But when you don't have to hustle everyday to beat the other guy, you can get lazy," one *Herald Examiner* editor said.

"And when the other paper is a distant number two," another editor said, "they look for any story they can to grab some attention—especially if it's a story the *Times* missed."

Thus, when the *Times* gave only one paragraph to the original Eulia Love story, *Herald* editors immediately made it "their" story.

As Stella Zadeh, then city editor of the *Herald,* said, "We were much more interested in it [the Love shooting] than if the *Times* had played it big on page one."

But the story was intrinsically a good one, and the *Herald,* sensing that, dispatched a young, black woman reporter the next day to the black neighborhood where the shooting had taken place.

"She was really interested in what happened—sympathetic," Zadeh said. "She found out about the $22 money order [in Mrs. Love's purse], and then we knew we had a good story, and [we] made the commitment to go after it."

James G. Bellows, then editor of the *Herald,* said he thought the *Times* also suffered in its early Love coverage from "long ago deciding that the minority communities weren't really their market."

Critics quote a statement that Otis Chandler, then publisher of the *Times* (and now chairman and editor-in-chief of the parent Times Mirror Co.), made on television in 1978 to the effect that the *Times* "could make the editorial commitment to cover these (minority) communities," but the *Times* is "not their kind of newspaper."

Said Bellows, "That kind of thinking trickles down . . . some stories won't get covered."

Times editors find that reasoning "preposterous." Chandler was not, they say, stating *Times* policy but relating a tragic and incontrovertible truth—that hundreds of years of discrimination and deprivation have left many in the minority communities with less education and sophistication than most of their white counterparts.

Times editors insist the paper tries to cover minorities, and they cite as proof a number of major stories on subjects of special interest to minorities. They also point to the paper's consistent editorial support of equal opportunity and affirmative action.

But the paper's circulation is still considerably lower in minority communities than elsewhere; the paper has no bureau in Watts or East Los Angeles and only 12 of the paper's 391 reporters and editors were black, none of them at the management level, at the time of the Eulia Love shooting.

What is probably more significant in the Eulia Love case, though, is the general attitude most newspaper people everywhere have toward violent crime in minority communities.

The attitude is not racism but cynicism: Violence is often so common in minority communities that it loses some of its news value.

Reporters and editors often tend to be interested in the less common and more glamorous murder at what they call "a good address"—in some wealthy suburb—and to callously dismiss a ghetto murder as "just another misdemeanor homicide."

Thus, it took more than three months for the fatal shooting of Eulia Love to make the front page of the *Los Angeles Times;* yet when a woman and two teenage boys were shot by a masked burglar in Beverly Hills on May 24, 1979, the story was on page one the very next morning, even before any of the victims had died.

"That story was overplayed because it was Beverly Hills," one *Times* editor said.

Said Mark Murphy, then metropolitan editor of the *Times*, "You see so many tragedies everyday, especially in the minority communities, that any sense of urgency in your mind becomes diminished. Then you become blasé about what's really a compelling story—like Eulia Love."

At the *Times* that "blasé" attitude often affects more than just the coverage of violence in minority communities.

"This paper isn't aggressive enough," Murphy said. "We tend to be a little . . . slow to react at times."

Times reporters who have spent much time at other newspapers say the atmosphere in the *Times* city room does not crackle with the same sense of fierce individual competition among reporters—or the same zeal to do battle with outsiders—that fuels many other newspaper staffs.

Some attribute this to the absence of strong competition here from another large daily paper and to a resultant emphasis at the paper on the major projects, overviews, features, and analyses rather than on daily news stories.

Other *Times* editors and reporters blame the "mellow, laidback" life-style of Los Angeles. Still others, like Murphy, say the problem is a lack of fire within individual reporters and editors—a deficiency exacerbated by the largely laissez-faire style in which the paper's metropolitan staff was run at the time of the Eulia Love shooting.

Some *Times* reporters agree.

Bill Boyarsky, chief of the paper's city-county bureau, said he remembers going to work with considerable disquietude the morning the *Herald Examiner* broke the first story on the Eulia Love autopsy. The *Times* had tried to get the story the previous day but had failed, and Boyarsky said, "I expected a call first thing from the [city] desk, saying, 'Where the hell were you guys on that one? . . . Why didn't we have it?' '' But no one called Boyarsky to complain about the slip-up.

That "indifference" colored the paper's early coverage of the entire story, Boyarsky said, and he—like many others at the paper—blames a lack of "social conscience" and "moral indignation" at the *Times*.

"I know we're not putting out a polemical sheet . . . the *People's World*," Boyarsky said, "but if you're going to cover urban affairs you should have some sense of injustice. I don't get that from our editors."

Some of those editors concede this. Murphy said he does not think the *Times* should be "a muckraking, hard-ass, crusading newspaper." Noel Greenwood, his top assistant at the time and, subsequently, his successor, said, "I'm not a great believer in righteous indignation when it comes to newspapering. It colors your judgment and distorts your perceptions. . . .''

But the problem with the *Times* coverage of the Love story, said editor William F. Thomas, was not so much a lack of indignation as a lack of recognition and reaction. "When a woman is shot to death by the police in her own yard in a dispute over a gas bill, you have to say to yourself, 'Holy Christ, we've got to get out there and find out what happened.' ''

Newspapers often fail to react quickly enough in such cases, though, and this was not the first time the *L.A. Times* had failed to do so. To avoid such failures, the *Times* had for two years been reassigning editors and restructuring the way such daily decisions and assignments are made.

"It's been a weak, penny-ante operation," Greenwood admits.

But habits and attitudes, as well as people, are involved, and change does not come easily.

Grahame Jones, one of the people involved in the city desk personnel changes, was day city editor at the time of the shooting. He said he saw a wire service story when he went to work the next morning, and thought, "That's a good story; we'll have to get someone on it."

When he saw that the *Times* had given the story only one paragraph that morning, though, Jones said, he changed his mind. "I figured no one thought it was much of a story."

Jones admits now that he should have "gone ahead on my own." But middle-level executives in other professions often do (or don't do) what they *think* their superiors want done (or not done) rather than doing what seems appropriate.

Jones did nothing. Neither did any reporter—not even the police beat reporter, who might routinely have followed up on the story himself.

Greenwood, who said he is not sure he was even aware of the shooting until the paper's reporter in Santa Barbara called it to his attention a few days later, said he subsequently told Jones twice to have the police beat reporter (a black) look into the story. But neither Jones nor the reporter recalls any such directive.

Boyarsky, meanwhile, had decided he should have one of his City Hall reporters, Doug Shuit—who had written other stories on police shootings—start investigating the story. He told Greenwood of his intentions.

"I figured they'd take care of it from then on," Greenwood says now. "They had carte blanche."

A few days later Shuit wrote a story on City Councilman Robert Farrell's call for a council review of police training in the use of nonlethal force. But his editors told him to keep the story short, and when he wrote it, they ran it on page thirteen of the third section.

"That told me they weren't very interested in it," Shuit said.

Why didn't Shuit argue with his editors, tell them it was a good, important story worthy of further development?

"It's not my style to fight," he said. "Maybe if another reporter was working the story. . . ."

Besides, Shuit and Boyarsky, like many reporters at the paper, thought that the paper was not anxious to print anything critical of the police. Years of contentiousness between the paper and two previous police chiefs seemed to have "softened the paper up so much, it put them on the defensive," Shuit said.

Times editors insisted they had published several stories critical of the police in the years immediately before the Love shooting, but the reporters' perceptions affected their response to the Love story.

"It's a kind of self-censorship," another *Times* reporter said. "I hear reporters say they *can't* write this story or that story because their editors don't want them to, but, in reality, the editors may not feel that way at all."

Shuit's reaction to the Love story was further complicated by his realization that the *Herald* had gotten a head start on it. Journalists often let such factors govern their behavior. A story is "our" story or "their" story. If it's "theirs," maybe "we" ignore it. Ed Kosner, editor of *New York* magazine calls this the "NIH [Not-Invented-Here]" syndrome.

In the Love case, Shuit said, "My attitude was that rather than chase a story the *Herald* already had, I wanted to do my own police-shooting story." So, encouraged by Boyarsky, he intensified an investigation he had already started on another police shooting, this one of an eighteen-year-old youth.

Shuit was not the only *Times* reporter working on the Love shooting, even in the early stages of the story. On January 13, Celeste Durant was assigned to cover Love's funeral. There was an antipolice demonstration afterward. She wrote a story about the funeral and the demonstration.

It never appeared.

Times editors said the story, as written, had several holes, "didn't advance things very far" and was not important enough for them to try to squeeze into a tight paper on a Saturday night.

But the *Herald Examiner* published a twenty-four-paragraph story on the funeral and demonstration.

Durant, a black, was angry; she accused her editors of everything from poor news judgment to outright racism—charges they all denied—and when she visited the *Times* City Hall bureau a couple of days later, she and Shuit discussed their unhappiness over the paper's coverage of the Love case.

Instead of going together to complain to their editors, though, they just decided their editors were not interested in the story.

In the weeks that followed, the *Times* carried several routine stories on the case but nothing major. Then, on March 30, Boyarsky read an *Esquire* magazine column critical of the paper's coverage of the Love case; among other things the column said, "The *Times* probably didn't give a damn . . . about Eulia Love and assumed its readers didn't either."

Boyarsky wrote a memo to his editors, pointing out that the *Times* had been first with some details of the story and that the *Herald* had been wrong on some others. But he admitted, "We were too late, with too little, on the Love story."

About the same time, a *California Journal* article also was critical of the paper's Love coverage, and editors at the paper were beginning to realize they had overlooked a major story.

"They'd blown it," said Kenneth Reich, a reporter who is one of the paper's most outspoken internal critics, "but I'll have to commend the editors for this: They weren't too proud to admit they'd been wrong. They were journalistically responsible . . . and went into it with a vengeance."

Two days after writing his memo, Boyarsky was placed in charge of a four-reporter task force, and on April 16, the day before the district attorney released his own report on the shooting, the paper published the results of their work—three stories, totaling more than 7,000 words, spread over parts of eight different pages.

It was a comprehensive, insightful, well-written presentation, and it was followed by several other stories in the ensuing weeks. The paper has also made it a point—a policy—since then to routinely pay more attention to all police shootings. In fact, under Greenwood and his top assistant, David Rosenzweig, the paper has greatly improved its coverage of the daily local news and its scrutiny of the police. So the mistakes made on the Eulia Love case have ultimately benefited the paper (and its readers).

But on the Love story itself, as one editor said, "We really screwed up. It was a big error by everyone concerned, from the very top editors down to the police reporter."

7

THE PULITZER PRIZES

It was the biggest scandal in the history of the Pulitzer Prizes: Janet Cooke, a twenty-six-year-old reporter for the *Washington Post,* was forced to surrender her Pulitzer Prize (and her job) after it was disclosed that her prize-winning story about an eight-year-old heroin addict named "Jimmy" was a phony. There was no eight-year-old heroin addict named "Jimmy."

The controversy that followed this disclosure in 1980 probably brought more public attention to the Pulitzer Prizes than any other event since the prizes were first awarded in 1917. Until the Janet Cooke affair, most members of the general public were probably only dimly aware of the prizes—primarily from having seen front-page stories announcing them each year and from reading "Pulitzer Prize–winning" attached to the front of many famous (and not-so-famous) names.

But even now, little is generally known of the Pulitzer Prize process itself.

When the Pulitzer Prizes are announced each spring, it is but the last step in an arduous, often arcane process.

Until 1977, for example, almost anyone could claim to have been nominated for a Pulitzer Prize. All he had to do was nominate himself. Although the vast majority of Pulitzer entries are submitted by individual newspapers, there are no rules requiring this. Anyone may send in an entry.

Now, however, entries are called "entries." To be "nominated," an entry must be selected as a finalist by one of the formal nominating juries.

In the arts—books, plays, and music—these juries are made up of experts in their respective fields as selected by the Pulitzer Prize Board and its secretary. These jurors are paid $250 each.

In the twelve journalism categories, each jury is made up of four to six newspaper people, also selected by the board and its secretary. (Like the board, they serve without pay.) The journalism juries meet for three days in early March at Columbia University—each jury in a separate room—and they select the finalists, whose names are then forwarded to the Pulitzer board.

Although the juries' nomenclature has changed from time to time, the juries—mostly journalism professors until 1947, virtually all editors now—have always been "nominating juries" in the sense that they serve as a screening committee, reducing the 60 or 80 or 130 entries in each category to a more manageable three to five finalists.

But juries have frequently balked at their role as merely preliminary judges. From 1975 to 1979, for example, despite a board request that they submit their nominations in alphabetical order, fifty-one of the fifty-six juries submitted them largely—often entirely—in order of preference, clearly specifying their choices for the ultimate winner.

The juries also submitted as few as one nomination and as many as ten. But since 1980 juries have been formally required to submit three nominations in alphabetical order.

Juries are still permitted to make more than three nominations in "exceptional cases" and to specify their preferences among the finalists, but the actual list of nominees must be alphabetical.

As in the past, all the juries' selections—in journalism and the arts—are voted on by the board during its annual meeting at Columbia in April.

The jury system, and the quality of the juries, has been improved considerably in recent years, but the Pulitzer board still makes the final decisions—and that means controversy. Even with all the recent improvements, for example, the board still overruled its juries' first choices nine times in the last four years. But at least this selection process is a little simpler than it used to be.

Until 1976 the board's choices were forwarded to the trustees of Columbia, who formally presented the awards. According to the terms of Joseph Pulitzer's bequest, they could refuse to honor any of these choices and give no awards in those categories, but they couldn't replace the Pulitzer board's choices with their own.

The trustees grew increasingly unhappy with this largely rubber-stamp role, especially in the early 1970s when the Pulitzer board voted to give awards for stories on the Pentagon Papers, President Nixon's tax returns, and American policy making during the Indo-Pakistani war.

Many trustees felt uncomfortable paying tribute to journalistic work based on information that many of them thought had been obtained illegally or improperly.

"In each instance I was able to persuade the trustees to

make the award as recommended by the [Pulitzer] Advisory Board," former Columbia president William McGill subsequently wrote to Joseph Pulitzer, Jr., chairman of the Pulitzer board.

But in all three cases, the trustees issued a disclaimer, saying, in effect, that they would not have made these awards had the choices been exclusively theirs.

Fearing further such disputes that "would only damage the Pulitzer Prizes and . . . do great harm to Columbia," McGill helped initiate discussions to remove the trustees from the Pulitzer selection process. On April 11, 1975, that was accomplished.

The awards are now made by the president of Columbia on behalf of the university, with all final decisions having been made by the Pulitzer board, which is no longer called the "Advisory Board," just the "Pulitzer Prize Board."

*   *   *

H E WAS one of the most respected newsmen of his generation—an editor, a publisher, and an entrepreneur. In 1947 he was selected as one of twelve editors to serve on the elite board that annually awards the Pulitzer Prizes. But it was a short-lived appointment. He attended the 1947 meeting, skipped the 1948 meeting, and showed up dead-drunk for the 1949 meeting.

"He told us he'd just come from spending all night in a whorehouse," recalls one board member who served with him. "Then he folded his arms on the table, put his head on his arms, and went to sleep."

Everyone ignored the slumbering editor until noon when he was awakened to attend the traditional luncheon with the president of Columbia University, which sponsors the Pulitzers. After lunch he went back to sleep for the rest of the afternoon while the rest of the board voted on the various awards.

At day's end, board member Arthur Krock, then chief of the Washington bureau of the *New York Times,* gestured toward his sleeping colleague and asked his fellow board members, "Do I hear a motion to accept [his] . . . resignation?"

Another board member replied, "But he hasn't offered to resign."

Krock: "He will."

The vote was unanimous. Krock then shook the fellow awake and took him outside for a walk. When they returned, the man resigned.

In the sixty-seven years since the first Pulitzer Prizes were awarded—under the terms of a bequest by Joseph Pulitzer, publisher of the *St. Louis Post-Dispatch* and the *New York World*—more than seventy editors have served on the Pulitzer board. Only two have served as briefly as the man with the dreadful hangover. None has been as powerful as Krock. But all have deliberated and voted in such secrecy that even an incident like a board member's day-long, booze-filled nap went unreported until I wrote about it in the *Los Angeles Times* thirty-one years later.

Although Pulitzer Prize–winners often learn unofficially of their good fortune through the journalistic grapevine before the formal announcement is made, board deliberations are so secret that not even Lee Hills, chairman of Knight-Ridder and a member of the Pulitzer board from 1970 to 1982, knew, when he won a Pulitzer in 1956, that he had actually been the third choice of the nominating jury that year.

When I told him, in 1979, that he had only won because the board had overruled the jury, he was stunned.

Much of the secrecy surrounding the Pulitzers—board members' votes aren't even officially recorded—has been cultivated by the Columbia journalism professors who have served as secretaries to the board and administrators of the prizes through the years.

This was particularly true of John Hohenberg, secretary-administrator from 1954 to 1976 and "a great believer in the sanctity of the closed door" in the words of Elie Abel, former dean of the Graduate School of Journalism at Columbia.

But Hohenberg has retired now, and over the last several years the secrecy shrouding the Pulitzer selection process has been pierced several times amid growing controversies concerning several recommendations made by various Pulitzer nominating juries that were overturned by the Pulitzer Prize Board itself.

As a result, jury reports more than three years old have now been opened to scholars and others of "serious intent," and several new rules went into effect for 1980—including a complete overhaul of the jury system, the addition of the first two blacks and the first woman (and first nonjournalist) to the Pulitzer board, and, for the first time, the announcement of the runners-up in every prize category when the prizes are awarded.

But these changes aren't likely to diminish controversy over the Pulitzers. There has always been controversy over the Pulitzers—and fear that controversy would somehow tarnish the prizes—and the Pulitzers have always survived, prestige intact.

As Hohenberg himself wrote in discussing the awards made in 1925, "It would have been a dull year if the Pulitzer Prize had not fomented a debate."

Among the most serious criticisms leveled at the Pulitzer process over the years:

- It is dominated by a few large Eastern establishment newspapers (primarily the *New York Times* and the *Washington Post*) and distorted by the friendships, logrolling, and gentlemen's agreements made by these papers' editors on the Pulitzer board.
- Papers published in the West, and small papers published

anywhere, are systematically and unjustly neglected when the prizes are awarded.
- Reform and innovation are all but impossible because the board is made up of conservative old men who pick their own successors, a self-perpetuating elite.
- Some deserving winners are deliberately bypassed in favor of inferior entries because the board wants to spread the prizes around.

In short, many critics charge, personal and political considerations often so compromise the award-making process that the Pulitzers don't deserve the almost mystical esteem in which they are generally held by journalists.

The Pulitzers are, indisputably, the most prestigious awards in American journalism—"the only ones that really count," in the words of one editor.

The Pulitzers are inevitably front-page news the day they're announced (even in 1945, when Germany surrendered the same day), and they're invariably invoked for years, even decades after when a "Pulitzer Prize–winning reporter" writes a book or makes a speech . . . or dies.

The $1,000 award that comes with each Pulitzer Prize is but a token of the award's actual value in terms of public and professional recognition. When *New York Times* columnist Russell Baker won the Pulitzer for commentary in 1979, he wound up on the cover of *Time* magazine.

"There's something magic about the Pulitzer," says two-time Pulitzer Prize–winning reporter James Rissen of the *Des Moines Register*. "It gives you prestige in and out of the profession. I often get invited to speak, and I'm expected to talk on all kinds of cosmic issues. Suddenly I'm an all-around expert."

A few years ago, I spent six weeks traveling around the country, looking into the entire Pulitzer process—interviews with every member of the Pulitzer board (four of whom were themselves Pulitzer Prize–winners), as well as with many past board members, jurors, winners, and other editors and reporters.

I also examined board minutes and nominating jury reports for every year available since the present system began in 1947.

What came from this now-updated and still-valid study is a surprising, fascinating, complex, often contradictory portrait of a process now influenced far less by politics and cronyism than its detractors charge—and influenced far more by caprice and sentiment than the general public might believe.

I found that:

- All things considered, small papers (especially very small papers) generally fare much better than is widely perceived, sometimes winning awards less for journalistic merit than because they are the sentimental favorites of big-city board members.
- Because the Pulitzer board votes on so many awards in so short a time—twelve journalism prizes and seven arts prizes in a two-day meeting (formerly a one-day meeting)—some decisions are remarkably quick and casual, even "capricious" and "haphazard," critics say.

    (On at least two occasions, the board has overruled jury recommendations because a board member happened to see a cartoon or a series of stories not mentioned by the jury, stuck it in his pocket that morning, pulled it out during the meeting, showed it around or read it aloud, and swayed enough votes to switch the award.)
- The machinations of a small group of men often dictated the Pulitzer Prize–winners of the 1940s, 1950s, and early 1960s. But the present Pulitzer board seems to have largely avoided these overt machinations.
- The *New York Times,* which has been represented on the Pulitzer board all but seven years since 1917, has benefited more than any other paper from board votes overturning jury recommendations for Pulitzers.
- The *Washington Post* has *lost* more Pulitzers on board over-

turns of jury recommendations than any other paper.

* The West is vastly underrepresented on the Pulitzer juries and the Pulitzer board—and in the number of prizes given out. ("Basically, the board members tend to read each other's papers, from Chicago east, and the prizes reflect that," says one former board member.)
* Cartooning has traditionally been the most controversial Pulitzer award, with more overturns of jury nominations (including four years in a row in the late 1970s), more repeat winners, and more years with no award at all than any other category.

    (Three explanations suggest themselves: (1) cartooning is a most subjective art; (2) unlike the various writing categories, cartooning does not require board members to spend much time pouring through voluminous entries if they want to overrule the jury; and (3) there are, by general agreement, only five or six top-flight cartoonists working at one time, and the board must always balance its desire to honor the best work and its desire to spread the prizes around. In the sixty-seven-year history of the Pulitzers, there have been only nine two-time winners in the nine writing categories and only two in the two photo categories. No one has ever won three Pulitzers for writing or photography. But there have been eight two-time winners—and three three-time winners—in cartooning.)
* The Pulitzer board has traditionally been dominated by what one former member calls "the elder statesmen of the journalistic establishment"—"tired, old stuffed shirts," in the less polite terminology of another editor. This may help explain why reform has historically come so slowly to the Pulitzer process.

The average age of the board is fifty-six, the youngest member forty-eight, the oldest seventy. More than half the board members are publishers, presidents, and chairmen, and most of the rest are editors-in-chief—"too far removed, really, from the day-to-day operations of the editorial process," concedes Clayton Kirkpatrick, former Pulitzer board member and former president of the *Chicago Tribune*.

One of the most interesting findings of my Pulitzer study is that the board's rejections of many jury recommendations in the late 1970s were not as uncommon as critics say.

There has never been a year in which the board did not overturn at least one jury recommendation, and the average is about three a year. In 1960 alone the board overruled seven of the eight jury recommendations—and in three categories that year the board gave Pulitzers to people not even listed as finalists by the juries.

In 1978 and 1979, when the board gave Pulitzers to individuals not among the jury finalists, there was considerable resentment among the jurors over this "unusual" snub of their recommendations. But it wasn't unusual at all. It happened forty-two times from 1924 to 1977—and in 1944 the board threw out all the jury finalists in seven of the eight existing categories and made their own awards, starting from scratch.

The greatest single controversy involving the Pulitzers, however, has always been the question of cronyism—politics. Reports have occasionally surfaced that this editor or that publisher had called a friend on the Pulitzer board to lobby for one of his paper's entries that year and that board members have lobbied each other for the same reason.

Most board members do know each other professionally—often socially—and they do sit together on award day, voting on the prizes, many of which involve each other's papers. Of course, any board member whose paper is nominated for an award must leave the room until discussion and voting in that category is completed. That means virtually every award is given with one or two, sometimes as many as four, board members not participating.

Nevertheless, the questions arise:

Do board members speak and vote for their friends' papers

even when they don't deserve a prize? Do they avoid voting or speaking against certain nominations, even if they find the nominations undeserving, for fear of hurting friends' feelings or alienating board members who might then speak or vote against *their* papers' entries in other categories? Do they—consciously or otherwise—trade off: "You vote for mine, and I'll vote for yours?"

"There's always a little of that kind of thing going on in any political board," said the late Turner Catledge, a Pulitzer board member from 1955 to 1967 when he was executive editor of the *New York Times*. But most present board members can cite several examples each of voting against their close friends or for their competitors, and they say the competitive instincts of most board members and the sometimes fierce give-and-take of the board room make logrolling all but impossible.

Board members insist there is no lobbying within the board for one's own paper, and they say there is virtually no lobbying from outside either. That strains credulity just a bit, and other sources do say there is occasionally some lobbying by outsiders—usually quite subtle lobbying.

Lobbying does appear to be minimal, though, and board members all agree that, whatever the result of the voting, there is surprisingly little grousing about defeat, gloating about victory, or worry about hurt feelings among board members themselves.

"If a guy comes back into the room and finds out he's just lost a Pulitzer, he just smiles and his heart is broken . . . and we go on to the next category," says board member Eugene Patterson, editor and president of the *St. Petersburg* (Fla.) *Times*.

Nevertheless, only twice in sixty-seven years (in 1923 and 1965) have Pulitzer Prizes been awarded without at least one going to a paper represented on the Pulitzer board, and interviews and statistical analyses make clear that, in years past, the board was often less than a model of equality:

- Newbold Noyes, Jr., a member of the board from 1963 to 1975, when he was editor of the *Washington Star-News,* says he was "surprised by how little politics there was on the board." But he admits there were times when, "as the editor of the other paper in town, I voted against the *Post* when I probably wouldn't have if I'd been from Dubuque."
- In the twenty-five years that Kent Cooper of the Associated Press served on the Pulitzer board (1931–56), AP won fourteen Pulitzers and rival United Press didn't win a single one. UP (now United Press International) won its first Pulitzer the year after Cooper left the board and has since won seven more.

  ("Cooper just saw to it that UP didn't win any Pulitzers," says Gardner Cowles, Jr., chairman of Cowles Communications when he was on the Pulitzer board from 1947 to 1958.)
- The *Baltimore Sun* won nine Pulitzers from 1928 to 1953 while its editor, Frank Kent, was on the board. But the *Sun* didn't win a single Pulitzer in the first twenty-five years after Kent left the board.

Unquestionably, the most dominant figure in the history of the Pulitzer Prize Board—"the Lyndon Baines Johnson of the board" in the words of one colleague—was Arthur Krock, a member of the board from 1940 to 1954 and a two-time Pulitzer Prize–winner himself.

"It wasn't so much that Krock used his influence to get prizes for his own paper [the *New York Times*]," says one board member. "He just insisted that the people he thought were best got the prizes, whoever they were."

Krock often boasted privately of his successful lobbying, both in journalism and the arts, even after he left the board (as in 1957 when he helped influence the selection of John F. Kennedy as the Pulitzer winner in biography).

"One year, when I was editor of the *Chicago Daily News,*

we were being considered for three Pulitzers,'' recalled the late John S. Knight, who won a Pulitzer himself in 1968. "I was on the [Pulitzer] board then, and Krock just took me out for a little walk and said I might want to be 'more restrained.' I got the message.

"I called . . . my executive editor back in Chicago and asked him which one [prize] we wanted to give up . . . and that's how the board voted."

Knight and other former board members say Krock and three or four of his friends on the board often had dinner together the night before the formal prize voting each year and reached a consensus among themselves on the major awards. The practice endured until the early 1960s, even after Krock left the board, they say.

"That little inner group really made the decisions," Gardner Cowles, Jr., says. "It seemed to me that most years they decided which awards would go to the *New York Times*, AP, the *Baltimore Sun*, and *St. Louis Post-Dispatch*, and they let the rest of us divide up the rest of the awards."

In 1940 four of the five Pulitzers awarded went to papers represented on the Pulitzer board. In 1944 and again in 1945 they won five of eight. In 1947 and again in 1951 they won six of eight.

From 1950 to 1961, the Pulitzer board overturned jury recommendations fourteen times on awards involving papers represented on the board. In eleven of the fourteen, those papers benefited from the overturns, winning prizes the juries hadn't thought they deserved.

There is always a built-in credibility problem with the Pulitzer board, though, even if board members are veritable saints in their altruism. The best papers are generally represented on the board, and the best papers should (and do) win most of the Pulitzers.

Newspapers represented by eight members of the 1979 board won forty-one Pulitzers while these men were on the board. But is that necessarily sinister? Or is it just plain fair and logical—

inevitable? After all, thirty-five of these forty-one prizes were won by the *New York Times, Washington Post, Philadelphia Inquirer, Chicago Tribune, Boston Globe, Milwaukee Journal,* and *Miami Herald*—seven of the ten papers on most lists of the best papers in the country.

Moreover, since 1961, board members' papers have won only four more Pulitzers than they've lost on board rejections of jury recommendations, and fewer than a third of all prizes have been won by board members' papers.

Clearly, times have changed since Krock's reign. In the last nine years nominating juries have put board members' papers in the finals 185 times, but the board has given those papers only forty-one prizes—voting against each other, in effect, 75 percent of the time.

Joseph Pulitzer, Jr., publisher of the *St. Louis Post-Dispatch,* is chairman of the Pulitzer Prize Board, but the *Post-Dispatch* hasn't won a Pulitzer since 1966. The *Chicago Sun-Times,* on the other hand, won five Pulitzers from 1976 to 1980 even though it had no representation on the board and its strongest daily competitor, the *Chicago Tribune,* had.

"People always talk to me about wheeling and dealing on the board," says John Hughes, a 1967 Pulitzer Prize–winner when he was with the *Christian Science Monitor,* and now the publisher of two small weeklies in Massachusetts. "It just doesn't happen. The fix isn't in now."

Thus, although some prizes are still won (or lost) for reasons other than journalistic merit—sentiment, tradition, geography, luck—no one man (or group of men) dominates the Pulitzer board today. Voting blocks shift constantly, depending on the issues involved in any particular award or procedural question.

Benjamin C. Bradlee, executive editor of the *Washington Post,* was the most outspoken, charismatic member of the Pulitzer board from 1969 until his resignation in 1979, and critics have suggested that his presence helped the *Post* win ten Pulitzers during that time.

But the *Post* has also "lost" more Pulitzers than any other paper. Eight times juries recommended the *Post* for Pulitzers only to have the board give the prize to another paper—and five of those overturns came while Bradlee was on the board, two of them in one year.

In 1973, Pulitzer nominating juries in local reporting, international reporting, and commentary all recommended the *Post* for Pulitzer Prizes. But the *Post*'s Watergate coverage was not recommended—ranked only third by the public service jury, in part because one juror thought the *Post* had "overindulged . . . on unattributed information."

The *Post*'s Watergate entry may also have suffered in the voting because the public service jurors came from Riverside, California; Salt Lake City; Kansas City; Chicago; and Portland, Maine—all outside the Washington–New York–Boston–Philadelphia political complex where Watergate was receiving more attention at that relatively early stage of the story.

But between the jury vote on March 9 and the Pulitzer board vote on April 12, Watergate conspirator James W. McCord, Jr., wrote to U.S. District Judge John J. Sirica, disclosing the White House cover-up effort, and the entire story began to unravel.

Suddenly the *Post* was no longer virtually alone in its aggressive pursuit of the Watergate story. The board voted unanimously (with Bradlee out of the room) to reverse the jury and give the public service award to the *Post*.

The board also ratified the jury's choice of *Post* columnist David Broder for the commentary prize.

But the board overruled the juries on the two other Pulitzers recommended for the *Post* and gave the international reporting prize to Max Frankel of the *New York Times* and the local reporting prize to the *Chicago Tribune* (which had been the public service jury's first choice).

Thus the *Post* won two and lost two—largely, some say, because the board did not want to give the *Post* (and Bradlee) an unprecedented four Pulitzers in one year.

"There was a strong feeling that four was too many . . . that we should spread them around," says former board member James Reston of the *New York Times*.

Bradlee says he went to the Pulitzer board meeting that year "prepared to resign" if the *Post* didn't win for Watergate, and even though it did win, the *Post* and Bradlee have often lost—before and since—on procedural matters as well as awards.

When, in 1979, the Pulitzer board discussed the addition of nonjournalists to the board, Bradlee's response was "over my dead body." He argued that "what makes the Pulitzer Prize so special is precisely the fact that it's journalists giving it to journalists."

The board, says Eugene Patterson, "listened to Bradlee, then voted his ass right down," approving "up to three" nonjournalists and immediately naming Hanna Gray, president of the University of Chicago, as the first.

"Anything Bradlee's for automatically lost, ten to two," Bradlee says, with an unhappy smile.

Indeed, for all Bradlee's charm and eloquence, not one of his fellow board members named him when I asked them to identify the three or four most influential members of the board during his tenure. Neither was Bradlee ever named to the board's special subcommittee that seeks out new members.

He's too abrasive. He offends people.

"They don't want any bomb-throwers or iconoclasts," he says.

Surprisingly, Reston was not very influential either.

" 'Scotty' [Reston] has this magisterial presence that has everything to do with him and nothing to do with the *New York Times*," one board member said late in Reston's tenure. "When he speaks, it's like E. F. Hutton: We listen. But he doesn't speak out that much anymore. He's old [seventy]. He doesn't carry many votes."

The consensus among board members when I interviewed them for my 1980 study was that their two most influential recent colleagues—both former Pulitzer Prize–winners themselves—have been Eugene Patterson (because he is articulate, intelligent, insightful, and forceful but neither stubborn nor dogmatic) and Lee Hills (largely because he devoted more time and energy to Pulitzer matters than any other board member).

It was Hills, for example, before his term expired in 1982, who helped overcome Bradlee's argument against including nonjournalists on the board—by discovering that the formal plan for the original awards, dated June 10, 1917, specifically said, "The Advisory Board shall also have the power to add to its numbers by the appointment of persons of distinction who are not journalists or editors."

Even Hills and Patterson have lost frequently in board votes, though:

- Patterson's *St. Petersburg* (Fla.) *Times* has been nominated for five Pulitzers in the ten years he's been on the board, but it won only one.
- In 1979, Patterson argued in favor of limiting the number of entries any one paper could make in any prize category, and he was resoundingly defeated.

Hills warned the board at that same meeting that if William Raspberry of the *Washington Post* and Roger Wilkins, then of the *New York Times,* were appointed as the first blacks on the board, it would confirm the widely held view within the profession that the *Times* and *Post* control the board.

The board appointed Raspberry and Wilkins anyway.

Hills's papers won thirteen Pulitzers while he was on the board, but they were in the finals thirty-four other times and lost. His best paper, the *Philadelphia Inquirer,* has won six Pulitzers since 1975, but it has lost twenty-one times when its entries were in the finals—three of them when they were the juries' first choices in various categories and the board voted (with Hills out of the room) to give the prizes to other papers. In fact, last year (1983), with Hills off the board but with Gene Roberts, executive editor of the *Inquirer*, on the board for the first time, the *Inquirer* made the finals in three categories—and won no Pulitzer Prizes.

Roberts is likely to become influential on the board because he is bright, persuasive, well-liked, and widely respected. But his influence is not likely to help his paper win more Pulitzers and could, in fact, have just the opposite effect. Roberts loves to win Pulitzers, but he is also a most ethical man—and both he and his fellow board members will probably bend over backward to avoid even the appearance of favoritism or cronyism.

"You've just got a bunch of hard-headed, independent men on that board now," William McGill, who sat on the board while president of Columbia, told me in 1979. "They're bosses. They're used to getting their own way. No one's going to lead them around by the nose."

"Independent" and "hard-headed" they may well be, but interviews and analyses of their voting patterns clearly show there has often been a remarkable degree of unanimity—and of sentimentality—in their award choices.

In 1979, for example, the weekly *Point Reyes Light* in Northern California became one of the smallest newspapers ever to win a Pulitzer Prize.

The *Light*, with a circulation of 2,700, was given the coveted Pulitzer public service award for its stories exposing conditions in Synanon, the drug and alcohol rehabilitation program.

But many members of the Pulitzer Prize Board—and of the nominating jury that recommended the *Light* to the board—told me they ultimately voted to give the prize to the *Light* more because it was a small paper whose editors had shown great courage, at considerable financial risk, than because the paper's Synanon stories were necessarily better than the three other finalists in the public service category.

Virtually everyone in the Pulitzer selection process agrees that the *Light*'s stories were excellent and worthy of Pulitzer consideration on purely journalistic terms.

"But if you took the names of the newspapers off the . . . entries, I would definitely have voted for the *Chicago Tribune* series on the problems of the aging," says Michael O'Neill, then editor of the *New York Daily News* and a member of the Pulitzer public service jury in 1979.

Several members of the Pulitzer board said they, too, might have voted for the *Tribune* series—or for one of the other finalists, the *Chicago Sun-Times* or the *Los Angeles Times*—had they not been influenced by the contrast between the size and resources of these papers and the meager, husband-and-wife operation at the *Point Reyes Light*.

"The job that couple did was damn good," one board member says, "but the guts they showed, with Synanon just a few miles down the road . . . that's what the Pulitzers are all about, that's what won the award."

Contrary to what is generally thought, by journalists and the public alike, Pulitzer Prizes in journalism are not given for "the best" work in each category but for a "distinguished example" of work in each category.

"If you just gave the award for the 'best' work," says board member James Reston, "money and size would count too much, and you'd give all the prizes to the same three or four or five papers every year. The prizes would just become the plaything of the big and rich.

"We not only want to reward excellence but to encourage others," Reston says. "I own my own weekly now, and I saw how that award [to *Point Reyes*] affected my young staff . . . the shudder of excitement and their feeling that, 'If we get these real estate bastards, maybe we can win a Pulitzer too.' "

Thus, contrary to widespread criticism in the industry, the Pulitzer Prize Board is often far likelier to lean in favor of small-town papers than in favor of the large metropolitan dailies that are widely thought to dominate the selection process.

"One of the natural characteristics of the journalist is sympathy for the underdog," says former board member Clayton

Kirkpatrick. "Whenever a smaller paper comes in with an entry of especially high quality there's a tilt on the board [toward that paper]."

This is but one of several ways in which Pulitzer Prizes are sometimes awarded on the basis of personal sentiment rather than sheer journalistic merit. Interviews with past and present members of the Pulitzer board and of the board's many nominating juries, and a detailed study of more than thirty years of jury and board selections, make it clear that the board sometimes also gives prizes to:

- Older journalists who are demonstrably past their peak but who deserved awards in earlier years and didn't get them. "We'd call this 'voting our guilty consciences,' " says one board member. (Two recent examples: sportswriter Red Smith of the *New York Times,* who won the commentary prize in 1976, and drama critic Walter Kerr of the *New York Times,* who won the criticism prize in 1978. Both were cited for the body of their work, as well as work in the specific year.)
- People who were recommended for prizes by juries but rejected by the board in previous years.

The board will also bypass deserving entries to give prizes to admittedly inferior entries so as to avoid:

- Giving more than one award to the same paper in one year.
- Giving a prize to someone who has won before.

But the most frequent "sentimental/emotional/romantic vote"—as one board member calls it—is clearly for the small paper over the big paper.

Virtually every member of the Pulitzer board told me of the special pleasure he felt in voting for the *Point Reyes Light* in 1979.

"There was ecstatic excitement all around the [board] table," William McGill, then president of Columbia University, told me.

That year may have been the most sentimental year for all the Pulitzers. Board members also gave prizes to the *Pottstown* (Pa.) *Mercury* (circulation 30,000) and the *Pottsville* (Pa.) *Republican* (circulation 28,000) in head-to-head competition with papers from Chicago, Philadelphia, and Washington.

But this is no isolated phenomenon. The board has also given Pulitzers over the last decade to small papers in Lufkin, Texas; Xenia, Ohio; and Anchorage, Alaska.

"I was chairman of the jury that gave the [1977 public service] award to Lufkin," says Norman Cherniss, executive editor of the *Riverside* (Calif.) *Press-Enterprise*. "If that same story had been in the *New York Times, Washington Post,* or *L.A. Times,* it probably wouldn't have gotten the award.

"Editors just have a special place in their hearts for small papers."

This sentiment is not new. As far back as 1923 the *Emporia* (Kan.) *Gazette* won a Pulitzer for editorial writing, and since then Pulitzers have been given to papers in Alice, Texas; Atlantic, Iowa; Fremont, Nebraska—even to the weekly *Hungry Horse News* in Columbia Falls, Montana, among others.

My study shows that when the Pulitzer board overturns a jury recommendation, it is almost twice as likely to reject a large paper in favor of a small one as it is to reject a small paper in favor of a large one.

There are other instances of Pulitzer by sentiment—however much most board members may publicly insist they are unaware of it.

"Sure, there are emotional factors that tilt our votes sometimes," concedes board member Eugene Patterson. "But we're not going to say that. We like to say we're Simon-pure."

Board members deny, therefore, that they try to even the scales for slights in previous years. But my study shows:

- Lenoir Chambers of the *Norfolk Virginian-Pilot* was the first choice of the editorial-writing jury in 1959. The board gave the prize to someone else instead. The next year Chambers wasn't even on the jury's list of the five best, but the board gave Chambers the prize anyway.

- Clark Mollenhoff of the *Des Moines Register and Tribune* was the first choice of the national reporting jury in 1956. He lost. In 1958 he was the jury's fourth choice. He won.
- Paul Conrad, then of the *Denver Post*, was the cartoon jury's first choice in 1963. He lost. The next year he won, and he won again in 1971, with the *Los Angeles Times*, even though he was the jury's fifth choice that year.
- Wendall Rawls, then of the *Philadelphia Inquirer*, was the first choice of one of the local reporting juries in 1975. He lost. He was the first choice again in 1977. This time he won.

"Lose once and your chances of winning next time the board sees your name are pretty damn good, even if you don't deserve it that [second] time," says one loser-turned-winner. "That's what . . . a board member told me."

An even better example of the role that sentiment plays in the Pulitzer process—better because some board members will admit to it, at least off-the-record—involves the board's tendency to avoid repeat winners, even when that means giving the prize to a less-deserving entry.

"The whole tilt," says one board member, "is to spread the prizes around, one to a customer."

For example, Russell Baker was the commentary jury's third choice in 1979—as he was in 1976. But in 1976 the jury's first choice was Red Smith, who had never won before. The board felt Smith was long overdue and gave him the prize. In 1979 the jury's first choice was Vermont Royster of the *Wall Street Journal,* and as the board moved toward giving him the prize, one board member reminded his colleagues that Royster had won before.

"It was then that the tide turned to Russell Baker," said the late Richard Baker, then secretary to the board.

Russell Baker won.

Newspapers themselves sometimes lose prizes because the board, in the words of one member, "finds it embarrassing to give two or three prizes to the same paper the same year."

This attitude has given rise to widespread rumors and howls of injustice. The publisher of one large newspaper claimed a few years ago that juries had recommended his paper for three Pulitzers, but that the board told him, "We decided you can only have one."

In this instance, according to my study, the claim was pure fantasy—wishful thinking, perhaps; the paper was nominated for, and won, only one prize that year.

But similar tales are still sometimes true. The *Philadelphia Inquirer* was a finalist in six categories in 1979 and the juries' top choice in two, but won only one prize. In 1975 the *Inquirer* won a Pulitzer for national reporting and was also the first choice of the local reporting jury. But the board gave the local award to another paper, and John Hohenberg (then secretary to the board) later admitted to jury members, in effect, that they had been overruled, in part, because the board didn't want to give the *Inquirer* two prizes in one year.

This unstated policy of trying to spread the honors around probably kept *Washington Post* cartoonist Herbert Block from winning his third Pulitzer until 1979—twenty-five years after having won his second. (He won his first in 1942.) In fact, "Herblock's" recent experiences with the Pulitzer board provide a unique insight into several aspects of the Pulitzer process.

In 1978 cartoonist Paul Szep of the *Boston Globe* was on the verge of winning *his* third Pulitzer. He was the jury's overwhelming first choice that year. (Szep "stands alone," the jury told the board.) But because Szep had won in 1974 and 1977 the board gave the prize to the jury's second choice, Jeff MacNelly, then of the *Richmond News-Leader,* who had won only once before (in 1972).

"There was a strong feeling on the board that there was no

way we were gonna let some young guy like Szep [then thirty-six] win three Pulitzers before Herblock [who was seventy]," says one board member.

The very next year Herblock won his third Pulitzer even though the jury had not nominated him as a finalist and many board members conceded he was well past his prime.

The jury's recommendation in 1979 was Robert Englehart, Jr., then of the *Dayton Journal Herald*. Englehart was, in fact, the jury's only nomination—despite jury instructions requiring the submission of at least three nominees.

But jury members felt Englehart was "head and shoulders above the rest," says Stanley Asimov, vice president of *Newsday* and chairman of that cartoon jury.

Board members didn't care much for Englehart's work—or for the jury's behavior.

"There was a feeling that this [submitting only one nominee] was a defiant gesture on the part of the jury," says Osborn Elliott, dean of the Graduate School of Journalism at Columbia and a nonvoting member of the Pulitzer board.

The board asked the jury to submit other nominees. Asimov —who insists the jury had not intended to "be provocative . . . or challenge the system"—polled his fellow jurors by telephone, and all agreed to stick with Englehart. So board members resumed deliberations on an alternative choice.

"We didn't have time to go through all the entries again," says Clayton Kirkpatrick. "But we all knew Herblock. We knew there would be a minimum risk [of criticism] if we chose him. With Herblock, we wouldn't be getting a lemon."

Many critics say that "play-it-safe" philosophy is precisely what's wrong with the Pulitzer process: the process too often rewards the conventional, ignores the radical, and resists change.

"The whole process tends to be too predictable, knee-jerk . . . incestuous," says Norman Isaacs, former chairman of the National News Council, a former Pulitzer board member, and a frequent Pulitzer juror.

The Pulitzer board, for example, has always been dominated by the Eastern establishment newspapers, and despite many recent procedural changes, it still has not fully taken into account the shift in population toward the West and Southwest and the improvement of some papers in those areas.

Of the more than seventy journalists who have served on the board since its inception, forty-six have come from the East, only eight from the West or Southwest. On the present board only three come from the Western United States. Thus, when board members decided that they must begin to include blacks, it was no surprise that they chose Roger Wilkins, then of the *New York Times,* and William Raspberry of the *Washington Post.*

(In fairness, it would be difficult to argue that they were not among the most deserving. But some critics have suggested that another black, Robert Maynard, publisher/editor of the *Oakland Tribune,* would have been just as deserving and would also have helped redress the geographic imbalance on the board.)

The board (and its secretary) also select the jury members, and while geographic representation is somewhat more equitable on the juries than on the board, the ratio between jurors from the eastern half of the United States and jurors from the western half over the last ten years has been 3½ to 1.

It's a self-perpetuating cycle: Predominantly Eastern board members pick predominantly Eastern jurors, who send predominantly Eastern prize-nominations back to the predominantly Eastern board, which picks predominantly Eastern prize-winners.

I am not suggesting there is an Eastern conspiracy against the West. Undeniably, more of the best newspapers are in the East than in the West. But the journalists who vote on the Pulitzer Prizes *are* "heavily influenced by their Eastern backgrounds and the fact that they see mostly Eastern papers," says one former board member.

"Of course, there's an Eastern bias," says James G. Bellows, who's edited papers in New York, Los Angeles, Miami, and Washington. "Stories that get mentioned in *Time* and *Newsweek* have a head start [for a Pulitzer Prize], and it's the East Coast papers that *Time* and *Newsweek* watch closely.''

Even some past and present Pulitzer board members acknowledge this bias:

"We kid ourselves when we think we see papers from all over the country," says Lee Hills. "There's a tendency to go with the familiar."

"Go with the familiar" indeed. In recent years, 90 percent of the jury nominations have been for papers in the eastern half of the United States. In the last fourteen years, 142 of the 160 Pulitzer Prizes have been won by papers in the eastern half of the United States.

The statistics are not all one-sided, though. The *Los Angeles Times* was represented on the Pulitzer board from 1957 to 1975, and even though the paper is a relative latecomer to the ranks of the nation's best newspapers, it has won eleven Pulitzers. Only the Associated Press and five other papers—two of them now defunct—have won more.

And the *New York Times?* Well, the *New York Times* is a special case. Consider the following:

It is April 1977. The Pulitzer Prize Board is discussing the nominations of its jury in international reporting. The jury's first choice: James Markham and Henry Tanner of the *New York Times*—the only *New York Times* entry to make the finals this year in any category.

But the board doesn't think their work, or that of any other nominee for international reporting, really deserves a Pulitzer Prize. Perhaps, they say, they should give no award for international reporting.

At that point, three board members recall, the late Richard Baker—then a Columbia University journalism professor who was serving as secretary to the board and administrator of the prizes—blurted out, "But that means the *Times* won't win anything this year."

No Pulitzer Prize for the *New York Times?* Heresy. After all, the *New York Times* has won more Pulitzers—fifty-two—than any other newspaper. Its closest competitors—the Associated Press (thirty-three), the *St. Louis Post-Dispatch* (seventeen), and the *Washington Post* (sixteen)—aren't even close.

In fact, on the day the Pulitzer Prizes are announced each year, the *Times* maintains an open telephone line from Columbia to its city room where executive editor A. M. Rosenthal always has champagne waiting, secure in the knowledge that he and his staff will have something to celebrate.

But the Pulitzer board didn't listen to Baker in 1977. The *Times* was shut out. Rosenthal didn't need his champagne.

Baker later said he didn't recall making the statement attributed to him about the *Times* that year. But he admitted being "a *Times* man," and he was acutely aware that many critics thought he was not the only "Times man" involved in the Pulitzer process.

There is a widespread feeling in newspaper circles that the *New York Times* wins the most Pulitzers not only because it is the best paper in America, but also because Columbia and the Pulitzers have a stake in the *Times*. And vice versa.

Consider:

- Columbia is in New York.
- Arthur Ochs Sulzberger, publisher of the *Times,* is on the Columbia board of trustees.
- Columbia's Graduate School of Journalism, where the Pulitzer offices are, has a library named for Sulzberger's father.
- For many years that school was "virtually an employment agency for the *Times*" in the words of one high-ranking *Times* executive.
- The *Times* was represented on the Pulitzer board every year from 1940 to 1980. In fact, the *Times* has been represented on the Pulitzer board every year but seven since the prizes began in 1917 (although, in fairness, it must be pointed out

that even in those seven years the *Times* won prizes—nine times—including two in each of the last three years).

"No one is suggesting there's a conscious effort to give the *Times* awards it doesn't deserve," says one board member. "It would be difficult even if someone tried. But there is something subliminal there. Everyone [on the board] knows that Columbia is scared of the *Times.*"

Two other possible explanations for all those Pulitzers the *Times* has won:

- The *New York Times* is the one paper all board members—and many jurors—read regularly.
- The *New York Times* IS the *New York Times,* and some jurors and board members may automatically vote for some of its entries, swayed by the quality, prestige, and mystique of the *Times,* and confident that no one could quibble with a vote for so august and excellent a newspaper.

Thus, only once in the last fifty years has the *Times* gone more than two consecutive years without winning at least one Pulitzer. Six times the *Times* has won two Pulitzers in one year.

In 1978 the *Times* became the first paper ever to win three Pulitzers in one year. But two of the three came when the Pulitzer board overruled the recommendations of its nominating juries: The *Times*'s international reporting winner had been that jury's fourth choice; the *Times*'s commentary winner wasn't even among the jury's three finalists.

The board often overrules the juries, of course. It always has. But a careful examination of the records shows that the *New York Times* has been the beneficiary of these overturns more often than any other paper—ten times since 1956.

The two papers that have been the second and third greatest beneficiaries of board overturns, however, have been the *Washington Post* (six) and the *Los Angeles Times* (five). Since the two *Times*es and the *Post* are generally regarded as the three best papers in the country, one could legitimately argue that the Pulitzer board has simply rectified jury oversights in the course of justly rewarding journalistic excellence.

Moreover, the *New York Times* has *lost* more than most critics realize. On five occasions the *New York Times* has *lost* Pulitzers when the board overruled jury recommendations—and in twenty-six of the sixty-three years since the Pulitzer Prizes began, the *New York Times* didn't win a single award.

In 1980 several board members told me they could not conceive of the Pulitzer board operating without a *New York Times* representative. But that's just what it's done the last three years.

A few board members even foresee the day when there will be no one from the Pulitzer family on the board even though a Pulitzer has always been chairman of the board.

But Joseph Pulitzer, Jr.—grandson of the founder of the prizes, publisher of the *St. Louis Post-Dispatch,* and chairman of the Pulitzer board since 1955—often seems uninterested in the Pulitzers, some board members say.

"Joe's a sweet man, a true gentleman," one board member says, echoing the sentiments of many. "He's not really a newspaperman, though. He's a dilettante, an art collector, a skier. He should be curator of a museum someplace."

"Joe's fought all the proposals for change in the Pulitzers as if his ancestors up in heaven would personally resent it," says Elie Abel, former dean of the Graduate School of Journalism at Columbia.

For several years, Pulitzer resisted proposals to announce the runners-up for the Pulitzer Prizes at the same time the winners are announced. Other board members said such an announcement would diminish controversy over the prizes and lessen the mystery and secrecy many of them considered inappropriate for a newspaper award.

But Pulitzer argued that announcing the runners-up would detract from the winners, and some other board members agreed.

It wasn't until 1980 that the board finally overrode these objections amid the most sweeping changes in the history of the awards.

Many of these changes involve procedures to improve the juries—with board members providing new nominees for the juries and helping to select the jury chairman.

Juries are the critical point in the Pulitzer process, most board members feel, and they blame poor juries for most of the recent controversy over board rejections of jury recommendations.

"I'm a little sick of talk of how perfect the jurors are and what assholes we [board members] are," Ben Bradlee told me when he sat on the Pulitzer board. "I'd say some of the juries need reforming as much as the board."

As with the board, the juries often suffer from a lack of new blood.

"Once you're on the jury list, you're there for life," says board member Richard Leonard, editor of the *Milwaukee Journal.* "That's why we're putting together a whole new list now."

The board secretary, who assembles the juries from these lists, tries to balance each jury with representatives of newspapers of varying sizes and locations. But he hasn't always succeeded.

In 1978, for example, the international reporting jury consisted of editors from Memphis; Atlanta; Shreveport, Louisiana; Charleston, West Virginia—all from the South, none with any foreign staff of its own.

The Pulitzer board rejected the jury's first three choices and gave the Pulitzer instead to the jury's fourth choice—Henry Kamm of the *New York Times*—for the first stories describing the plight of the Cambodian boat people.

"That jury was just plain ignorant," says one board member. "You couldn't possibly give that award to anyone but Kamm."

Other board members and several jurors say juries too often lack the knowledge and sophistication necessary to properly evaluate the entries in their categories.

But putting the juries together is no easy task primarily because, until relatively recently, board rules prohibited anyone from serving on a jury for a category in which his newspaper had an entry.

"About the only jury I can put anyone from the *New York Times* on is cartooning," a former board secretary once complained.

Now the juries operate much as the board itself operates. A journalist may sit on any jury, but if an entry from his newspaper is being discussed as a potential finalist, he leaves the room until after the vote is taken.

Amid all the criticism of the Pulitzer process, however—ranging from the composition of the juries to the decision of the board—critics often overlook how seriously the jurors and board members take their Pulitzer responsibilities.

Judges realize that the awarding of a Pulitzer doesn't only confer an honor on an individual and a newspaper, it also sends a message to the profession. Thus, they worry about whether various potential winners actually measure up to Pulitzer standards—journalistic and ethical.

Sometimes board members give no award at all in a particular category if they think Pulitzer standards have not been met. Other times they just give the awards to someone other than the jury's recommendation.

In 1967, when the international reporting jury voted 4–1 to give Harrison Salisbury of the *New York Times* a Pulitzer for his stories from Hanoi, the board was bothered by some "reportorial deficiencies" in Salisbury's stories, as well as by his failure to attribute some casualty figures to Communist sources.

"We also knew that several other papers had requests in to go to Hanoi," says Newbold Noyes, Jr., who was on the board then as editor of the *Washington Star-News*. "We didn't think he should get a prize just because he was the first they [Hanoi] said yes to unless he'd done a better job than anyone else could have done there, and he hadn't."

There may have been yet another reason for the board's discomfiture with Salisbury—a hawk-dove split among board members. "They [the majority] just thought it was unpatriotic for him to have gone to Hanoi in the first place," says Charles Bailey, then editor of the *Minneapolis Tribune*.

Don Maxwell of the *Chicago Tribune*, whose selection to the board had been urged by Turner Catledge of the *New York Times*, helped lead the fight against Salisbury.

After prolonged discussion the board voted 6-5 against Salisbury.

John Hughes, who won the prize instead for his *Christian Science Monitor* stories on Indonesia, precipitated an even more acrimonious debate himself in 1978. That year the first choice of the commentary jury was television critic Gary Deeb of the *Chicago Tribune*. But Hughes, who had been elected to the board in 1977, thought William Safire of the *New York Times* deserved the prize for his columns on the financial dealings of President Carter's adviser, Bert Lance.

Safire wasn't even on the jury's list of three finalists, so Hughes had someone dig his columns out of the original entries, and he passed them around during the board's lunch break. When deliberations resumed after lunch, the board was split.

Ben Bradlee led the opposition to Safire, calling the former speechwriter for President Nixon "a hit-man of the first water [who] went bail for Nixon."

Bradlee grudgingly conceded that Safire's columns on Lance were "damn good," but he insisted the rest of his work was "damn bad." Editor Thomas Winship of the *Boston Globe* agreed.

In fact, almost everyone on the board was hostile to Safire—politically, journalistically, some even personally. But most agreed that his work on Lance was admirable and that political differences did not justify denying him the award.

"He went after Lance; he did the tough, unpopular job when

the rest of us crapped out," says Eugene Patterson. "That's operating in the true Pulitzer spirit."

Safire got the award on a 10–2 vote, but only after Bradlee succeeded in having the award citation limited to "for commentary on the Bert Lance affair," the first time in the history of the commentary prize that the winner was not cited for his entire year's work.

A year later, the board had another ethical debate. The jury on local investigative reporting had nominated the *Chicago Sun-Times* as one of four finalists for its articles exposing graft and corruption in the city. To get that story, *Sun-Times* reporters had operated a bar incognito for four months.

The question: Are deception and misrepresentation in the pursuit of a story legitimate journalistic techniques?

Again Bradlee was against giving the award. This time Patterson agreed. Both argued that newspapers cannot demand honesty of those they write about if they are less than honest themselves. Other board members insisted that some important stories can be reported only by using these methods. Clayton Kirkpatrick urged the board to give the prize to the *Sun-Times,* even though his own paper was the *Chicago Tribune.*

"It was one of the most valuable and enlightening discussions I've ever heard," says board member Warren Phillips, then president (and now chairman) of Dow-Jones & Co.

The debate was "civilized but impassioned," says William McGill, then president of Columbia.

Patterson and Bradlee won the debate. The *Sun-Times* lost the Pulitzer.

Curiously, there is another ethical question that many journalists outside the Pulitzer process raise, but that Pulitzer jurors and board members themselves brush quickly aside: What of the paper that deliberately sets out to win a Pulitzer from the moment a story is conceived, assigned, written, and published?

Some contend this distorts the journalistic process, that papers then ignore or underplay other, potentially more important stories and give their "Pulitzer stories" more frequent and prominent play than they deserve.

"You can build a big reputation pretty fast with a few Pulitzers," one editor says. "That's what the *Philadelphia Inquirer* has done." (The *Inquirer* won six Pulitzers from 1975 to 1980.)

But Winship echoes many close to the Pulitzer process when he says, "Any story good enough to be considered for a Pulitzer is a good story by any standards. Hell, I've never known a guy who had a better instinct for what will win prizes than Gene Roberts. But his [prize-winning] stories were all good, important, valuable, well-played. . . . What's wrong with that?"

Pulitzer board members are more concerned about another problem—one of logistics, not ethics. That problem is the proliferation of entries for the Pulitzer Prize.

In the beginning, entries often had to be solicited for the board. By 1954 there were 200 entries in eight journalism categories. Last year there was a record 1,264 entries in twelve journalism categories (plus almost 600 others in the arts categories).

Until 1979 the juries generally met at Columbia the first Thursday and Friday in March to read and judge all the entries. But they could no longer finish the job in that time, especially since "everyone was rushing to catch a plane by two o'clock Friday afternoon to get home for the weekend," in the words of one frequent Pulitzer juror.

So juries now meet the first Monday, Tuesday, and Wednesday in March. But the work load is still heavy. Jurors may have to read more than a hundred entries—each consisting of ten or fifteen long, complex articles, buttressed by testimonial letters, often assembled in scrapbooks so large "you damn near get a hernia just holding them," says a former secretary to the board.

Lee Hills says he had a study made several years ago and he

found that all the entries in one single category chosen at random totaled 3 million words—the equivalent of more than thirty novels—all to be read in three days.

One explanation for this avalanche: Many big papers submit several entries in each category.

In 1978 the *Baltimore Sun* submitted eleven entries in the international reporting category alone. The previous year the *Chicago Sun-Times* submitted seven entries in one category and six each in two others. From 1975 to 1979 the *Boston Globe* submitted four or more entries in a single category thirteen times.

The Pulitzer board has discussed prohibiting multiple entries but finally decided only to "informally discourage" the practice—beginning with the papers represented on the board, many of whom are among the worst offenders. "Flooding the juries with an excess of multiple entries is frowned upon," newspapers were told in the 1980 Pulitzer announcement. "More than three entries by a newspaper in a single category is discouraged."

Gene Roberts is opposed to this.

"In any contest," he says, "a judge can quickly rule out a lot of entries that don't even come close to measuring up, and as soon as you find one or two really good entries, you use them as a standard for the rest. Judging just doesn't take that long."

Veteran jurors agree that 50 percent to 75 percent of the entries in every Pulitzer category can be dismissed almost immediately. "They're just ego trips for the reporter or the paper," says one juror. But jurors would prefer fewer entries so they could spend more time reading and choosing among the very best. Roberts insists, however, that ". . . you can't say you're honoring the best if you place any restrictions on what can be entered."

Roberts still remembers that the *Inquirer*'s Donald Bartlett and James Steele won the 1975 Pulitzer Prize in national reporting for stories Roberts didn't even nominate. "I nominated them for something else," he says. "Another editor here nominated them for that. If we'd been limited to one entry per category, they wouldn't have won a Pulitzer and it would've been my fault.''

But critics of the multiple entry system say that is Roberts's job as editor—to make difficult decisions and live with their consequences.

"An editor shouldn't dump his newsroom political problems on the Pulitzer juries," Patterson says. "He usually knows his best entries, and he should pick them. If that hurts somebody's feelings, well, that's why editors get paid."

Most likely this question will come up again if the board's attempt to discourage multiple entries does not significantly reduce those entries. If so, the board is probably better prepared than ever before to deal with it or with virtually any other issue.

Until recently, about the only time board members discussed Pulitzer procedures was near the end of the day they met each year to vote on the prizes. Occasionally they met for a day in the fall or appointed interim subcommittees to deal with procedural matters, but that was not sufficient to respond seriously to most proposals for reform. Board members now have several such subcommittees, and they also meet regularly every fall just for this purpose.

All the recent changes in Pulitzer procedure should help credibility. But no matter how many reforms the board institutes, controversy will probably always surround the Pulitzers. The descriptions of the awards are purposefully general, and critics have "long despaired of discovering the criteria upon which the . . . prizes are awarded," as one writer put it.

Moreover, luck always plays an important role in the prize process. Much depends on what the competition is in any given category in any given year. What's good enough to win in one category one year might not be good enough to even make the finals in another category or another year.

"In a lot of ways, it's just a big crap shoot," says one editor.

Besides, Pulitzer judging, like all judging, is subjective. So are the views of the people whose work is being judged. As A. M. Rosenthal, a Pulitzer Prize–winner in 1960 and now executive editor of the *New York Times,* said when asked if he thinks the Pulitzers are generally equitable:

"I think that when we win, the Pulitzer board has shown great acumen, and virtue has been rewarded. When we don't win, I think there's been a goddamn . . . injustice, and the board's a bunch of anti-Semitic . . . jerks."

8

THE USE AND ABUSE OF THE ENGLISH LANGUAGE

My late wife, Ellen, regarded the English language as a treasure and a trust—something to be used wisely and precisely and never to be betrayed. She delighted in the richness of the language, in exploring its every nuance, and I think it is safe to say that I first fell in love with her through her letters—which left me, alternately, marveling, smiling, and scurrying to the dictionary. Ellen routinely used such words as *pasquinade, marmoreal, japanned, lucubrations, megrims,* and *peccavi* in both correspondence and conversation, as well as in her own writing—feature stories for *TV Guide* and book reviews for the *Los Angeles Times* and *Philadelphia Inquirer*—and she reserved her most searing and scornful glances for those editors who had the temerity to suggest that she might wish to choose a simpler word from time to time. Thus, you can well imagine the horror with which Ellen greeted the arrival at our door each morning of the daily newspaper (in our case, the *Los Angeles Times*) with its appalling ration of staccato, monosyllabic constructions, imprecisions, garbled syntax, misused words, misspellings, and assorted other abuses of the English language. "How can you work for such a paper?" she asked me more than once.

Finally, in part to maintain my own integrity in her eyes, I decided to research and write a story on the use and abuse of the English language by the daily newspaper. After analyzing newspapers for about two months I found (and wrote on the front page of the *Los Angeles Times*)—to Ellen's immense delight—that the *Los Angeles Times* may just be the worst major newspaper in America in its abuse of the English language. But I also found that most other newspapers also mangle the language with great (and appalling) regularity. And, finally, I found that there are a great many readers who share Ellen's (and my) horror at this dreadful state of affairs.

I received several hundred letters from all over the country on my story, and virtually all of them thanked me for my efforts and expressed outrage at various language mistakes in their own daily newspaper, examples of which they provided by the score.

To this day, two years later, I still receive a letter every week or two from somewhere in the United States mentioning my story and enclosing a newspaper clipping with yet another offense against the language (often but not always from the *Los Angeles Times*).

Did my story embarrass editors and reporters at the *L. A. Times?* Some of them. Did it make them angry? Some of them. Did it make them more vigilant? Not noticeably. In the days and weeks that immediately followed the publication of my story, the paper mistakenly used *ringer* (for *wringer*), *emersed* (for *immersed*), *wrangle* (for *wangle*), *wretching* (for *retching*), *hoards* (for *hordes*), *knicked* (for *nicked*), *aesthetic* (for *aesthete*), *sunk* (for *sank*), *equitably* (for *equably*), and *he* (for *him*).

The *Los Angeles Times* also continued to misspell words at a rate that would alarm even a tolerant kindergarten teacher, and it managed to say such things as "data shows" (it should have been "data show"), "anyone may send their" (it should have been "his" or "her"), and "there are only a handful" (it should have been "there is only a handful").

This was not just an unfortunately aberrant period. While writing this introduction, I saw such horror stories as *credulity* (for *credibility*), *imminent* (for *eminent*), *descendancy* (for *descent*), *karat* (for *carat*), *peddling* (for *pedaling*), and—yet again—*he* (for *him*) in my morning paper. Today, not five minutes ago, I noticed that the major story on the front page of the paper managed to misuse both *perverse* and *bemused*.

As Ellen would have said, "It's unconscionable."

*   *   *

ALDEN WOOD is the fifty-six-year-old vice president of a Boston-based insurance company. In his spare time, he enjoys racing sports cars and playing drums in a jazz quartet. But his real passion is the use (and increasing abuse) of the English language, especially in the nation's press.

Wood's interest in language began, he says, when he was eight years old, and his parents told him about an uncle who led a glamorous life as a writer. Now, Wood is in charge of his company's advertising and public relations program; he teaches a college course in language usage and writes a monthly column on language abuse for a business communications newsletter.

In recent years, Wood says, he has seen a significant decline in proper language usage in newspapers, magazines, and books. And he is not talking just about misplaced commas or subtle syntactical mistakes that could be attributed to typographical errors or the pressure of deadlines.

No, Wood's columns, and his files, are filled with the most egregious and embarrassing media mistakes:

- A *Boston Globe* story referred to a man who had been arraigned "on charges of negligible homicide." (*Negligent* homicide would have been correct; no homicide is *negligible*—at least not to its victim.)
- A *San Francisco Examiner* story was headlined: "Climber peaks inside volcano." (It should have been *peeks*—unless the climber had a spiritual or sexual epiphany inside the volcano.)
- The *St. Louis Globe-Democrat* published a front-page headline that said: "Europe to soft peddle Iranian sanctions." (It should have been *soft-pedal*—unless the sanctions were for sale.)

Wood says he is appalled by these errors, and other language buffs in other cities—a growing breed these days—agree with him. So do most newspaper and magazine editors.

In fact, interviews nationwide have disclosed enormous concern among editors about the deterioration in the use of language in their publications. There is no doubt, they say, that in the last decade, reporters and copy editors at even the best publications have increasingly displayed an ignorance of (and an indifference to) the basic rules of English usage.

Bad grammar. Misspellings. Incorrect punctuation. Poorly constructed sentences. Misused words. Mixed metaphors. Non sequiturs. Clichés. Redundancies. Circumlocutions. Imprecision. Jargon.

Many reporters are making more language mistakes than ever, and many copy editors—whose job it is, among other things, to correct these mistakes—are not correcting them. On occasion, copy editors even change grammatical sentences to *un*grammatical sentences. (One *Boston Globe* reporter insists that he wrote a sentence that began, "Those who were"—and a copy editor changed it to "Them that was. . . .")

"Language misuse in American newspapers is a disgrace," says Eugene Patterson, editor and president of the *St. Petersburg* (Fla.) *Times.*

"I'm amazed at the fact that . . . so many mistakes are made," says Richard Leonard, editor of the *Milwaukee Journal.*

"There are more mistakes in everything I read," says Eleanor Gould Packard, associate editor of the *New Yorker.*

As befits what is generally regarded as the best-edited publication in America, the *New Yorker* itself still seems almost free of language mistakes. But Packard says even the *New Yorker* is "having trouble finding people [with a proper command of the English language] to come in and work as editors."

Newspaper and magazine editors are not alone in their concern about this problem. NBC newscaster Edwin Newman, theater and film critic John Simon, and political columnist William Sa fire have all written books on the subject, and Safire writes a weekly column on it for the *New York Times.*

Language mistakes extend far beyond the press, of course. Political speeches, business memos, and athletes' post-game comments are so filled with the torture of the English language that misuse almost seems the standard of the day.

Alexander M. Haig, Jr., was so careless in his use of the language during his years as Secretary of State that the British daily *The Guardian* parodied one of his speeches in 1981; *Time* magazine accused Haig of "conducting a terrorist campaign . . . against the English language." Haig regularly used incorrect— and nonexistent—words, turned nouns into verbs and adjectives, and indulged in such obvious redundancies as "careful caution."

"The effect of government generally on the language and on writing and on journalism is horribly corrupting, polluting . . . ," Allan M. Siegal, news editor of the *New York Times,* said during Haig's tenure in Washington. "I think, for instance, that if General Haig is secretary of state long enough, no child will be safe; no one in this country will grow up speaking anything like standard English."

Concern about declining language standards is not new. Jonathan Swift complained about the same decline in the eighteenth century, and George Orwell warned, in 1946, "The English language is in a bad way. . . . Modern English, especially written English, is full of bad habits."

As Thomas R. Lounsbury, dean of American grammarians at the turn of the century, wrote in 1908:

"There seems to have been in every period in the past, as there is now, a distinct apprehension in the minds of very many worthy persons that the English tongue is always in the condition approaching collapse, and that arduous efforts must be put forth persistently to save it from destruction."

Jim Quinn, in *American Tongue and Cheek,* cynically dismisses as opportunists those contemporary pop grammarians who worry in print about the decline of the language. "There is hardly an aspect of American life that has not made the best-seller list after somebody was lucky enough to discover it was in the last stages of decline," Quinn says.

But there are several differences between the circumstances involved in the decline in language standards today and in earlier generations. One difference is that previous declines were largely limited to people who didn't write for a living; today, misuse of the language by professional writers has become pervasive in everything from comic strips (recent mistakes there include *priviledge*/for *privilege, burgler* for *burglar,* and *who's* for *whose*) to serious literature and academic treatises.

A few years ago, the *New Republic* devoted most of a page to mocking the misuse of language in a new book by Graham Greene—described by his publisher as "the most distinguished living writer in the English language."

But it is in daily newspapers that the most frequent and most flagrant language mistakes are being made:

- The *Milwaukee Journal* published a story about foreign tourists who "pour over English lessons." (They'd learn more, and stay dry, if they *pored* over their lessons.)
- The *San Jose Mercury-News* noted: ". . . Dunn said this could be settled like gentlemen between he and Wright." (*Him* was no gentleman.)
- The *New York Daily News* said a basketball player had a *flare* about him. (He actually had a *flair*—unless, perhaps, his car broke down on the highway one night.)
- From the *Oklahoma Journal:* ". . . in whom's office she worked."

How does the English language fare today in newspapers generally regarded as the nation's best?

The *Washington Post* has mentioned a company that *has become* the first utility to place a new unit. Another *Post* story described efforts to keep Northern Virginia's *principle* reservoir from drying up. (It should have been *principal;* as the *Post's* ombudsman at the time, Bill Green, pointed out in a memo to *Post* editors: "If there's a reservoir of principles out there, let's declare the thing a national monument and surround it with marines. It may be the best resource available.")

A *Los Angeles Times* reporter described actor Jack Nicholson as "looking like an all-night coach passenger who had just awoke. . . ." (It should have been *awakened*.) Another *Times* reporter wrote that someone *collaborated* a congressman's statement. (It should have been *corroborated*.) A *Times* copy editor incorrectly used the word *disinterest* in a headline across the top of a page. (*Disinterest* means *lack of bias;* the editor meant *lack of interest* or *apathy*.)

A careful reading of major newspapers around the country

shows that there are probably more language errors in the *Los Angeles Times* than in any other paper of its caliber.

In part, this may happen because—for many years, in some departments of the paper—reporters have had more freedom (and copy editors less authority) than their counterparts on most other major papers. This has led to a certain laxity among reporters and copy editors alike—a condition that the paper's top editors say they have been trying for several years to correct.

Nevertheless, in one single week, the *Times* incorrectly used *he* for *him, whom* for *who, was* for *were, were* for *was, would* for *will,* and *which* for *that*—and also misused *equitably, plethora,* and *swirl,* in addition to making many other mistakes.

In three separate stories published earlier, over a four-day period, one *L.A. Times* reporter misused *resilient* for *resistant, magnet* for *magnate,* and *premiere* for *premier.* A few weeks later, this same reporter, in a single story, misspelled *persistent, occurrence,* and *publicly* and made several other mistakes in grammar, usage, and punctuation.

But even the *New York Times,* which probably makes fewer language mistakes than any other paper, is making them with increasing frequency, editors and grammarians say.

The *New York Times* has, more than once, used *fortuitous* as a synonym for *fortunate.* (The preferred meaning of *fortuitous* is simply *accidental,* whether for good or ill.) The paper's staff has also constructed sentences so carelessly that in one story a man was said to have given birth to a child; in another story the FBI was made to sound as if it were offering to help kill young children. Other *New York Times* stories have misused *refute, acronym, yolk, arrested, fulsome, dilemma, barrage, ironically, mitigate, burgeoning, fact, myriad, proliferating, who,* and *whom.*

"You can't expect on a newspaper the stylistic writing of a fine novelist or historian," said the late Alfred Friendly, former managing editor of the *Washington Post.* "What you can expect is clarity . . . and accuracy . . . [rather than] laziness and sloppiness. You should strive for good writing to indicate that the [reporter] covering the story . . . is an educated lady or gentleman and not a plumber from off the streets.''

Some critics contend that sloppy grammar is the product of sloppy thought and that carelessness with language leads to carelessness with facts. But most editors say their reporters, even the younger reporters who most often make language mistakes, are generally very careful with facts and with the conclusions they draw from them.

''They're brighter and better reporters, in many ways, than their predecessors,'' one editor says. ''They just don't know grammar.''

Why not?

One explanation, many editors agree, is the influence of television—''the nonlanguage and aboriginal grammar of commercials, commentators, sports announcers, athletes, assorted celebrities, and just about everyone in that word-mongering and word-mangling medium,'' in the words of John Simon.

People speaking spontaneously on television are, understandably, more likely to make mistakes in language usage than are people who write their comments and then edit them. Spoken English is also more casual and less precise than written English, and people accustomed to watching and listening to television, rather than reading books, hear more colloquial and improper English, and they absorb it and repeat it.

This is true of jargon, as well as of grammatical errors.

Politicians have always spoken a special jargon—an obfuscating bureaucratese—but in previous generations, reporters often sanitized or carefully excerpted these remarks before printing them. Now, politicians (and other public figures) are in our living rooms every night, in full rhetorical flower, saying ''energy-wise, economy-wise, and environmental-wise'' and ''I cannot relate to that material possessory consciousness.''

During the Iranian hostage crisis, then-President Jimmy Carter said, on national television, "The government of Iran must realize that it cannot flaunt, with impunity, the expressed will and law of the world community."

But *flaunt* means "to make a gaudy, ostentatious, conspicuous, impudent, or defiant display." Carter meant *flout*—"to mock or scoff at; show scorn or contempt for."

Television and politicians are, however, only two factors in the declining quality of language use in the press. Technological changes in newspapers themselves are also responsible. Many newspapers now use computerized typesetting devices and video display terminals—desk-top consoles with small, television-like screens—instead of typewriters.

One Eastern editor says these changes have virtually eliminated proofreaders at his paper, "and that's eliminated the daily competition we used to have, with proofreaders delighting in catching mistakes made by the high-priced reporters and copy editors. Now all those mistakes show up in the paper."

Another editor, in the Midwest, says reporters seem less conscious of language mistakes when they view their stories on a video screen than when they have them typed out in front of them on paper.

But most editors agree that the primary reason for the decline in proper language usage in their profession is a decline in the quality of language instruction in the schools.

Although some editors say this deterioration began as long ago as the 1930s and 1940s, with a gradual de-emphasis on learning by rote, most editors say the deterioration, or at least its rapid acceleration, is much more recent. They date it from the mid-1960s.

It is the young men and women who have gone to school since then, the editors say, who are writing much of the careless, ungrammatical prose that so often sullies today's newspapers.

Dozens of studies seem to support this theory.

One study, for example, shows that average scores on the Scholastic Aptitude Test (SAT)—the test widely used as a college entrance exam—dropped steadily from 1963 to 1980; the decline in test scores for verbal skills was especially precipitous.

Some critics attribute this, in part, to the virtual disappearance of Latin from the school curriculum.

"Fifty years ago," one critic writes, "*half* of all students in public high schools were studying Latin." By 1978, the figure was 8 percent.

There are other explanations for what Paul Cooperman, in his book *The Literacy Hoax,* calls "a sharp and widespread decline in the primary academic skills of America's students" since the mid-1960s.

Studies show that students are now assigned less reading— and easier reading. They are given fewer writing assignments. They are less frequently taught to diagram sentences.

"Less thoughtful and critical reading is now being demanded and done in high school, and . . . careful writing has apparently gone . . . out of style," said a committee charged with studying the declining SAT scores.

Why?

Editors have several theories:

- Classes are larger. Newer teachers are less skilled, and lazier, having themselves been given an inferior education. Students, accustomed to watching television, are more difficult to motivate and more resistant to authority.
- Editors also complain about "misguided attempts to make education more 'relevant' and to encourage 'individual expression,' " instead of teaching basic language skills.

Most editors and critics see all this as a natural (but much-to-be-lamented) by-product of student-inspired campus reforms in the 1960s.

Even a political liberal like Thomas Winship, editor of the *Boston Globe,* blames what he calls "this illiteracy crisis" on, among other things, the increased academic permissiveness of the sixties. "We're finally getting in the newsrooms the children of the sixties, the children who had the misfortune of going through school . . . when they forgot to teach them English . . . forgot to have them do any kind of work," Winship says.

"I'm afraid it was . . . progressivism running haywire, running amok. We . . . gave kids . . . their head to seek their own intellectual ground. . . . I think we just gave them, really, too much educational freedom."

Or, as John Simon puts it, "Students themselves became the arbiters of what subjects were to be taught, and grammar, by jingo (or Ringo), was not one of them."

Winship and others praise 1960s activists for their "tremendous contributions to society," but along with these contributions came an "anything-goes, do-your-own-thing" ethic that many editors insist has contributed significantly to a deterioration in language instruction and usage.

Another editor offers this admitted oversimplification of the 1960s mind-set on the rejection of all authority:

"I can wear my hair long, I can go without a tie, and I can say *different than* [instead of *different from*]."

Edwin Newman says many people who knew better deliberately misused language in the sixties in an effort to disassociate themselves from the Establishment, to mark themselves as anti-Establishment—as opposed to those who led us into Vietnam and oppressed our minorities and polluted our environment.

"In the sixties you had probably millions of people who didn't *want* to use English well," Newman says. "They were making their points by having a limited vocabulary, by being able to say little more than 'you know' and 'I mean' and 'wow' and a few other expressions . . . because this was a political position and, as they saw it, a humanistic position."

Henry Grunwald, editor-in-chief of Time Inc., agrees with Newman. "We even had . . . in the sixties and seventies the kind of attitude that correcting somebody's grammar was an elitist act and, given certain situations, even a racist act," Grunwald says. "This . . . had quite a real impact on our education, which was not very good to begin with . . . not disciplined enough . . . , and there's no doubt that this has had an impact on the kind of writing you get in magazines and newspapers [now]."

Teachers who were themselves radicalized in the 1960s compounded this problem. These teachers "suspected that competition was immoral, grades undemocratic, and promotion based on merit and measurable accomplishment a likely way to discriminate against minorities and the poor," *Time* magazine said in 1980.

Allan M. Siegal, news editor of the *New York Times,* says that because of the attitudes about language that were developed in the 1960s, editors who are concerned about the language are made to feel defensive today.

"On this paper now," Siegal says, "for someone to be a language buff is regarded almost as an eccentricity or a curiosity. . . . That fact is noted about him or her the way it would be noted that the person is a model railroad buff. Why should it be a curiosity that professional . . . writers and editors have a particular passion for the language? That wasn't true twenty-one years ago . . . when I started to work for the *Times.*"

What can newspaper editors do to reverse this attitude, to encourage good language habits?

Siegal reads the *New York Times* in bed every morning, green pen in hand, and he marks every mistake he finds—grammatical, factual, stylistic, or otherwise; he tears out these stories and has his secretary send them to the offending parties.

Siegal says he finds about half a dozen language mistakes a day in his paper, and he is blunt in his criticism of them. His scrawled comments have included "Ugh," "An abomination," "3rd-rate copy-editing," and "Illiterate."

Several times a year, Siegal also assembles and distributes

to the staff a more detailed report on mistakes (and triumphs) that have appeared in the paper.

The late Theodore Bernstein originated this report, called "Winners & Sinners," in 1951, and Siegal took it over seven years ago. It has since been copied by many papers. The *Washington Post,* the *Boston Globe,* the *Milwaukee Journal,* the *San Jose Mercury-News,* the *Miami Herald,* and several other papers now periodically circulate similar reports to their staffs.

The *Los Angeles Times* also began distribution of a "Style & Usage Report" in 1980, but so far it has been much less comprehensive, much less frequent, and much less ambitious than those at many other papers.

Some papers are going far beyond these occasional bulletins in their attempts to improve newspaper writing, and correct language usage is only one of their objectives.

Too much newspaper writing is "graceless, awkward . . . a chore to read, instead of a pleasure," says Eugene Patterson of the *St. Petersburg* (Fla.) *Times.*

Other editors say newspaper stories are too often dull, boring, long-winded, unclear. Editors are clearly concerned that the accessibility, immediacy, and impact of television are far more inviting than the black and white columns of a newspaper. They are trying to combat that by encouraging newspaper writing that is clearer, more direct, more forceful, and more graphic, as well as more grammatical.

In 1977 the *St. Petersburg* (Fla.) *Times* hired Roy Peter Clark, an English professor at Auburn University, as a writing coach for its staff. Now Clark conducts writing seminars at the Modern Media Institute in St. Petersburg, and newspapers through the country send reporters and editors to him for help. Clark's interdisciplinary approach involves conversations with poets, novelists, and academicians, as well as with other reporters and editors.

"A recent . . . study [by the Gannett newspaper chain] shows that writing problems are a major reason why readers turn off on newspapers,'' the late Ed Orloff said when he was assistant managing editor of the *San Francisco Examiner*.

"The more colorful, dynamic, and stimulating the writing,'' the study said, "the more the paper is read, and the more satisfied the reader becomes.''

With that objective in mind, more than thirty papers—large and small, independent and chain, in all parts of the country—have organized various kinds of writing programs for their staffs in recent years. They have conducted one-day or one-week writing seminars or they have hired part-time professors or full-time editors to serve as writing coaches, working with two or three reporters at a time to improve their prose style and their mastery of the language.

One editors says he noted "a marked improvement" in (writing) quality within a year after he hired a writing coach.

Many reporters say writing coaches force them to think more about the act of writing—to become as aware of grammar, structure, transitions, and figures of speech as they are of sources, statistics, and deadlines.

Too many reporters do not even think of themselves as writers, says Alan Richman, assistant managing editor for writing at the *Boston Globe*. "[To them] writing is just taking whatever they've got in their notebooks and putting it in the paper. They don't necessarily think they're exercising a craft.''

Nevertheless, some editors worry that the use of writing coaches may lead to an overemphasis on flashy writing at the expense of responsible reporting—that form will become more important than content, that reporters will spend more time searching for colorful metaphors than for verifiable facts. Most editors seem to think, however, that this danger can be averted and that a renewed emphasis on good writing—clear, vivid, accurate, grammatical writing—is long overdue in American newspapers.

As an incentive, many newspapers are now giving cash awards for the best-written stories each month.

Editors at Knight-Ridder newspapers also have developed a comprehensive, 3½-hour test for prospective copy editors; editors at Knight-Ridder's *Philadelphia Inquirer* say the testing program, combined with efforts to encourage better writing, has produced a steady improvement in the quality of the paper's prose. *Inquirer* reporters have won several major writing awards in recent years.

"By and large, most papers don't put the sort of emphasis on this that I think they should," says Gene Foreman, managing editor of the *Inquirer*. "There is simply not a high priority on good writing and precision editing. . . . There is a prevailing attitude that the important thing is to get the news first and get it right, and I certainly don't quarrel with this. But since we are earning our living with language we have a responsibility to be very careful about its usage and [to] observe all the rules of the language."

*   *   *

Get a dictionary. Here are the dozen words that newspaper editors say their papers most often use incorrectly: *dilemma, egregious, enormity, fortuitous, fulsome, hopefully, ironically, penultimate, portentous, presently, quintessential,* and *unique.*

Here are the pairs of words that newspapers most often mix up and misuse: *abdicate* and *abrogate, adverse* and *averse, affect* and *effect, alleged* and *intended, allude* and *elude, allusion* and *illusion, breach* and *breech, composed* and *comprised, convince* and *persuade, continually* and *continuously, disinterested* and *uninterested, flaunt* and *flout, gantlet* and *gauntlet, imply* and *infer, lay* and *lie, lectern* and *podium, nauseated* and *nauseous, noisy* and *noisome, pore* and *pour, precipitate* and *precipitous, prostate* and *prostrate, rebut* and *refute, who* and *whom.*

People who write, and edit, for newspapers also seem to have a curious problem with the word *successfully.* They often use it when it's unnecessary, redundant, as in "successfully withstand" *(New York Times),* "successfully capture" (United Press International), and "successfully avoided" *(Time* magazine).

Redundancy, in fact, seems to be an occupational hazard for journalists, as witness "planning ahead" *(Boston Globe),* "apparent heir apparent" (United Press International), and "ominous portent" *(Los Angeles Times).*

Editors also complain frequently about:

- Such vogue words as *parameter, thrust, viable, dialogue,* and *perception.*
- Such mixed metaphors as "The smell of war returns to Washington, and this time I am listening seriously" *(Washington Post).*
- Non sequiturs (" 'Born in Argentina, he was an ardent golfer' is my favorite," says Rene J. Cappon, general news editor of the Associated Press).
- A singular subject with a plural verb or vice versa. (From *Ways of Escape* by Graham Greene: "The day of the Lee-Enfield and the Maxim gun were more favorable to the European than those of the dive bomber and the Bren." No, "the day . . . *was* more favorable than *that* of. . . .")

Worst of all, perhaps, many reporters seem unable to construct a simple sentence that says what they want it to say, with all the right words in the right places:

- A *Binghamton* (New York) *Evening Press* story said, "Yesterday, a car battery exploded in his face while helping a stranded motorist."
- A *Boston Globe* story said, "She died in the home in which she was born at the age of eighty-eight."
- A *St. Petersburg* (Fla.) *Times* story said, "A thirty-year-old St. Petersburg man was found murdered by his parents in his home late Saturday."

Such mistakes are neither infrequent nor inconsequential. In the St. Petersburg story, for example, sloppy sentence construction made it appear that a man had been murdered by his parents. In fact, he was murdered by someone else. His parents found his body.

It would be difficult to overestimate the pain, grief, and embarrassment that the parents could have suffered because of this mistake.

But many reporters and editors remain largely indifferent to the rules of grammar and the nuances of language.

In fact, one *Los Angeles Times* copy editor recalls editing a story that said someone had "died in his home, Post Office Box 320-A," and when he pointed out to his superior that this construction made it appear that the man had died in a mailbox, his superior just shrugged and said he didn't think it was worth changing.

9

THE EDITORIAL CARTOONIST

Some scholars trace the roots of contemporary editorial cartooning as far back as twelfth-century Japan, but a more common starting point is sixteenth-century Italy, where artists Annibale and Agostino Carracci created the word *caricature* to describe their *ritrattini carichi* ("loaded portraits").

William Hogarth of England and Honoré Daumier of France were the early giants of what became modern editorial cartooning in Europe—Daumier was jailed in 1831 because of his caricature of King Louis-Philippe—and Benjamin Franklin is largely credited with drawing the first American political cartoon (in 1754).

But it was Thomas Nast's slashing cartoons in *Harper's Weekly* in the 1870s that truly established the political cartoon as an art form in the United States. Nast's attacks on William "Boss" Tweed's Tammany Hall political machine in New York helped break the machine and send Tweed to jail.

"Stop them damn pictures," Tweed once ordered underlings after seeing a particularly harsh Nast cartoon. "I don't care so much what the papers write about me. My constituents can't read. But, damn it, they can see pictures."

Tweed tried to bribe Nast to go "study art" in Europe, but Nast refused and continued to draw. A brilliant and effective symbolist, he popularized not only the Tammany tiger but the Democratic donkey and the Republican elephant, and for most of the next century, cartoonists continued to rely heavily on symbols and/or labels in their drawings.

"The first quarter of the twentieth century was the golden age of the political cartoonist," one historian wrote in 1954. "The issues were simple enough to be easily interpreted, and there was enough elemental violence in them to satisfy the satirist."

But when the depression struck, cartooning suffered along with virtually everything else. Issues became more complicated, personal caricature and personal invective diminished, and cartooning entered a long decline.

Despite the work of a few fine cartoonists, that general decline did not really end until after the largely regimented, patriotic cartoons of World War II and the stultifying apathy and cold war fears of the 1950s gave way to the controversial sociopolitical issues of the 1960s and 1970s.

Bill Mauldin, who had been the best among the very few good World War II cartoonists, joined Herbert Block ("Herblock") and Paul Conrad in setting early examples for a new generation of cartoonists.

Committed liberals all, they drew strong cartoons on Vietnam, civil rights, and, later, Watergate.

Herblock probably had the most public impact of the three. It was Herblock, a three-time Pulitzer Prize–winner, who coined the term *McCarthyism* when he was among the very first journalistic critics of Senator Joe McCarthy during the 1950s Communist witchhunts. It was also Herblock who so consistently savaged Richard Nixon—he of the sinister scowl and five o'clock shadow—that Nixon was quoted as saying, during his 1960 campaign for the presidency, "I have to erase the Herblock image."

What makes Herblock and Conrad so unusual and so important, even today, is that both have often seized on important issues before they were at the forefront of public consciousness. Thus, they educate as well as comment; they help establish an agenda and a moral tone for public debate.

Lyndon Johnson and *Mad* magazine were also enormously influential in the regeneration of editorial cartooning in the 1960s and early 1970s.

"In large measure, Lyndon Johnson brought life back into the form," says Jules Feiffer, playwright and cartoonist for the *Village Voice.* "If Johnson hadn't given us Vietnam, and there hadn't been an emerging generation of talented art students who were thinking of going into illustration, maybe, or advertising and, instead, went into editorial cartooning because of their opposition to the war, lots of . . . interesting people . . . wouldn't have been in the business."

Mad magazine, Feiffer once wrote, was "the editorial voice of the paranoid teenager. . . . [It] taught kids from puberty that the adult world was to be sneered at. *Mad*'s irreverence, generally aimed at safe targets, legitimized for these young, would-be cartoonists a cynicism that later prepared them to address America at war.

"The effect of Lyndon Johnson's war on a generation of artists raised on reading *Mad* magazine was combustible," Feiffer wrote in an introduction to a collection of cartoons by an antiwar member of that generation, Doug Marlette of the *Charlotte Observer*.

But the single greatest influence on cartooning in the 1960s was Pat Oliphant.

When Oliphant came to the United States from Australia in 1964, he quite literally changed the shape of American editorial cartooning.

Until Oliphant arrived, most American cartoons were vertical in format; he—and, now, almost everyone—prefers horizontal cartoons, which provide more opportunity for story-line development and which are more in keeping with the viewing habits of readers accustomed to looking at television, billboards, and the movie screen.

But Oliphant's influence was even greater in terms of style and tone. He uses far fewer labels than most traditional American cartoonists did. He draws ordinary people and ordinary scenes. His humor is more subtle and irreverent. His drawing style is looser, more freewheeling. He is more iconoclastic, less ideologically predictable; his targets are on all sides of the political spectrum. He is less doctrinaire and more whimsical than Herblock, Conrad, and Mauldin.

"Oliphant's arrival on the scene sparked a lot of awareness among people who had pretty set ideas about what editorial cartoons were," says Tony Auth, Pulitzer Prize–winning cartoonist of the *Philadelphia Inquirer*. "A lot of people who would not have considered themselves editorial cartoonists suddenly were able to entertain the possibility because the definition was broadened."

Oliphant thus introduced a whole new style of cartooning to the United States. That style subsequently influenced Jeff

MacNelly and ultimately gave birth—albeit in a somewhat bas-
tardized form—to much of the cartooning that dominates the
American editorial page today.

*   *   *

W HEN Steve Benson was a kid, he decided he'd like
to be a fireman or a policeman when he grew up.
Then he grew up. He decided to be a weather-
man instead.

But an aptitude for mathematics is essential to the study of
meteorology, and Benson "was never very good with math,"
he says. So, at age twenty-one Benson had to change plans again.

"I decided," he says, "well, if I can't use my head, I'll go
into editorial cartooning."

Benson is thirty now. He is the editorial cartoonist for the
Arizona Republic in Phoenix. Despite his facetious remark about
not using his head, he is an intelligent and articulate fellow—
and, like most cartoonists, a formally trained artist. But Benson
is also, according to many of his peers, a prime example of what
is wrong with editorial cartooning in America today.

Benson is one of a large and growing number of young editorial cartoonists who are widely accused by their more established peers, and by many editors and syndicate executives alike,
of not using their heads (or their imaginations), of being imita-
tive (rather than original), amusing (rather than provocative).

Perhaps "80 percent to 90 percent of [today's] cartoonists
. . . don't have an idea in their silly little heads," Jules Feiffer says.

Since many of these cartoonists often emulate—consciously
or subconsciously—the work of two-time Pulitzer Prize–winner
Jeff MacNelly, many other cartoonists have taken to calling them
"MacNelly clones" or "MacBensons" (a name coined by another two-time Pulitzer Prize–winning cartoonist, Paul Szep of
the *Boston Globe*).

There are now dozens of "MacBensons" on newspapers across the country, and their collective impact on the state of the cartooning art has been enormous.

Over the last decade, and especially in the last three or four years, cartoons of strong political comment, drawn by artists of passionate moral commitment, have increasingly given way to cartoons of mild topical humor drawn by "MacBensons"—"gag-writers for the Johnny Carson show," as MacNelly himself calls them.

"I don't see too many cartoonists taking strong stands on anything," says Don Wright, two-time Pulitzer Prize–winning cartoonist for the *Miami News*. "We have far too many younger cartoonists who've lost sight of what should be motivating an editorial cartoonist, and that is issues," he says. "They look at it primarily as an opportunity for a gag of the day, dimly related to some issue."

Strong stands on issues are important to Wright, so much so that, perhaps more than any other cartoonist, he actively participates in his paper's daily editorial conferences and joins in the discussion of the paper's editorial stands and political endorsements, almost as if he were an editorial writer.

Other cartoonists, many of whom deliberately avoid their papers' editorial conferences in an effort to preserve their own independence, nonetheless agree with Wright's criticism.

Some of these cartoonists attribute the "gag-of-the-day" syndrome to newspaper efforts to compete with television situation comedies and the false bonhomie of television newscasts. Other cartoonists say the new syndrome simply reflects the contemporary political climate. The nice-guy presidencies of Gerald Ford, Jimmy Carter, and Ronald Reagan have not generally produced the visceral issues and the concomitant moral outrage generated by Lyndon Johnson (over Vietnam) or Richard Nixon (over Watergate).

Paul Conrad, two-time Pulitzer Prize–winning cartoonist for the *Los Angeles Times,* insists, however, that newspaper editors who are afraid of offending their readers are more to blame than politics or television for the blandness of so many editorial cartoons these days.

"For far too long," Conrad says, "editorial page editors were writing crap. . . . They didn't say anything. . . . Here comes this new breed [of cartoonist] doing funny illustrations that really don't state an opinion. . . . This gives the editor the best of all worlds. Now he's got something to go along with his editorials."

Conrad abhors such thinking. He is an angry man and he thinks all cartoonists should be angry all the time. If their cartoons take such strong positions that they make readers—and their subjects—angry, too, so much the better.

Conrad is not alone in enjoying the howls of anguish from his targets. Just as Conrad reveled in being named to Nixon's "enemies list," so Paul Szep could barely contain his delight in 1982 when Governor Edward J. King of Massachusetts filed a $3.6-million lawsuit against him and the *Boston Globe* for "false and defamatory" cartoons and columns.

But not every cartoon can be a brutal knockout punch that engenders lawsuits and permanent personal enmity. No cartoonist (no matter how talented) can be that consistent, and no reader (no matter how sympathetic) will remain that interested.

"If everyday I delivered a haymaker, readers would become numbed, immune, bored," says Doug Marlette, cartoonist for the *Charlotte Observer* and the only cartoonist ever to win a prestigious Nieman Fellowship to study at Harvard. "I like to mix it up—one day offering the yin of an apocalyptic warning, the next the yang of a little topical whimsy."

Whimsy—humor—has long been an integral part of the editorial cartoon, of course, but in years past, most of this humor was satire, parody—sometimes subtle, more often savage, almost invariably cynical and ideological. But now, with some notable exceptions, humor for humor's sake has largely replaced humor that made an ideological comment.

Some newspaper editors say that ideologically based cartooning is an anachronism today, a throwback to the days when newspapers were more openly partisan on their news pages as well as on their editorial pages.

Today's cartoonist, these editors say, reflects a growing desire by newspapers to avoid knee-jerk, doctrinaire editorial positions in favor of a more evenhanded approach—a trend evidenced by, among other things, the development of op-ed pages to provide a forum for views that differ from those of the paper. Cartoons that rely on shallow stereotypes and doctrinaire ideology clearly do not serve this purpose.

But a cartoon is, by definition, one-sided and, in the strictest sense, unfair. A cartoon can't say "on the other hand. . . ." A cartoon makes one point—quickly, strongly, unqualifiedly.

"We violate all the rules of journalism," MacNelly concedes. "We misquote and slander . . . and distort . . . and everything else. [But] the interesting thing is the political cartoonist usually, if he's any good, gets a hell of a lot closer to the truth . . . than a responsible reporter."

Still a cartoon is black and white, literally and figuratively, and most cartoonists with strong ideological commitments tend to see life in these simple terms. As Anthony Day, editor of the *Los Angeles Times* editorial pages, puts it, "If you're convinced that God speaks to you every morning, life is very simple." In fact, some editors liken cartoonists to children because of this obsessive oversimplification. "Only kids and cartoonists see the world in such stark terms," says one editor.

This is probably the major reason the *New York Times,* alone among major newspapers, has no staff editorial cartoonist.

"Our own editorial expressions are carefully honed as to tone and quality of argument," says Max Frankel, editor of the paper's editorial pages. "It's hard not to imagine an editorial cartoon being hotter . . . and distorting the net result."

(For the last several years, the *New York Times* has been publishing a selection of cartoons by various artists every Sunday, but even those cartoons are not generally among the most forceful available, either in style or viewpoint.)

(The paper tries so hard to be fair, some critics say, that these weekly cartoons are often—in Jules Feiffer's words—"the least interesting work by the least interesting people [or] . . . the worst work by the best people; almost never will it be first-rate work by first-rate men.")

Although most cartoonists tend to see themselves as analogous to columnists, most newspapers publish several columnists of varying styles and political persuasions everyday; a few papers have two staff cartoonists—the *Chicago Tribute* now has three—but the vast majority have only one. Even if a paper regularly publishes the work of various syndicated cartoonists as well, which most papers do, many readers tend to see the staff cartoonist as the voice of the paper.

That can be particularly discomfiting to editors if the cartoonist is stridently doctrinaire or stylistically savage—or both. To minimize that misperception by readers, many papers (including the *Los Angeles Times*) have moved their cartoonists from the editorial page to the op-ed page; there, it is assumed, the cartoonist will be more clearly perceived as speaking only for himself, like a columnist, not for the newspaper.

Even that separation is not enough for some editors, though, and now, more than ever before, editors can (and do) choose their cartoons from a growing number of artists who illustrate the day's news humorously rather than commenting on it harshly (and, to some, offensively).

Many of these cartoonists are in their twenties and early thirties, and a large percentage of them have been heavily influenced by MacNelly and, subsequently, by Mike Peters of the *Dayton Daily News,* the 1981 Pulitzer Prize–winner.

When MacNelly began cartooning for the *Richmond News-Leader* in 1970, he brought to the drawing board a truly inspired sense of humor and a fresh drawing style—what *Newsweek* once characterized as a "distinctive, goofy gracefulness" that differed markedly from the more brutal approach of a Conrad or a Szep.

MacNelly is "the best draftsman ever to pick up a pen" in the perhaps hyperbolic words of Szep himself, and other cartoonists echo Szep's praise.

MacNelly also brought to American cartooning a conservative political philosophy.

Traditionally, the best cartoonists in this country have been liberals. In fact, Conrad (among others) argues that a conservative cartoonist is a contradiction in terms. "Conservatives don't have a sense of humor," he says.

But MacNelly is both conservative and funny. Even liberals admire his work, and by 1981 he was syndicated to almost 500 papers. Then, at the age of thirty-four, MacNelly retired. Why? He wanted to concentrate on a comic strip he had developed. He also had some personal problems. Most of all he was bored and frustrated—artistically as well as politically.

"The stuff that Reagan was trying to accomplish was stuff that I'd been yelling about for ten years," he says, "so I was basically in a rooting position" and cartoonists would much rather roast than root.

Worse, MacNelly says, doing five cartoons a week made him feel he was on a treadmill—"a slave to the front page.

"I really think that's why I quit. . . . I just said . . . this is not the way you should be doing a creative enterprise. . . . I'm not proud of what I'm turning out. . . . I was just doing it to fill space."

Many cartoonists, and many columnists, feel the same way. In fact, they liken the pressure of a daily cartoon or column to that of making love to a nymphomaniac. As soon as you're done, you have to start all over again.

Some cartoonists try to escape this pressure by taking a midweek day off now and then. Some take off for much longer. Editor Thomas Winship of the *Boston Globe* gave Szep four months off in 1981 because he thought he had grown stale after almost fifteen years of daily cartooning.

Garry Trudeau quit his *Doonesbury* strip early in 1983 saying he needed time to rethink and modernize his characters.

MacNelly was off for about ten months, and he, too, has now started over—for the *Chicago Tribune*. But this time MacNelly is drawing only three cartoons a week.

There was some speculation that other newspapers might not be willing to make that accommodation for MacNelly and that his syndicate might have trouble selling his cartoons as widely as before. The concern was largely unjustified. MacNelly now appears in more than four hundred papers. But even if Mac-Nelly had not returned almost to his pre-retirement peak of popularity, there would have been no shortage of MacNelly-like cartoons. There are still all those MacNelly clones out there; their work looks somewhat like MacNelly's—and it's much cheaper.

A newspaper pays for a syndicated cartoon based on a variety of factors: the circulation of the paper, the competitive situation in the paper's hometown, the size of the territory for which the paper wants exclusive rights to the cartoon, the negotiating skills of the newspaper editor and the syndicate salesman, and, of course, the popularity of the cartoonist.

The fee can range from less than $5 a week to more than $100 a week. Most major metropolitan papers generally pay $50 to $75 a week for a top cartoonist, but since there are, proportionately, few major papers and few top cartoonists, the average fee is about $10 to $20 a week.

(The syndicate and the cartoonist generally split these fees 50/50, although a few of the best, more established cartoonists get more than 50 percent, and some newspapers insist on a percentage of their staff cartoonist's share of any syndicate fees.)

A major newspaper might have to pay $125 for MacNelly, for example, but might be able to buy one of his imitators—or a package containing several of his imitators—for $25.

Critics say, however, that while the MacNelly clones try to copy MacNelly's drawing style or sense of humor, they largely ignore his ideas, his political commentary.

MacNelly's world view is "a kind of . . . forgiving . . . generally pleasant view . . . a nice, warm sense of humor," says cartoonist Jim Borgman of the *Cincinnati Enquirer*. "A lot of us MacNelly clones misunderstood that to think of that approach as being less opinionated than the older stuff."

Increasingly, many young cartoonists are making the same mistake when they emulate Mike Peters, the fun-loving, perpetually ebullient cartoonist who appears occasionally on the NBC "Today" show.

Peters says he feels as strongly about most issues as do such cartoonists as Conrad, Szep, and Herblock ("my idols"), but much as he would like to, he can't draw their kind of "mean, biting, nasty" cartoon.

"I am, by nature, a fairly happy . . . funny guy," he said, and his cartoons—like the elaborate pranks he often plays at home and in the office—reflect that.

Even more than MacNelly, Peters seems—especially to the casual eye—to be drawing funny pictures, with funny captions, utterly devoid of political or social commentary. Sometimes that's exactly what he is doing. But often he is using humor to make a political comment—as in his widely praised 1980 cartoon showing George Washington ("I cannot tell a lie"), Richard Nixon ("I cannot tell the truth"), and Jimmy Carter ("I cannot tell the difference").

As with the MacNelly clones, too many of Peters's imitators fail to see, or to be influenced by, his political insights.

The result: vast numbers of cartoons that are occasionally amusing, seldom provocative or inventive, and almost never offensive. Moreover, a great many of them look alike, almost as if they had been produced by Xerox rather than by individual artistry.

Instead of doing what the best cartoonists do to start each workday—reading several newspapers and magazines, thinking about issues and ideas, trying to transfer feelings from gut and brain to paper—these cartoonists sit in their offices wondering, "What would MacNelly or Peters draw today?"

Sometimes, of course, similarities between cartoons—and between cartoonists—are purely coincidental. There are a finite number of visual images available, and given the limitations of the medium and the mind-set of most cartoonists, it is not unlikely that several cartoonists will, on occasion, draw similar cartoons on similar subjects.

When Egyptian President Anwar Sadat was assassinated, for example, many cartoonists drew dying doves of peace. Pure coincidence. When the movie *Jaws* was popular, almost every cartoonist in the country, it seemed, drew a shark devouring something. Pure coincidence.

But some similarities seem to transcend coincidence. Cartoonist John Lara was fired by the *Register* in Orange County, California, and dropped by the Field Newspaper Syndicate in 1981 after several of his peers assembled a package of his and MacNelly's cartoons that made it appear that Lara had copied some of MacNelly's ideas and artwork.

Similarly, Dave Simpson of the *Tulsa Tribune* was dropped by United Feature Syndicate about five years ago after he was accused of copying ideas and artwork from MacNelly, Oliphant, and several others—accusations that his syndicate editor says Simpson did not deny.

Most young cartoonists—most young artists—are influenced to some extent by the contemporary masters, of course. But in time, if they're good—original rather than derivative—they evolve their own style.

"Artistic style doesn't come overnight," Steve Benson says. "Often it takes many years to develop and represents the selective ingraining of influences from many sources."

MacNelly himself readily admits to having been greatly influenced in his early days by Oliphant, and Oliphant concedes his own early debt to British artist Ronald Searle.

As Benson rightly argues, "Such evolution is at the heart of the creative process."

But too many of today's younger cartoonists seem in danger of stagnating, not evolving. They have achieved some success—recognition, syndication, remuneration—by emulating MacNelly (or Peters or someone else), and they're not about to change.

The cartoonist whom other cartoonists singled out most often in this regard during my 1982 interviews was Jack Ohman, then with the *Columbus* (Ohio) *Dispatch* and now with the *Portland Oregonian*. Ohman's work was syndicated to about fifty papers until MacNelly "retired" in 1981. Then, because the two men were stylistically and ideologically similar—and because they shared the same syndicate—the syndicate offered Ohman to all of MacNelly's clients (about 70 percent of whom accepted).

Suddenly, at age twenty-one, Ohman found himself rich and famous—syndicated to 350 papers nationwide, earning more than $100,000 a year, featured in *People* and *Newsweek* magazines—and, later, hired away from the *Columbus* (Ohio) *Dispatch* by the *Detroit Free Press* before going to Portland last year.

Since MacNelly returned, Ohman has lost about 55 percent of his newspapers, his syndicate says. But many cartoonists say such defections could ultimately benefit Ohman. These cartoonists, some of whom admit to being jealous of Ohman's instant success, say Ohman still lacks political and artistic maturity; the pressure of trying to satisfy MacNelly's client list could prevent him from ever maturing into a talented cartoonist in his own right, they argue.

Even syndicate executives admit that the early riches of syndication can inhibit a young cartoonist, make him reluctant to engage in the kind of experimentation that would enable him to develop his own style.

A young cartoonist working for a single paper (or a small group of papers) can take chances—try new techniques, take controversial stands, tinker with various styles. But the easiest way for a cartoonist to become rich and famous is to have a syndicate sell his work to a lot of papers. The easiest way for the syndicate to do that is for the cartoonist to draw in the currently popular style and to be as predictable and as inoffensive, as bland, as possible.

It's "absolutely true" that someone who does gag cartoons can be more easily syndicated than someone who does strong editorial viewpoint cartoons, says Don Michel, executive vice-president and editor of the Tribune Company Syndicate.

So, many of today's cartoonists do gag cartoons—thereby incurring the scornful wrath of their more talented (and more committed) peers.

A cartoonist's job is to "kick ass and take names," Pat Oliphant says, and when Oliphant first came to the United States from Australia, he tried to do that in a style new to this country. He says he hoped this would show other cartoonists that they, too, could develop individualistic styles and visions. Instead, he growls, most of today's cartoonists are just mimics, "stamping out hubcaps . . . scared to try [anything different]."

Oliphant is one of the most influential, widely syndicated, highly regarded, well-paid cartoonists in the world today. He is also one of the most outspoken.

With the disdainful iconoclasm that is so characteristic of his cartoons, Oliphant is quite willing to disparage, by name, many of the most respected cartoonists in the country. To Oliphant, Peters is "a disaster . . . a lightweight joker. . . . I couldn't take him seriously"; Conrad is "a knee-jerk limousine, doctrinaire liberal . . . with not much to say"; MacNelly is someone who "never made what I would call a really strong statement in his career."

Oliphant waxes particularly wrothful on the subject of MacNelly—at least in part, one suspects, because *Newsweek* put MacNelly (rather than Oliphant) on the cover when it did a major story on cartooning in 1980.

Oliphant felt so slighted that he not only sneers openly at MacNelly, he has also refused to permit *Newsweek* to reprint an Oliphant cartoon since that issue was published.

Although the vast majority of cartoonists would disagree with Oliphant's denigration of MacNelly, Conrad, and Peters, Oliphant is certainly not alone in his willingness to deride others among his peers. Not surprisingly, men who earn their living by ridiculing other people in print aren't notably reluctant to ridicule their fellow cartoonists as well.

But there is also a great deal of camaraderie among some cartoonists. A number of them speak frequently to each other on the phone—encouraging and nourishing and admiring each other—and Pulitzer Prize–winners Szep and Tony Auth of the *Philadelphia Inquirer* have lobbied quite vigorously (albeit unsuccessfully so far) to get a Pulitzer Prize for Jules Feiffer.

In fact, except for Oliphant, even the most virulent critics of the modern editorial cartoon concede that there are more excellent cartoonists working today than ever before. Despite Oliphant's opinion in several cases, interviews with more than fifty cartoonists, editors, and syndicate executives nationwide produced general—indeed, almost universal—agreement on the best of the breed: Oliphant himself, MacNelly, Conrad, Don Wright of the *Miami News,* Szep, Peters, Auth, Herblock.

(Herblock's inclusion on the list seems less a testament to the quality of his work today than to the great respect his peers have for his artistic excellence and his artistic and ideological consistency and courage for more than forty years. But Mauldin is also venerated for his work in the 1940s, 1950s, and 1960s, and almost no one contends that he is doing first-rate work now.)

Most cartoonists place Feiffer, Trudeau, and caricaturist David Levine in the top rank, too, although none of the three is an editorial cartoonist in the same sense as the others on the list. Marlette, Jim Borgman of the *Cincinnati Enquirer,* Wayne Stayskal of the *Chicago Tribune,* and three or four other cartoonists are generally ranked just behind the top group, and there are perhaps half a dozen other new young cartoonists whose ability and potential are also widely admired.

But there is overwhelming agreement among most of the top cartoonists, and among the men who syndicate and publish their work, that while there are more first-rate (and potentially first-rate) cartoonists now than ever before, there are also far more second-rate, third-rate, and twelfth-rate cartoonists than ever before.

On that point, almost everyone agrees, Oliphant is absolutely right in his sweeping excoriations and in his lament that what makes most of today's cartoons so bad is that so many of them look alike and so few of them take strong stands.

Complaints that the editorial cartoon has lost its bite are not new. They have been made periodically since the turn of the century. But the blandness of today's editorial cartoons is more noticeable because it is more pervasive. Now it is a case of the bland leading the bland.

There are 185 active editorial cartoonists in the United States now, perhaps 50 percent more than a decade ago. More smaller papers than ever have their own cartoonists, and more cartoonists, especially young cartoonists, are in widespread syndication than ever before.

But quantity has not brought variety.

"There's a whole host of cartoonists doing the same stuff, and it's very boring," said Robert Englehart, cartoonist for the *Hartford Courant,* and most of the best cartoonists agree. Imitators of MacNelly and Peters have become so ubiquitous that the few young cartoonists whose styles differ markedly from theirs are finding it increasingly difficult to be syndicated.

Of all the promising younger cartoonists mentioned favorably in interviews for this study, for example, the one most often praised for his originality was Ben Sargent, thirty-five, a reporter-turned-cartoonist appearing, until recently, in only about seventy-five papers, far fewer than many less-talented cartoonists.

"Sargent's work is very hard to sell to editors right now . . . because it looks . . . different, and editors aren't that secure in their own taste and knowledge of what's a good cartoon," David Hendin, Sargent's editor at United Feature Syndicate, said three years ago.

In 1982, Sargent won a Pulitzer Prize. So far it doesn't seem to have affected his work. But syndications can beget homogenization in subject matter as well as in style. To attract syndication, many young cartoonists are quite willing to change their drawing styles, avoid controversy, and all but ignore local issues (in favor of cartoons on more recognizable and, hence, more salable national issues).

In recent years, syndication has made cartooning a most lucrative field for young artists. MacNelly, for example, will probably earn at least as much from syndication as he will from the *Chicago Tribune* (where he was hired at a reported $100,000 a year). There are eight or nine other cartoonists whose combined income from salary and syndication tops $100,000 a year. The lure of syndicate riches—the pressures and potential of grand success—is so great now, said cartoonist Gene Basset of United Feature Syndicate, that "a lot of the young guys are willing to practically sell their souls to get syndicated."

In fact, Basset said, it's precisely because he *wasn't* willing to sell his soul that he lost his job in 1981 after nineteen years with the Scripps-Howard newspapers.

Basset said his editor, B. J. Cutler, began censoring his cartoons, insisting on a more conservative approach than the liberal Basset was willing to provide, even telling him just how to draw (and how not to draw) various figures.

Basset's departure is officially classified as a resignation, but one source very close to the situation said he was actually fired. (Cutler refused to discuss Basset.)

No cartoonist, no matter how established or how talented, is completely independent of his editors, though. Some editors, because of their own political views (or those of their publishers, friends, advertisers, or community leaders), exercise great control over cartoonists, even requiring that cartoons reflect the paper's lead editorial each day (or, at least, not take a stand diametrically opposed to the editorial).

Perhaps that's why so many cartoonists prefer to be apolitical—or just to draw gag cartoons.

Even on the best, most independent papers, though, an editor will occasionally reject a cartoon because he considers it in bad taste or grossly unfair or libelous. That, editors say, is their job: to make the final decision on what the newspaper publishes. Thus, while the best cartoonists are given virtually a free hand within those few limitations, they do have to get the formal approval of their editors for each cartoon, either in rough draft or final form.

Most cartoonists make almost a daily ritual of showing rough sketches to various reporters or editors or editorial writers whose judgment and taste they respect. If one of these people suggests a change or says, "I don't get it" or "I don't like it," most cartoonists are appreciative. But if the editor of the editorial page or the editor of the paper rejects a cartoon outright, the cartoonist may erupt in a towering fury.

Once, during Watergate, Paul Conrad said his editors at the *Los Angeles Times* rejected three anti-Nixon cartoons in a single day. They thought he was in a rut. He said he got so angry he stalked out of the office and didn't come back for three days. His editors said they suggested he go home and relax for three days. Either way, his cartoons didn't appear in the *Times* for three days.

Paul Szep has reacted with similar anger when editors at the

Boston Globe rejected his cartoons. On three separate occasions, he said, he's just gone off and played golf for a few days to cool down.

Szep now appears to have one of the most volatile editor-cartoonist relationships. Until 1981, Szep reported to the paper's editorial page editor, who reported to editor Thomas Winship. Winship has great admiration and affection for Szep, so Szep generally enjoyed extraordinary latitude. But the *Globe* got a new editorial page editor, Marty Nolan, in 1981, and Nolan reports directly to the paper's publisher, not to Winship. Nolan has decided that Szep was "coddled" before. No more.

"I'm less indulgent toward Szep," he said. "I spike him. . . . I think he's wonderful. I love him. But he can be a pain in the ass."

Szep was a particular "pain in the ass" to Nolan last year when he drew a cartoon of President Reagan having a telephone conversation with Russian leader Yuri Andropov. The cartoon showed Reagan saying, "Hey, Yuri. . . . Guess who's getting a new MX missile system to help arms reduction and world peace?" Andropov, scowling, replied with a two-word phrase in Russian. The phrase, as Nolan quickly learned from members of Boston's Russian-speaking community, had several possible translations—all sexual, all generally regarded as vulgar, and at least one meaning, roughly, "suck my cock."

Szep said he didn't know what the Russian words meant; he said he had just asked a Russian-speaking reporter at the *Globe* to tell him a basic Russian profanity. Nolan, unimpressed with this defense, suspended Szep for two weeks (later reduced to one week) without pay.

"Szep is brilliant when he's brilliant," Nolan said, "[but] . . . you can't just be savage . . . you can put a swastika on a guy's jockstrap and it'll get attention. . . . He reduces the paper's credibility with people by tastelessness."

Szep most often "lacks taste," Nolan said, when he draws

the pope. Any pope. So Nolan ordered him to stop drawing the pope. Forever.

Szep said he and Nolan just aren't on the same "satiric wavelength" and he attributes Nolan's edict on pope cartoons to Nolan's Catholicism, a charge Nolan denies.

But questions of taste—particularly on religious issues, bodily functions, and sexual imagery—tend to cause more friction between editors and cartoonists everywhere than do matters of politics and ideology.

A decade ago, when then-Vice President Spiro Agnew was castigating the media, Conrad drew a cartoon of Agnew urinating on a pile of newspapers. His editors refused to publish it. Bad taste, they said.

A few years ago, when capital punishment was being debated in North Carolina, Doug Marlette of the *Charlotte Observer* drew a Good Friday cartoon of Christ carrying an electric chair on his back to Gethsemane. His editors refused to publish it. Sacrilegious, they said.

The best cartoonists are probably not rejected outright more than once or twice a year. More often an editor will suggest a slight modification in wording or drawing to tone down or eliminate a potentially offensive cartoon. But cartoonists know that rejection is often possible and on occasion, when they've drawn a cartoon they think might be rejected, some try elaborate ploys to outmaneuver their editors.

A cartoonist might show his editor a rough draft, get it approved, then make subtle but significant changes in the final drawing. Or he might show his editor cartoons that are certain to be rejected, then show him a questionable cartoon that might appear acceptable by comparison.

Another favorite ruse of some cartoonists is telling their editors they don't have an idea for a cartoon until so late in the day that it will be too late to draw another cartoon if the first one isn't approved.

Nolan said Szep used to try that delaying tactic until Nolan gave him an ultimatum: Any cartoon not submitted by Nolan's deadline wouldn't be published that day.

"I said, 'You better get that muse cranked up a little earlier,' " Nolan said. "I'm not going to stay all night waiting for an inspiration of genius. Genius can wait twenty-four more hours, till the next day's paper. . . . I think he can meet some of the basic minimum requirements of a daily newspaper and not offend his artistic soul too much."

Relations between editors and cartoonists often fluctuate wildly (and cyclically) especially if the cartoonist is a Szep (or a Conrad), someone with strong political convictions and a strong drawing style. During some periods, arguments seem constant. At other times, editor and cartoonist get along famously.

When I first interviewed M. G. Lord of *Newsday*, for example, she was clearly unhappy with her editors. "Being twenty-six is a real pain for a cartoonist when your editorial board is fifty," she said. "You don't see eye-to-eye." But later, on the telephone, Lord spoke fondly and understandingly of her editors. The difference? In recent weeks they had been seeing eye-to-eye with great regularity.

Lord, one of only four women drawing cartoons for daily papers in the United States, has often fared better than some other young cartoonists in editorial battles. The reason: She had a rather well-developed political sensibility when she joined *Newsday;* her politics did not surprise her editors.

Many of today's young cartoonists are apolitical, at least when they begin. Unlike their predecessors in the 1960s, who often turned to cartooning to express their political viewpoint, the cartoonist of the late 1970s and early 1980s often cares no more about what political viewpoint he espouses than about what artistic style he adopts. If he subsequently changes and becomes political, his editors may not like it.

Lee Judge, cartoonist for the *Kansas City Times*, readily conceded that when he started out as a cartoonist he had no interest in politics. "I just wanted to be like Jeff MacNelly and get on the cover of *Newsweek* and make a million dollars," he said.

Judge was twenty-three when he started work—first part-time, then full time—for the *Sacramento Union*. That was in 1976. In 1979 he moved to the *San Diego Union,* and over the next year, as he matured, his political philosophy began to develop (or perhaps more accurately, it began to manifest itself more frequently in his cartoons).

"As I began to understand more about the business," he said, "I began to realize that supposedly we're here to say something."

But Judge was (and is) liberal. The *San Diego Union* was (and is) conservative. In mid-1980 the *Union* fired him.

Borgman had a similar beginning but, so far, a happier ending.

Borgman said he had little interest in politics when he joined the *Cincinnati Enquirer* in 1976 at twenty-two, so he was "as content to say one thing as the opposite thing" in his cartoons. When Borgman's editors occasionally suggested he take a particular political position, he was quite willing to do so, he said. He liked to draw and he was having fun, so why not?

But like Judge, Borgman found that as he began to read more and to educate himself politically, his cartoons were increasingly at odds with his paper's editorial page.

Then Borgman got a good job offer from another paper. He said he used that offer to win more freedom from his editors.

Thomas Gephardt, editor of the *Enquirer*'s editorial page, said Borgman's increased freedom after his job offer wasn't as "cut and dried" as that. Gephardt insisted that Borgman was granted wider latitude primarily because he had become more established in Cincinnati and was more accepted by the paper's readers.

Now, in fact, *Enquirer* editors sometimes seem downright pleased—and proud—when a Borgman cartoon makes people angry. When the paper published several of his best cartoons in its Sunday magazine, the accompanying story spoke primarily of the "tide of phone calls" that come in "on a day when a particularly controversial Borgman cartoon appears."

What kinds of cartoons bring in a "tide of phone calls"?

On this, most cartoonists and editors agree. At the top of the list, most of them say, are cartoons critical of Israel. No matter how consistently a cartoonist supports Israel, the instant he draws one cartoon critical of Israel, the angry calls, letters, visits to his editors, and accusations of anti-Semitism begin.

"Any time you do Menachem Begin the telephone turns into the Golan Heights," one editor said.

People who feel strongly about abortion, gun control, the death penalty, and virtually any religious issue also are likely to become enraged when a cartoonist disagrees with them.

Almost every cartoonist who has been drawing for more than a couple of years can tell at least one frightening story about angry reader response. Borgman said an angry reader once threatened to move his house off its foundation. Tony Auth said an angry reader once came banging on the front door of his house at one o'clock in the morning. Kate Salley Palmer of the *Greenville* (S.C.) *News* said she has heard reports that the Ku Klux Klan is out to get her.

Paul Conrad has had similarly strong reactions to his many anti-abortion cartoons—in part, one suspects, because his opposition to abortion, which stems largely from his Catholic training and beliefs, stands in stark contrast to his liberal views on most other issues. His liberal readers feel betrayed by his refusal to take the liberal stand on abortion, too, and they resent his savage imagery of dead babies and pickled fetuses in jars.

But Conrad draws strong, often brutal, cartoons on a variety of issues, and enraged reader reaction is not unusual. On three or four occasions, he said, he has received death threats. Once, an irate reader placed a rabbit, with its head neatly severed, near Conrad's back door. Twice he has received packages that he thought might contain bombs. Both times the police bomb squad was called.

Conrad laughs about the "bombs" now: One package was filled with dog manure, the other with horse manure.

No wonder many editors say a good strong cartoon brings out the animal in all of us.

10

THE RESTAURANT CRITIC

For much of my adult life, I tended to regard eating in much the same way I regarded getting gas for my car—something to be done automatically when the tank was empty, with as little thought and as little expenditure of time and money as possible. If I thought about it at all, I probably figured the differences between French, Italian, and Chinese cuisine were of no greater consequence to me than the differences between the gas pumped by Mobil, Texaco, and Arco. Thus fortified with ignorance and indifference, I generally skipped breakfast, wolfed down a cup of yogurt at my desk (or ran around the corner to the nearest hamburger stand) for lunch, and either ate a simple meal at home or visited the neighborhood pizza parlor or steakhouse for dinner.

But about ten years ago—coincidentally, just about the time the OPEC nations were making "Fill 'er up" more a plea for mercy (and a surrender to extortionate demands) than a routine request—I began to develop a genuine interest in eating. In a very short time, that interest became a preoccupation and then an obsession—so much so that now when I travel (for business or pleasure) I make my restaurant reservations for each night of the trip before I make my airplane and hotel reservations. I also take my own food (and wine) on airplanes—

having purchased various delicacies at carefully selected gourmet shops in each city I visit. When I go to France every summer, I plan the trip around restaurants, and I write to each restaurant three months in advance to make dinner reservations for every night of the trip.

At work, colleagues who stop by my desk now to ask that most casual of questions—"Free for lunch?"—know that I'm not likely to answer with a simple "Yes" or "No." Instead, I'll say, "What are you in the mood for?" . . . whereupon I will pull open the bottom, right-hand drawer of my desk and whip out my frequently updated list of acceptable lunchtime restaurants—which currently includes two fancy French restaurants, a steakhouse, two Italian restaurants, a seafood restaurant, a soul food barbecue pit in Watts, a Jewish deli, my favorite sushi bar, an assortment of Oriental restaurants, a Mexican restaurant (with a corner table that has been turned into a shrine for customer/novelist/ex-cop Joseph Wambaugh), and what must be the only hamburger stand in the world with valet parking and $42 bottles of French wine.

I've never been able to figure out what transformed me from someone utterly indifferent to food to someone so obsessed with the subject that, for one recent birthday, my son gave me a wheel of Brie, my daughter gave me chocolate, my wife gave me an expensive bottle of wine, and a friend sent me a card that began:

> Chocolate mousse and escargots
> Vichyssoise and red Bordeaux
> Crepes suzette
> Vinaigrette
> For zee birthday feast, you bet!

Given this obsessive interest in food, it was only a matter of time before I decided to write about restaurant critics. My editor, Bill Thomas, didn't much like the idea, though. The subject, he said, was fine; Thomas just wasn't sure I could do it objectively.

"You think you know so much about food and restaurants," Thomas said, "that I'm afraid all I'll get is 'David Shaw's list of the ten best restaurants and ten worst restaurant critics in America.' "

I resented that suggestion. After all, I know much more about sports than I do about food. As I told Bill, I'd been an avid sports fan since long before I realized that fettucine Alfredo was not the name of a Chicago mobster, and he had not questioned my objectivity when I proposed writing about newspaper sports pages. Agreed. I proceeded with my assignment. It was great fun. And a great education. Of course, my own, all-consuming interest in the subject did lead me to write far more than I should have. When I turned my four-part series of stories over to Bill, he said he liked them but couldn't possibly publish them all; I had written a small book. He said he wanted me to cut the total, 20,000-word package by about 75 percent. I gulped and said I'd do my best. I cut it 40 percent. He told me to make a couple of more small cuts. We compromised on those, too. The stories ran—and I think I maintained my objectivity (i.e., I had been fair and had not permitted my personal opinions to influence my reporting). Despite my personal feeling, for example, that Lois Dwan, my paper's own restaurant critic, has the critical faculty of an amoeba, I faithfully reported in my story that the other critics, restaurateurs, and gastronomes I interviewed made her a consensus choice as one of the five best restaurant critics in the country. Of course, that is more a comment on the abysmally low state of the art than on her perceived excellence, but that's another matter (one I dealt with in great detail in the original story and in the chapter below).

Dwan, as I pointed out in that story (and below), is honest, knowledgeable, conscientious, and a good writer. But she is also, as I pointed out, unwilling to say a restaurant is bad. How can anyone be a critic and not criticize? How can a reader trust a critic and be guided by a critic if the critic seems to like everything? I raised these questions in my original story, too. Dwan, I am told, was furious. I say "I am told" because she didn't say a word to me. Still hasn't. Not even when we pass in the hallway. She did send me a brief, snide note more than a year later, though, correctly pointing out that I had misspelled a word in another story. I wrote back, quite sincerely, thanking her and inviting her to lunch, hoping to bury the hatchet. Her reply: "That would be impossible."

Several other restaurant critics—and friends of restaurant critics—were also quite angry over my story. One was a man who had been my best friend. In fact, I'd been the maid of honor (honest!) at his wedding. But we had started to drift apart before I began work on this story, and by the time I finished it, our relationship was finished, too.

I was very critical of him in the story, as you'll see. He deserved the criticism. He was guilty of all I wrote—and more. But he wasn't a big-time restaurant critic. He didn't work for one of the major newspapers or magazines or radio or television stations. He worked, still works, for a regional monthly magazine and a small local radio station, and he published his own annual guide to the restaurants of Southern California, so he has a certain following. I had to include him in my story for that reason and also because people in the restaurant industry knew of our relationship. Had I left him out or gone easy on him, I would have opened myself to charges of conflict of interest, of protecting a friend. So, in my original story, I came down especially hard on him.

My editor suggested I had written too much about him, in fact. "I know you want to demonstrate your integrity," he said, "but you don't have to go overboard." I cut the material on my friend in half. But that still left plenty—most of it devastating—and my friend became my ex-friend.

Do I wish I had written about drama critics or music critics or art critics instead? No. Besides, I wrote about film critics earlier and encountered hostile reactions there, too—especially after I quoted someone as saying the man who was then the *Los Angeles Times* film critic was "the Will Rogers of film criticism; he never met a film he didn't like."

Critics in all the arts—and I include food, haute cuisine, as an art form—have a great deal in common, and many of the lessons to be drawn from this chapter on restaurant critics apply equally to critics in literature, drama, and music.

Can a critic do his job fairly, for example, if he socializes with the people he is criticizing? This is a special problem for book critics because many of the same people who write books also write book reviews. Thus, I recall attending a New York dinner party at which the guests included David Halberstam (author of *The Best and the Brightest* and *The Powers That Be* and a Pulitzer Prize–winning reporter when he worked in Viet-

nam for the *New York Times*) and Gloria Emerson (also a former Vietnam War correspondent for the *New York Times*).
Nothing unusual in that except that Halberstam had recently reviewed (very favorably) Emerson's new book and Emerson
was about to review (very favorably) Halberstam's new book.

Other questions critics must face: How much do you have
to know about your field—and must you actually be able to
perform in it (cook? paint? sing?)—to be a good critic? How
influential are critics? Can they help a new restaurant get
started? Yes. Can they close a Broadway play? Sometimes.
Can they keep a bad book from being a best-seller? No.

Can a critic be so consistently negative that he has little influence? Yes. Can he be so consistently complimentary that he
has little influence? Sure. (The former *Los Angeles Times* film
critic who "never saw a film he didn't like," is a fine prose
stylist and an intelligent and decent man, but when he moved
from reviewing films to reviewing books, he became the Will
Rogers of literary criticism; it sometimes seemed that he'd
never met a book he didn't like either—and no one I knew
paid any attention to his views on books or movies.)

There is also the question, of course, of conflict of interest.
Can you trust a film critic who's trying to sell his own film
scripts to the very movie moguls whose productions he is supposed to be reviewing? How about an art critic who serves as
a middleman on an art acquisition? Or a music critic whose
spouse or child was rejected by the local symphony or ballet
company? Or a restaurant critic who serves as a menu consultant to local restaurants?

As I said, the problems are similar in every field. But restaurant criticism may be the most interesting because everyone eats—and everyone thinks he knows a little something about food.

*   *   *

A FEW YEARS AGO, a Chicago restaurateur made what sounded like "a fascinating proposal" to Fran Zell, then the restaurant critic of the *Chicago Tribune*. He suggested that she cook dinner in his restaurant one night and invite a half-dozen restaurateurs to eat it and criticize *her* cooking for a change—in the *Tribune*.

Like most restaurant critics, Zell thinks of herself as a good cook. She accepted the challenge.

Big mistake.

Zell's six-course menu, wrote one restaurateur, was "a cop-out . . . bland . . . [it] lacked sophistication, consistency, and balance."

Zell's beef was "overcooked," said another restaurateur; "a major disappointment," added a third.

And her *pasta al pesto?*

"In my restaurants, we cook the pasta before we serve it," sneered yet another of Zell's dinner guests. "It's sort of a tradition."

But Zell, although clearly chastened by all this criticism, insists she does not regret her experiment.

"The meal was a flop," she says, "but I learned a lot about what it's like to cook under pressure. I became more understanding about what a restaurant goes through."

Judging from the comments made by other restaurateurs I've interviewed, that is just the kind of lesson most restaurant critics should learn.

In an effort to assess the influence, qualifications, integrity, methods, and reputations of the nation's restaurant critics, I interviewed restaurateurs, restaurant critics, and gastronomes and read thousands of restaurant reviews in newspapers, magazines, and guidebooks. The overwhelming consensus of everyone, including the critics themselves, was that too many critics know too little about what they are eating and writing about.

Among other major findings:

- Generally, critics can neither make nor break a restaurant. But they can help a new, small, or out-of-the-way restaurant get off to a good start, and they can hasten the demise of a poor restaurant.
- There is often a strong cause-and-effect relationship between the quality of the restaurant criticism in a given city and the quality of restaurants in that city.
- Critics sometimes have more influence on restaurateurs than on readers. Many restaurateurs say they have changed menus, recipes, personnel, and policies in response to critical reviews.
- Many critics sacrifice their credibility because they are reluctant to write negative reviews, and a few critics sacrifice their credibility because they are almost always negative.
- Restaurant critics should (but often do not) dine anonymously, avoid personal or business relationships with restaurateurs, refuse free meals, visit a restaurant at least three times before writing a review, and return periodically after a review to see if food or service have changed appreciably.
- In many publications, good reviews or listings often seem contingent on buying an advertisement.
- There has been a tendency among many critics to see expensive French restaurants as, almost by definition, the best restaurants and to ignore or downgrade other cuisines.

But the one point made most frequently by my interviewees was that most restaurant critics are ill-informed and ill-prepared to do their jobs.

Restaurateur after restaurateur provided examples of critics making serious mistakes. Critics have written that they liked (or disliked) certain dishes at certain restaurants, but the restaurants had never served those dishes. Other critics have called dishes by the wrong names. Or ascribed to them the wrong ingredients. Or the wrong origins.

One Los Angeles critic, served what must have been the first order of mussels he'd ever seen, said he didn't realize the restaurant served "black clams." A Philadelphia critic praised the sauce on one veal dish in a restaurant but criticized the sauce on another; the sauces were exactly the same.

I encountered this pervasive ignorance firsthand on several occasions. The most egregious came during a lunch interview with Larry Lipson of the *Daily News* in Los Angeles. Lipson, who writes what is probably the only daily restaurant column in the country, looked at my entrée when it arrived, and said, "That's a good-looking piece of lamb."

He was offered a bite.

He poked, probed, nibbled, swallowed, and said, "Gee, now I can't tell if that's beef or duck."

It was pork.

Unlike France, where fine dining in restaurants (and thus, serious restaurant criticism) has long been an integral and respected part of the culture, restaurant criticism in the United States largely consisted, until quite recently, of little more than superficial tip sheets based primarily on free meals and *quid pro quo* purchases of advertising.

"I'm the fifth generation to run Antoine's," says Roy Guste, Jr., of New Orleans, "but I'm the first generation to have to deal with true restaurant critics. Until a few years ago, all you had to do to get a good write-up was entertain the writers and pay for what they ate and drank."

To most restaurateurs, that was (and is) a good bargain, and many still encourage it, or at least accept it, with smaller papers that are unwilling (or unable) to pay for their critics' meals. "I'll pick up a reviewer's check for a $100 or $200 dinner sometimes," says Geril Muller of Ambrosia in Newport Beach. "I can get a nice write-up, and that's better, and cheaper, than [buying] an ad.''

Serious restaurant criticism is an expensive matter for a publication. The better critics spend $800 to $1,200 a month on meals. The *New York Times* often spends twice that. Mimi Sheraton, formerly restaurant critic for the *New York Times,* says she once spent $830 on a dinner for four. But the most reputable larger publications now insist on paying for their critics' meals.

Craig Claiborne is almost universally credited with bringing honest, serious food criticism to the United States when he reviewed restaurants for the *New York Times* from 1959 to 1972. Claiborne, himself a fine cook, studied at a respected Swiss hotel school for a year and also worked in a hotel and in a restaurant before becoming a critic.

"Craig really invented food criticism in this country," says Calvin Trillin, who has written about food (among other things) for the *New Yorker* and *Nation* magazines.

But for many years, Claiborne was an exception. At most papers the restaurant column appeared in the food section, which was (and in most papers, still is) dominated by press releases from the food industry and by what one former food editor calls "dull, limited, lowbrow recipes that tell you eighty-three ways to make tuna casserole."

Most newspapers routinely assigned restaurant reviews to sportswriters, real estate columnists, or anyone else who wanted a free meal or had earned the editor's favor.

Although that practice has not vanished altogether, it has diminished considerably in the last decade at the biggest, most reputable papers. Until then, restaurant criticism just was not a very high priority for most newspapers—and with some justifications. Eating well, eating in restaurants, just was not the national pastime it has recently become.

The typical American, wrote John Hess in his 1977 book, *The Taste of America,* traditionally began life eating "a synthetic, sweetened bottle formula . . . was weaned on starchy

baby foods loaded with sugar and monosodium glutamate and
. . . grew up on soda pop, candy, corn flakes, ketchup-doused
hamburgers, and instant coffee.'' Many Americans seemed to
feel like the housewife who told a television interviewer a few
years ago, ''Food is for health; why does it have to taste good?''

But now, as the *Chicago Tribune* said in 1980: ''Gourmet
cookbook sales are skyrocketing. Gourmet cooking classes are
filling up as quickly as they're offered. City magazines all across
the country are regularly featuring restaurant stories on their
covers—and regularly finding that restaurant reviews are among
their best-read stories.

Why the burgeoning interest in eating—and in restaurants?
More than anything else, the breakthrough in air fare reductions
that has, for the first time, made European travel affordable to
vast numbers of Americans has increased people's exposure to,
awareness of, interest in, and taste for different and better foods.

Now, suddenly, in the words of James Ward, restaurant critic
for the *Chicago Sun-Times,* ''Next to one's private parts, the
palate is the dearest thing there is.''

People want to dine out more often now—sometimes at considerable expense, on exotic combinations of food—and they need
reliable, knowledgeable restaurant critics to guide them. So most
big-city papers now publish at least one restaurant column a week.
Some have two or three. Even many suburban papers now have
their own restaurant columns.

A. J. Liebling, who wrote about food (among other things)
for the *New Yorker* in the 1940s and 1950s, once said, ''The
primary requisite for writing well about food is a good appetite.''

Most critics and restaurateurs would amend that to say ''a
good palate''—good taste, developed by eating well over a long
period of time. But if taste is the primary requirement for a restaurant critic, what are the other requirements? Must a critic be
a good cook? Should he or she have worked in a restaurant?

''I can't imagine a serious, good critic not cooking,'' says
Gael Greene of *New York* magazine, and most such critics agree.

One critic, Patricia Unterman of the *San Francisco Chronicle*, even cooks at (and has a part ownership in) her own restaurant.

In fact, several critics say they often find they can better understand why a dish in a restaurant did not taste right if they go home and cook it themselves.

But no one would seriously argue that a music critic must be able to sing or an art critic to paint. What's the difference?

"Standards are more defined in art and music; they're less precise in food," says Jack Shelton, who wrote a widely respected restaurant newsletter in San Francisco in the late 1960s. "You almost have to learn by doing sometimes with food." Moreover, in music and art, most readers acknowledge their ignorance and their need for expert guidance. But everyone eats, and most people can at least broil a steak, so they think they know something about food; most critics say their own ability to cook well—and to understand the importance and origins of raw products and the subtle intricacies of sauces and food presentation—is necessary to establish their credibility with readers.

That credibility is not easy to come by for a variety of historical reasons.

"Let's face it," says Gene Roberts, executive editor of the *Philadelphia Inquirer,* "until a few years ago, some of the worst prostitutes in our business were connected with food criticism."

It was not uncommon for a restaurant critic to dine at a restaurant as a guest of the restaurant's public relations man, then print the public relations man's press release as a "review"— under the critic's byline. Neither was it uncommon for newspapers to trade favorable reviews for advertising.

Both practices are still followed at many smaller newspapers. Phyllis Richman, restaurant critic for the *Washington Post,* says some restaurateurs are still so accustomed to paying for good reviews by buying ads that when she called one restaurateur to tell him that her review would be appearing that Sunday, he mistook her for a suburban critic and said, "Oh, no, not again. I can't afford another review so soon."

Until last September, The *Long Beach* (Calif.) *Independent Press-Telegram,* for example, actually labeled as "advertising" all the pages containing its twice-weekly restaurant reviews.

Tedd Thomey, who has been reviewing restaurants for the Long Beach paper for thirty years, does include nonadvertisers in the reviews about one-third of the time, but he seldom wrote negative reviews of any restaurants.

After Knight Newspapers took over the Long Beach paper in 1974 (becoming, in the process, Knight-Ridder Newspapers), Thomey was directed to write more critically. He did so—until a number of restaurants canceled their ads after receiving unfavorable reviews.

"About a year ago they [the paper's editors] told me to go back to what I was doing before," Thomey told me in 1980. But the paper decided to try respectability again, beginning last September. The "advertising" label was removed from the restaurant pages—a weekly, tabloid section called "Stepping Out"— and Thomey was again told to write honest, critical reviews. That may be easier said than done after all these years. The most serious criticism I could find in the early issues of the new "Stepping Out" section was Thomey's lament that he was served a Scotch and water after having ordered Scotch on the rocks in one local restaurant. One early section that Thomey's editor sent me to demonstrate the paper's new policy featured a front-page review of a mediocre Italian restaurant that Thomey pronounced "fabulous . . . superb . . . the answer to every restaurant-goer's dream."

At some other suburban papers, restaurant reviewers actually sell restaurant ads themselves. Thomey does not, but Eleanor Day of the *Pasadena* (Calif.) *Star-News* and Marge Finken of the *South Bay* (Calif.) *Daily Breeze* do. Their reviews are not labeled as advertising, but both Day and Finken concede that they review advertisers' restaurants about 70 percent of the time— and in Finken's case it's more than 80 percent, judging from a random sample of her columns.

Both Day and Finken say—indeed boast—that they never write unfavorable reviews. "I don't like to tear places down," Finken says.

Even on some large metropolitan newspapers, there is often a symbiotic relationship between the restaurant critic and the advertising department.

Joel Connelly says he quit as the restaurant critic of the *Seattle Post-Intelligencer* in 1978 because of "a continuous battle with the advertising department over anything critical I said in my column."

The threat of canceled advertising is omnipresent in any publication with a serious restaurant critic. Generally, only the most reputable (and profitable) publications resist the pressure.

Washingtonian magazine continues to give critic Robert Shoffner his freedom, for example, even though a Georgetown restaurant canceled its $22,000 advertising contract after Shoffner wrote that its corned beef hash "resembled nothing so much as a bowl of Alpo."

Although most large, respectable publications now insist that their critics dine anonymously, pay for their meals, and maintain a strict independence from the advertising department, there have continued to be frequent violations of this ethical ideal in recent years, costing many critics their credibility.

The editor of the *Dallas Times-Herald* says he fired his restaurant critic several years ago for eating free meals in restaurants and then billing the paper twice for each meal.

Los Angeles magazine fired critic George Christy in 1974, in large part because of what editor Geoff Miller calls "persistent reports that he was going to restaurants after he reviewed them and allowing them to be the host for him and his friends at dinner."

Jean Leon of La Scala in Beverly Hills says Christy was "famous for not paying his check. He'd just show up without a reservation . . . with six or eight people, and he'd demand a table and . . . eat . . . and be insulting and demanding and degrading to the waiters and then get up and walk out and not even leave a tip.''

Bruce Vanderhoff of Le Restaurant in Los Angeles says Christy also ate at his restaurant many times without paying.

''George Christy has always written nice things about us,'' Vanderhoff says, ''but he was everything a restaurant critic should not be. He ate here probably twice a week for . . . more than a year . . . and he always insisted on a specific table, ordered expensive wine . . . stayed late . . . and the only 'tip' he'd give would be a copy of the magazine for the boy who parked his car.''

Christy denies all charges against him. They are, he says, ''monstrous lies.''

Christy, now a columnist for the *Hollywood Reporter,* says he never goes to a restaurant without a reservation, never demands a specific table, and never behaves improperly. He says he paid for his own meals when he was a critic, except when restaurateurs ''insisted'' on picking up his check or when ''I had to ask friends to take me to dinner because my salary and expenses were . . . so low.''

Restaurateurs roar with laughter at these protestations of innocence.

Other critics have a somewhat different problem with their jobs: They become too personally involved with the restaurants they are writing about, and they lose credibility. That is what happened to Richard Collin, once the respected and influential critic of the *New Orleans States-Item.*

Collin, who had raved about a neighborhood Italian restaurant named Turci's (''unsurpassed in New Orleans or in Italy itself''), got into trouble when he helped put together a business deal to save the restaurant when it was about to shut down in 1973.

At first Collin was just an intermediary in the deal, doing his ''civic duty,'' he says, ''to save a New Orleans institution.'' But when the new owners of Turci's hired Collin's wife as a consultant, problems quickly developed. Mrs. Collin quit—unpaid—and Collin subsequently dropped Turci's to a new category in his ratings: "some good food but not a recommended restaurant."

It was a scandal in New Orleans, where people take their food very seriously indeed. Collin, who left the *States-Item* in 1980 but still publishes an annual dining guide, insists he was "only guilty of . . . misjudgment . . . hubris [and] naiveté" in the Turci's incident. But New Orleans restaurateurs say his credibility was permanently damaged.

In Los Angeles a similar fate has befallen Paul Wallach, who writes a monthly restaurant column for *Westways* magazine, publishes an annual dining guide, and conducts a daily radio talk show largely devoted to restaurants.

Wallach's guide is the most encyclopedic of any local restaurant guide in the United States and contains reviews of more than a thousand restaurants. But Wallach told me often in 1979 and 1980 that he had never eaten in many of the restaurants he reviews in the book. He relies largely on reports from friends and on reviews written by other critics.

"I wanted to publish a comprehensive book," Wallach says, "and it would be humanly impossible for anyone to eat in a thousand restaurants. I have to do it this way."

But Wallach does not admit in the introduction to his book that he does not eat at all the restaurants he reviews, and he often uses "I" and "we" in the reviews.

In the 1979 edition of his dining guide, for example, Wallach wrote of one restaurant, in part, "Best of all [are] the oyster loaf and the French dishes with a Creole flavor . . . although we do like the baked ribs with red beans and rice. It's all here and it may be the best Creole in town."

But it was several months after this review was published before Wallach ate at this restaurant for the first time, and he didn't have oyster loaf, baked ribs, or red beans and rice that night. I know because Wallach and I were, at the time, very close friends, and I was with him in the restaurant that night.

Moreover, Wallach has a particularly symbiotic relationship with the restaurant industry. He has done food and wine endorsements. He has hosted "epicurean" dinners at various restaurants. His income from his radio program has been directly based, in part, on how many restaurant commercials the show broadcasts.

Thus, since he praises most restaurants, even the most pedestrian—on the air and in print—restaurateurs and other critics question his credibility.

Wallach says he realizes that "some criticism can be justifiably directed at me" because of the commercials on his radio show, but he neither sells nor reads the commercials himself, and he insists there is absolutely no requirement that a restaurant advertise in order to be mentioned favorably.

In fact, Wallach not only praises many restaurants that do not advertise, he also, on rare occasions, criticizes restaurants that do advertise. Nevertheless, it seems obvious that no restaurant critic should have his income based, even in part, on restaurant commercials. If not his integrity, certainly his credibility is at stake.

What kinds of restaurant critics do have credibility today?

In some cities, the most influential restaurant critic works for the city magazine. Nowhere is this truer than in Chicago where *Chicago* magazine's Allen and Carla Kelson publish one or two long restaurant reviews every month, plus as many as fifty pages of restaurant listings (actually short reviews) that are frequently updated and rewritten by a staff of eight to ten carefully selected reviewers.

Many city magazines—*Los Angeles* and *Philadelphia,* for example—publish reviews that are independent of advertising, but they include only advertisers in their monthly back-of-the-book listings. *Chicago* magazine and a few others do not limit their monthly listings to advertisers.

Reviews in *Chicago* have such impact that one restaurateur

says his business fell 50 percent after a negative review, and another restaurant opened two new branches to handle business generated by a favorable review.

Even the critics for Chicago's two daily newspapers concede that *Chicago* magazine is the city's most influential forum for restaurant criticism.

By a wide margin, however, the most praised restaurant critic in America in the course of my 1980 interviews was Gael Greene of *New York* magazine.

Several other prominent restaurant critics credit Greene with initially awakening their interest in food criticism, and several restaurateurs said they had changed recipes and policies after she had criticized them.

André Soltner, chef and owner at Lutèce in New York, widely regarded as the finest restaurant in the United States, said he got angry with Greene once when she wrote that one of his desserts tasted "grainy." But he subsequently decided she was right, "so I changed the classic recipe."

Critics and restaurateurs alike repeatedly singled Greene out as the one critic who best gives readers a clear and inviting sense of the joy of eating. Over and over again, they spoke of Greene's "wonderfully sensual palate" and of the enticing, sexual imagery of her restaurant reviews.

Greene writes of "voluptuous" sweetbreads and "the bursting juiciness" of goose liver and, in a 1983 article on the best French restaurants in *New York*, of "seductively good" desserts. In fact, after that article was published, one reader wrote to *New York* to say, "Gael Greene's descriptions of French restaurants would put a porn writer to shame." Indeed, in reading Greene's restaurant reviews, one can almost envision her writing while making love to a great French chef on a bed of fresh *foie gras*. No wonder her first literary ventures apart from restaurant reviews have been novels heavily rooted in erotica. As she once wrote of herself, "I have dedicated myself to the wanton indulgence of the senses."

Greene is not without her flaws, of course, and even she admits that she is sometimes too kind when writing about restaurateurs she has come to know and like. Other critics say Greene's writing style has become so rococo—and her own persona so intrusive at times—that her criticism has lost some credibility.

"Gael's style was always more important than what she said about the food itself," says Robert Shoffner. "Now the food is third—after her style and Gael herself."

The visibility and cachet of *New York* magazine has helped Greene achieve both her credibility and her celebrity much the same way as some newspaper restaurant critics have developed their good reputations, in part because they work for the biggest paper in town and thus command the biggest audience. Nevertheless, there is a strong consensus among critics, restaurateurs, and gastronomes on just who, in addition to Greene, are the best critics: Mimi Sheraton, former *New York Times* restaurant critic, who has now agreed to contribute occasional pieces for *Time;* Phyllis Richman, *Washington Post;* Lois Dwan, *Los Angeles Times;* Robert Shoffner, *Washingtonian;* Patricia Unterman, *San Francisco Chronicle.*

But all the critics, even the most respected, generally are perceived as having serious weaknesses.

Dwan, for example, is widely respected for her longevity on the job, for her knowledge, for her willingness to explore different cuisines, and for her practice of visiting most restaurants three times before reviewing them. But she is widely criticized for becoming too friendly with some restaurateurs and, most of all, for not being sufficiently critical in her reviews.

Dwan praises virtually every restaurant she writes about. On those rare occasions when even she cannot, in good conscience, praise the food, she praises the decor or the service or the prices or the silverware. This makes it very difficult to use Dwan as a reliable guide. If she writes about six different French restaurants over the course of several months and praises them all, it's almost impossible to know which she actually thinks is best—

or if any one is actually worth going to. In one year, I recall, she reviewed more than fifty restaurants, and it would be difficult to say that any single review was actually negative. Could Los Angeles—or even Paris—possibly have fifty new, excellent restaurants in a single year?

Although Dwan has occasionally offered less-than-fulsome praise in the last couple of years, a genuinely negative review by her is still singularly uncommon. Indeed, when she did write a strongly critical review of the newly relocated Perino's restaurant last year, the *Times* felt compelled to publish—adjacent to a subsequent restaurant column—a more-than-800-word letter from the president of the restaurant, pillorying Dwan.

Unlike many critics, Dwan uses no three-star or four-star rating system to make distinctions among different levels of "good." To her, virtually every restaurant—except the new Perino's—seems equally good, and she even seems loath to compare the different "goods" (for fear, I guess, of hurting someone's feelings). In raving about the best Italian restaurants in New York early in 1983, for example, she wrote, "I should not—could not—compare New York Italian with Los Angeles Italian," and, later, "I would be hard put to name the best Italian meal I had in New York." Why? Isn't that one of the principal functions of a critic? Wouldn't any interested reader immediately wonder: (1) How *do* those great New York restaurants compare with my favorites in Los Angeles? and (2) Which *one* Italian restaurant should I go to next time I'm in New York? Legitimate questions. But Dwan provides no answers. To make comparisons is to imply criticism, however mild, and Dwan seems to equate criticism with negativism . . . and she avoids both as if they were somehow dishonorable.

"I think Lois finds it very hard to write a negative review," says Bruce David Cohen, restaurant critic for *Los Angeles* magazine, who says he likes and admires Dwan nonetheless. "Most of the time you don't know at the end [of her review] if you really should go to the restaurant or not."

Carole Lalli, formerly of *New West* and the *Los Angeles Herald Examiner*, says Dwan just doesn't have the temperament of a critic. "She's too much of a lady to say something unkind. She wants to be kind and fair and polite."

In part, this may be because Dwan is seventy years old and has been reviewing restaurants for the *Times* for seventeen years.

"She's not the gutsy thirty-two-year-old who's gonna . . . tear you up anymore," says Michael McCarty of Michael's Restaurant in Santa Monica.

Dwan herself attributes her largely positive reviews to "still being influenced, I guess, by my original charge . . . here: to tell people where to go to eat, not where *not* to go."

But that argument, says critic Richard Collin, echoing several of his peers, "is just a euphemism for being afraid to write the tough reviews that might make you unpopular [with restaurateurs]."

Many of the same people who criticize Dwan for being too kind to restaurants also criticized Mimi Sheraton for being too harsh.

Sheraton left the *New York Times* last fall, but her replacement—Marian Burros—is too new at this writing to be evaluated. Moreover, Sheraton's long tenure at the *Times* gave her great, and continuing, influence. She was the most thorough and one of the most knowledgeable of all the critics. She has studied cooking and traveled widely in France; she usually ate in a restaurant four to six times before reviewing it; and she returned after her reviews to see if either food or service had changed appreciably. She did everything she could to avoid being recognized and given special treatment in a restaurant.

In New York, Sheraton's impact, on restaurateurs as well as readers, was extraordinary. When she gave Lutèce only three stars (out of four) in 1977, the chef says he was "emotionally destroyed for two or three months. I couldn't create a new dish that whole time."

But Sheraton's taste was too traditional for me. In New York and in France, she generally raved about the more classic French restaurants, those that still serve heavy sauces, and she was downright scornful of several of my favorite practitioners of the lighter, more natural *nouvelle cuisine*. Sheraton also tended to like heavy, Germanic food—virtually all of which I find as undistinguished as it is undigestible.

And I was dumbfounded when she gave her top four-star rating to a Japanese restaurant last year. I like sushi, too, but four stars?

Many critics and restaurateurs also say Sheraton often seemed more interested in price, value, and quantity than in quality. They say she was too "destructive," too much "a housewife clipping coupons . . . a heavy-handed consumer-columnist-cum-laboratory-technician," a dour inspector general rather than someone who appeared to enjoy eating.

Sheraton's exhaustively detailed critiques on dish after dish after dish "make my eyes glaze over," one critic said. "Eating is supposed to be fun, but I never have the sense that Mimi is having fun."

Culinary knowledge, high standards, and harsh judgments are necessary to good restaurant criticism, of course, but some critics worry that as restaurant criticism is becoming increasingly sophisticated, it is becoming increasingly clinical.

"The grown-up food writers . . . seem to ignore the central question: Does it taste good? Did it make your tummy feel good?" says Calvin Trillin. "Never mind if it was the authentic recipe, made with the proper ingredients, as good as you had in Paris; did you *like* it?"

Craig Claiborne agrees. In New York, a few years ago, sitting with a group of gastronomes sampling and comparing and discussing three kinds of Russian caviar, Claiborne grumbled:

"This is why I don't like restaurant reviewing. I'd prefer just to eat one of these and enjoy it and say how good it is, rather than talking about 'Is it too gray or too black or too big and where do you rate it on a scale of one to ten.'

"In our expertise we've forgotten the sheer pleasure of . . . eating."

Although many people think the life of the restaurant critic—being paid well to eat well—sounds like a dream come true, many critics quit precisely because they (like Claiborne) find themselves spending so much time tasting and comparing and taking notes that they can no longer enjoy dining out.

"Besides, you have to eat a lot of shitty food between the great food," says Nga Hillenbrand, who once wrote restaurant reviews for *Chicago* magazine.

Most critics also have to worry constantly about their weight. Sheraton had to take a five-month leave of absence in 1980 because her 5-foot-5-inch body had ballooned to 197 pounds. Phyllis Richman spent a week at a diet spa in 1983 for similar reasons.

Many critics find themselves not only stuffed at the table but bored and frustrated at the typewriter as they search for new words to describe old dishes. So they lapse into such silly, anthropomorphic (and ultimately meaningless) descriptions as "a profound chocolate mousse" and "discreet escargots" and "a sullen flan" and "a rather impeccable little salad" and "the food had become much more self-possessed."

But Colman Andrews, who occasionally writes about food for several publications, probably expresses the dilemma of the full-time restaurant critic most vividly. "I can't imagine anyone who really likes food wanting to write a regular restaurant column," he says. "It's like being put out to stud. The basic activity is very pleasurable, but if you have to do it when and with whom you're told, it loses a lot of its charm." (Restaurant criticism, like studship, has a certain ineffable allure, though. Andrews recently resumed writing a weekly restaurant column for the *Los Angeles Times*—"only temporarily," he assured me. "I decided to do it once more while I can still perform.")

And what of the restaurateurs themselves? What do they say about the critics?

One restaurateur—Michael O'Keefe of the Water Club in New York—was so unhappy with Sheraton last year that he asked her to leave his restaurant before she could even order.

"The public loves something, then a critic comes along and says it's not good," O'Keefe explained. "I think the system is unfair."

The system is not unfair. Readers don't have to listen to the critics and often they don't. But Sheraton was unfortunate enough to be recognized—one of the primary occupational hazards of the professional restaurant critic.

When Jim Quinn was reviewing restaurants for *Philadelphia* magazine in the 1970s, he weighed about 225 pounds and wore his hair halfway down his back—sometimes tied in a pony tail.

"The possibility of his doing an anonymous review was almost nonexistent unless the maître d' and his entire staff were blind," says Philadelphia restaurateur Peter Von Starck.

In fact, most big-name restaurant critics *are* almost invariably recognized in the most important restaurants in their cities and in 35 to 50 percent of all the restaurants they visit.

But there are many smaller restaurants in every city where critics can avoid recognition if they make an effort to do so. The best critics generally make that effort. They know that if a restaurateur recognizes them, they will probably receive special treatment—better food and better service than the average customer is likely to receive.

When restaurant critic Allen Kelson of *Chicago* magazine goes to a restaurant, he wears a tiny microphone clipped to his tie and attached to a tape recorder in his jacket pocket. Then, when he wants to remember something about the meal, he just talks to his wife across the table and the tape recorder picks it up.

"If I took notes," Kelson says, "a waiter might guess who I am."

Other restaurant critics use other ruses to avoid being recognized. They make reservations under friends' names and pay their bills with credit cards issued in other names. They disguise themselves with wigs, hats, glasses, scarves, different hair styles and colors. They send their dining companions into a restaurant first and do not join them until they are seated. They refuse to have their pictures taken. They wear masks for public appearances.

All serious restaurant critics agree that they should not let restaurants know in advance that they are coming. But a few critics think that because a restaurant cannot, at the last minute, change its raw products or make new sauces or soups, it is unnecessary—indeed ridiculous—to resort to disguises or hidden microphones.

"The mere fact that a critic walks into a restaurant doesn't mean that genius suddenly invades the kitchen," says Shoffner.

Dwan agrees. So does Christian Millau, co-author of France's prestigious *Gault Millau* restaurant guide. In fact, Millau argues, a restaurateur making a special effort to impress a critic often makes mistakes in his zeal to do well.

I saw this phenomenon firsthand while interviewing Sheraton in a restaurant where she was well-known and fussed over. When I ordered cold asparagus vinaigrette, the nervous waiter served me hot asparagus hollandaise. When Sheraton ordered rare duck, the chef cooked the duck well-done.

Almost every critic I interviewed told of similar experiences—of soup hastily poured on the table without benefit of a bowl, for example, and of dinners delayed interminably because the chef and maître d' kept throwing dishes away trying to give the critic something perfect.

Nevertheless, most serious restaurant critics agree that they should do everything possible to avoid being recognized in a restaurant.

Restaurants *can* give a critic the best piece of meat or fish available. They *can* make sure everything is cooked properly and served hot. They *can* pretend to be out of something that is not particularly good or fresh that night. They *can* replace stale rolls and hold back the dried out, end cut of *pâté*. They *can* make special dishes. They can even make some *nouvelle cuisine* sauces on the spot.

Above all, restaurateurs *can* be more attentive, prompt, and polite.

"There's no question about it," says Gael Greene. "I always get the best treatment, the best piece of whatever is being served when they know it's me."

Greene remembers one meal at which she thought her lamb was disappointing, but the person sitting next to her raved about his lamb. Greene knew the chef and later asked him about the discrepancy.

"He was crushed," Greene recalls. "He said, 'But *he* must have gotten the plate I sent out for *you*.' "

In some cities restaurateurs are so determined to spot—and cater to—critics that there is a virtual black market in photographs of critics. The photos are posted in the kitchen or the reservation book.

Phyllis Richman of the *Washington Post* says she has been told that her posted photo is accompanied in some kitchens by signs offering a $50 reward to the waiter who points her out—and threatening dismissal of any waiter who serves her but does not alert the kitchen to her presence.

"If the waiter tells me such-and-such a critic is on table two," says one Chicago chef, "you can bet that nothing's leaving that kitchen unless it's as perfect as I can make it."

Restaurateurs cater to any valued, regular customer, of course. That's good business practice. But a critic is more than a valued, regular customer; a critic is a surrogate for an enormous number of other potential customers, and many restaurateurs not only cater to the critics, they clearly live in fear of them.

Adriano Rebora says that when he opened Adriano's in Los Angeles in 1978, "I was scared to death of what the critics would say. I'd seen them put restaurants out of business before, and I didn't know if I'd kill them or kill myself."

A former *New York Times* editor remembers eating with two colleagues at a Chinese restaurant in New York one night when Claiborne, then the paper's restaurant critic, dropped by to speak with one of the editors.

"The proprietor recognized Craig," the editor says, "and he started jumping up and down, and I thought he was going to expire on the spot. I'm sure he saw his entire career flash before his eyes."

Do restaurant critics really have that much influence on the success or failure of a restaurant?

Almost everyone agrees that a good review can help a small, new, or out-of-the-way restaurant get off to a good start. Almost half the restaurants polled in 1980 by John Cornyn and Associates in Portland, Oregon, said business had increased as a direct result of a good review.

Most new restaurants are undercapitalized, and if they have to depend on word-of-mouth, they often fail. In Los Angeles County, most new restaurants don't last a year.

"One restaurateur told me a good review . . . is worth $100,000," Richman says.

But after that initial push, it's up to the restaurant itself. People will come once out of curiosity after reading a favorable review; they won't return regularly if they don't like the restaurant themselves.

Sometimes a rave review can be more damaging than helpful. A new restaurant may not be able to handle large crowds or to perform well consistently. Or a restaurateur may try to capitalize on good reviews by squeezing in extra tables and booking too many reservations, thereby overtaxing his staff.

That's what happened after La Guillotine in Los Angeles received rave reviews early in 1977.

"We have 42 seats and we figured we could handle 80 people a night," says chef Ken Frank. "All of a sudden we were doing 120."

The kitchen was rushed. Service slipped. The restaurant became too noisy and too crowded for enjoyable dining. Angry, Frank quit. Not long after, La Guillotine folded.

In an effort to avoid such incidents, many critics say they now telephone small restaurants several days in advance to let them know a favorable review is coming—"so they can get ready for it," says one critic.

But good reviews are no more a guarantee of success with restaurants than they are with books, movies, or plays. Every serious critic can name several restaurants that folded or languished despite critical acclaim.

In fact, Frank now owns and cooks at La Toque, on the same site as the old La Guillotine, and even though he again received highly favorable reviews, his restaurant is still not a big moneymaker.

"There are so many intangible factors in the restaurant business," says one New York restaurateur. "Location. Timing. Personality. Luck. Mood. A good review alone won't do it."

Neither will a bad review necessarily damage a restaurant.

When Jimmy's opened in Los Angeles in 1978, one critic used such words as "inadequate," "indifferent," "wimpish," "soggy," "lukewarm," and "supercilious" to describe her dining experience there.

"But I still do 200 lunches a day; 180 to 200 dinners [Monday, Tuesday, and Wednesday] nights; and 300 dinners Thursday, Friday, and Saturday," says a very happy Jimmy Murphy.

Again, it's a question of intangibles; in the case of Jimmy's, a well-known, high-profile restaurateur created his own following, and the reviews were meaningless.

Similarly, established restaurants with a regular clientele are almost impervious to critics. Institutions like Chasen's in Beverly Hills, Antoine's in New Orleans, Bookbinder's in Philadelphia, and Trader Vic's in San Francisco have been severely criticized by some critics, but they continue to do very well.

Although some new restaurants *are* hurt by the critics—Patrick Terrail says Ma Maison in West Hollywood almost went out of business after the critics panned it when it opened in 1973—critics can generally close down only a bad restaurant that is already near collapse or, sometimes, a small new restaurant. That's why critics are usually quite careful about reviewing small new restaurants. If such a restaurant is bad, most critics won't write about it at all.

But larger, ambitious, well-publicized restaurants are fair game no matter how bad they are. The only question is how soon a critic should write his review. Some critics say a new restaurant should be given four to eight weeks; others say four to eight months.

Most restaurateurs argue that, unlike a Broadway play, restaurants do not have the luxury of out-of-town tryouts or previews to polish their performances and test their staffs before formal opening night reviews. Thus, they insist, they should be given a grace period.

But as critic Jim Quinn points out, "Plays charge lower prices for previews and out-of-town performances. Restaurants don't cut their prices the first few weeks."

Neither do restaurants cut their prices if the chef is out of town or if the maître d' is sick or if the best meats and produce aren't available.

Critics do realize, though, that even the best restaurants can have off-nights. That's why the best critics try to go to a restaurant two or three or four times, usually with two or three friends each time, before reviewing it. Unfortunately, return visits for a single column is expensive and time-consuming, and most critics—even some respected critics on major publications—say they generally visit a restaurant only once before writing a review.

The best critics find that unacceptable. So do restaurateurs. Many restaurateurs argue, in fact, that a critic has no right to review them at all, no matter how many meals they eat in their restaurants.

"Restaurateurs are like aging movie actresses: very sensitive [to criticism]," says Chicago restaurateur Jovan Trboyevic.

That they are.

Shoffner says he received a telephone death threat after writing a scathing review of one Washington restaurant. Ward says someone threw a load of manure into his yard—accompanied by a note that read, "Stop writing that shit"—after he criticized a Chicago restaurant.

Several restaurateurs have sued newspapers for libel over reviews. Almost all have lost. The courts have generally held that restaurant criticism is fair comment, protected by the First Amendment.

The most outspoken of all restaurateurs on the subject of critics is Nick Nicholas, owner of Nick's Fishmarket in Chicago and the organizer of an advertising and circulation boycott against publications with tough critics.

"No one is running around criticizing tailors or shoe stores," Nicholas says. "Why restaurant critics? Hell, it's my restaurant. I could serve bouillabaisse in an ash tray . . . or put my cream on the table in a shoe if I wanted to. You don't like it? Tough. Don't come back. But don't write anything bad about my place."

A few critics agree with Nicholas, and even the toughest critics insist they would be delighted if they *could* constantly be discovering and telling their readers about wonderful new restaurants. The problem, they say, is that most restaurants aren't wonderful, and to pretend they are would undermine the critic's credibility, mislead the reader, and, ultimately, contribute to a deterioration of overall restaurant quality.

"We used to have a critic on the *[Washington] Post* who seemed to like every restaurant he visited," says Bill Rice, former *Post* restaurant critic and now editor of *Food and Wine* magazine. "His ratings were [drawings of] smiles. Four smiles was tops. He routinely gave more four-smile ratings in Washington than *[Guide] Michelin* gave in all of France.

"When I asked various restaurateurs why they did certain

things so poorly, they just shrugged and, in essence, said, 'Hey, I got my four [smiles].' There was no incentive for them to try to do better.''

Many restaurateurs say that good, tough, knowledgeable critics help set standards for restaurants. Other restaurateurs say they often meet with their staffs after a critical review and discuss ways to improve food and service.

Good critics often inspire otherwise timid restaurateurs to experiment in the kitchen. Critics also encourage timid readers to experiment—to eat new kinds of foods in new kinds of restaurants.

As diners become more sophisticated and try more variety, they provide still further encouragement (and money) to enable chefs to experiment even more. "If the critics don't talk about your new dishes and new sauces, people are afraid to try them sometimes,'' says Rene Lannoy, maître d' at Le Gourmet in Los Angeles.

Thus, many restaurateurs credit Claiborne's reviews in the *New York Times* in the 1960s with helping to spark major innovations and improvements in that city's French and Chinese restaurants.

Restaurant critics are more influential in New York than in any other American city, but restaurateurs say good critics have also contributed greatly to improved cuisine in many other cities.

Critics have been especially influential in Los Angeles in recent years, in part because Los Angeles doesn't have a long tradition of fine dining and in part because people must often travel long distances to restaurants here.

San Francisco has long been regarded in some quarters as a great restaurant city, but by the time I was researching this material in 1980, Los Angeles had better, more innovative French restaurants than San Francisco—in part because Los Angeles critics embraced and wrote knowledgeably about French *nouvelle cuisine* in the mid- and late 1970s.

San Francisco critics generally did not do that, and most French restaurants there not only remained wedded to the heavier, richer, more traditional French cuisine, they just rested on their old, once-deserved reputations until only very recently.

(More recently, however, Alice Waters of Chez Pannisse in Berkeley and Jeremiah Tower and a few other innovative San Francisco area chefs have begun to breathe new life into their kitchens, helping give birth to what has come to be known as "California French cuisine." Once again, one can dine well and innovatively in the Bay area.)

There are, of course, many other reasons for the recent differences in Los Angeles and San Francisco restaurants, but restaurateurs in both cities say the critics have played an important role in terms of their influence on reader and restaurateur alike.

As critics become more sophisticated, so do readers. The more sophisticated readers learn to trust the better critics. In fact, reader and critic almost seem at times to be playing a cryptic, as well as a symbiotic, game together.

Virtually every restaurant critic has personal biases, for example, likes and dislikes that his or her regular followers come to recognize and to take into consideration when trying to decide whether to listen to the critic's advice on a particular restaurant.

"You have to learn how to read a critic very carefully," says Michael McCarty of Michael's in Santa Monica. "It's almost a code sometimes. If Lois [Dwan] spends the first five paragraphs of a review talking about the neighborhood of the restaurant and its decor, I know she doesn't really like the food all that much, even if she praises it later [in the review]."

Some critics even seem to forget their readers altogether and write just for their peers.

"They spend more time talking about the texture of the bernaise sauce than . . . about the total dining environment," says Bill Rice.

Much of this culinary snobbism manifests itself in the critics' bias toward French food—*haute cuisine*.

There are, of course, reasons for this bias.

"The predisposition to think French food is the best is justified," says critic Colman Andrews.

Andrews is right. But many critics have long minimized, or ignored, Italian, German, Mexican, and other ethnic cuisines, and some restaurateurs (especially Italians) say this neglect has discouraged them from experimenting with new dishes. Even when critics do write about non-French foods, they often judge them according to French standards and tastes, say several Italian and Chinese restaurateurs.

There are signs that this is changing. Major newspapers have published long, explanatory articles in recent years on Korean, Thai, Brazilian, and Indian foods, among others; the best critics now try to evaluate such restaurants on their own merits, based on what they are trying to achieve within their own class and cuisine.

Inflation has helped speed this process. Most people can't afford to eat at expensive French restaurants, at least not very often, and while they may get vicarious pleasure from reading about them, they also need help in choosing other, more affordable restaurants.

Many papers now have weekly columns on moderately priced neighborhood restaurants as well as on the better-known temples of fine dining.

"You can't base your reviews on only the best food in town," says Gene Roberts, executive editor of the *Inquirer*. "You also have to write for people who don't have that kind of money and aren't all that intense about food and just want to go out and have a good time."

Don't people go to restaurants primarily to eat, though?

Not necessarily

"For most people," says critic Sherman Kaplan of radio station WBBM in Chicago, "the food can be superb, but if the service is lousy, they don't have a good time. If the food's mediocre and the service is great, they can still be happy."

Some other critics agree. They say food quality should count for only about 50 percent of their total appraisal of a restaurant.

"You have to look at ambiance and decor and service," says George Lang, a New York restaurant consultant. "Otherwise you've just got a trough mentality . . . like cavemen."

But most serious restaurant critics insist food quality is paramount.

"I go to a restaurant primarily for food," Sheraton told me. "The creation of a beautiful restaurant is wholly desirable, but too many restaurateurs use fancy decor to take your eye off [the food]."

Thus, while Sheraton wrote about ambiance and service in her reviews, her four-star rating was based almost exclusively on the food.

Most other critics who use a star system follow a similar policy. But none of them, including Sheraton, seem to like using stars. They say they do so only because their editors and their readers insist on it.

"When you use stars, you have the impossible task of trying to compare imcomparables," says one critic. "How can you use the same rating system for a fancy, full-menu, northern Italian restaurant and a small neighborhood Thai place where the father does the cooking and his kids wait on tables?"

In Los Angeles, the most controversial restaurant rating system is the four-star system used by the Restaurant Writers Association.

The association is made up primarily of restaurant writers from smaller publications, a number of whom also sell advertising. With very few exceptions, the twenty or twenty-five members of the association are the kind of writers who never actually criticize restaurants.

None of the city's serious restaurant critics—those representing the *L.A. Times, L.A. Herald Examiner,* and *California* or *Los Angeles* magazines—belong to the Restaurant Writers Association. Most consider it, and its annual awards, a joke and an embarrassment.

Although Dwan was one of the co-founders of the association, she dropped out several years ago, and she, too, now considers its awards "by and large, not valid . . . ridiculous."

But Dwan continues to publish a list of all the association awards every year, and many restaurateurs say that gives them undue credibility.

"Most people just assume the Restaurant Writers Association includes all the restaurant writers, including the important ones who don't belong," says John Hammerton, maître d' at Perino's until he went to La Couronne.

Restaurateurs and some serious critics resent that. Even restaurateurs who have been honored by the association are disturbed by its apparent public credibility.

"They [association members] are asses who don't know a damn thing about food and should be ignored," says Piero Selvaggio of Valentino in Santa Monica, voted "Restaurateur of the Year" by the association in 1978–1979.

The Restaurant Writers Association isn't the only organization whose star ratings of restaurants elicit little respect among the *cognoscenti.*

Mobil announces five-star restaurant ratings throughout the United States each year, and they, too, are widely criticized.

The Mobil ratings seem more concerned with the cleanliness of the restaurants' restrooms than with the quality of their food. (Actually, Mobil may know something. I saw a survey last year that said for most diners, the two most important considerations in choosing a restaurant are the cleanliness of the restaurant—and the cleanliness of its bathrooms.)

"Mobil guides are useless," says Calvin Trillin, who has written three food books. "I've always thought the Mobil [restaurant] inspectors seem like guys who ran good service stations and were promoted for their efficiency but don't know a thing about food.''

For many years, *Holiday* magazine also published an annual restaurant guide. When the program began in 1953, it was virtually alone in the field, and for many years its awards, although flawed, carried a certain prestige.

But in recent years, especially since the magazine and its awards program were absorbed by *Travel* magazine in 1977, few people take the *Holiday* awards seriously.

Why are the *Holiday* awards now held in such low repute?

- The budget is now too small to permit enough visits to enough restaurants to make the awards credible.
- Like Mobil, *Travel/Holiday* tends to honor large, established restaurants.
- Too many restaurants are honored each year for the awards to mean anything. (Are there really more than 300 top-rated restaurants in the United States as *Travel/Holiday* claims? The *Guide Michelin* says there are only eighteen in all of France.)

One of the biggest reasons most knowledgeable food people are critical of the *Travel/Holiday* awards is that the man in charge of the program is not himself highly regarded.

"I have known and not respected Bob Balzer's taste for many, many years," says James Beard, probably America's preeminent food authority.

Robert Lawrence Balzer, who contributes to the *Los Angeles Times* and other publications, has been in charge of the *Travel/Holiday* awards for almost a dozen years, and even though his severest critics concede that the limited financing of the awards program forces him to operate under a severe handicap, they fault him personally on several counts.

These critics say Balzer is too friendly with too many restaurateurs. Indeed he is sometimes picked up by restaurateurs at the airport when he comes to town, and he sometimes stays in the restaurateurs' homes (or in their hotels) and is feasted accordingly in their restaurants.

By Balzer's own estimate, restaurateurs pay for his meals about 50 percent of the time.

Critics also say that Balzer, a recognized authority on wine, just isn't that knowledgeable about food and what knowledge he does have is compromised by his admitted unwillingness to be critical.

With all the shortcomings of the *Travel/Holiday* and Mobil awards, there is only one national restaurant guide in this country that even approaches adequacy, according to most critics. That book is *Where to Eat in America* by Bill Rice and Burton Wolf.

But because there is no comparison between restaurants in different cities in the book, and because the book was compiled from the reports of individual, independent critics in each city, the book lacks a uniform standard of judgment.

The best French restaurant in Indianapolis or Salt Lake City isn't likely to be as good as the best French restaurant in New York or Los Angeles, for example, but there is no way to determine that difference from this book.

Rice readily admits that. "If possible," he says, "I wouldn't dine in Salt Lake City ever in my life. But if I were in Salt Lake City, it wouldn't do me any good to talk about how much I'd love to be eating in Lutèce [in New York] that night. This book is designed to help you if you're in Salt Lake City."

But *Where to Eat in America* ultimately suffers from the same flaw as both the Mobil and *Travel/Holiday* awards. Many of its top choices—Antoine's in New Orleans, Scandia in Los Angeles, Le Trianon in San Francisco, La Maisonette in Cincinnati—are just not as good as they (or their reputations) once were. The awards to such restaurants tend to be self-perpetuating.

Why is there no national restaurant guide in the United States with even a fraction of the prestige and influence of the *Guide Michelin* and *Gault Millau* in France?

The most obvious difference between national restaurant

guides in the United States and France is, of course, that even with the recent, dramatic increase in eating well—and eating out— in the United States, fine dining is just not the cultural imperative here that it has traditionally been in France.

But most American restaurateurs, restaurant critics, and gastronomes say there are other reasons for the absence of a truly reliable national restaurant guide here.

* The sheer size of the United States (more than seventeen times larger than France) would make the cost and logistics of such a guide almost prohibitive.
* French restaurant guides deal almost exclusively with French restaurants. A comprehensive guide in the United States would also have to cover Italian, Mexican, Chinese, Japanese, Creole, and so many other ethnic and regional cuisines that finding and coordinating enough experts would be difficult; establishing a single standard of comparison for rating purposes might be impossible.
* Despite regional differences, tradition has dictated generally accepted standards of excellence for restaurants throughout France. (Of *Gault Millau*'s twelve top-rated restaurants in France in 1983, for example, ten also received *Michelin*'s top rating.) But the very diversity of the United States, combined with its lack of a long-standing national gastronomic tradition, have so far prevented the development of such uniform standards here.

"I'd trust a two-star restaurant in France," says Jay Guben, who used to operate a school for prospective restaurateurs in Philadelphia. "I'd have a pretty good idea what I was getting. But a two-star restaurant in Pittsburgh or Philadelphia?" He shrugs. "Who knows?"

Epilogue

About ten or twelve years ago, a *Los Angeles Times* reporter heard an ugly rumor: A group of white vigilantes in a local suburb was organizing to mount a violent attack on the city school district's interracial, crosstown busing program scheduled to begin the following fall. The reporter told his editor. The editor suggested he and another reporter look into the story.

A week or two later, the reporters returned with their findings: There was, indeed, such a vigilante group. But it was a very small group—just a handful of embittered parents. The reporters said there would no doubt be organized opposition to the busing program—as there had been in other major American cities, most notably Boston—but they thought the most significant opposition would be largely legal and political, not violent. The vigilantes, they thought, wouldn't attract much of a following. The reporters' suggestion: Ignore the self-styled vigilantes, for the time being at least.

The editors agreed. The story on the vigilantes was never published.

I don't generally believe in withholding stories from the public. Newspapers exist to publish—to inform, not to conceal—no matter how often (and how loudly) people in government and in corporate America (and elsewhere) trumpet their displeasure and invoke claims of "national security" or "the prerogatives of a free-market economy" to justify their attempts to keep information from the press (and from the public). I think the *New York Times* should have published its Bay of Pigs story

296

before that ill-fated invasion. I'm glad the *New York Times* (and other newspapers) published the Pentagon Papers. I'm glad the *Washington Post* published what it did on Watergate. I'm glad a whole range of newspapers, in the late 1960s and 1970s, published the stories they did on subjects ranging from pesticides to unsafe automobiles to chemical pollution to corporate skulduggery here and abroad.

But I'm also glad the *Los Angeles Times* did *not* publish its story on the white vigilantes. To do so would have unnecessarily, and dangerously, exacerbated tensions in the community. One story on the vigilantes in the *Times* would no doubt have triggered other stories elsewhere. These stories would have increased the visibility of the vigilantes and brought them new recruits. Their initial feeble threats of violence might have gained credibility. The danger they posed might have become a self-fulfilling prophecy. Instead, the vigilantes were left to rise—or fall—on their own. They fell. The community rejected—ignored—them. They were never heard from. By withholding its story, the *Times* had performed a valuable public service: It had helped keep violence out of what was already a nasty debate. The paper's decision was a classic example of intelligent and responsible restraint, and it was made possible not only by the presence of intelligent and responsible editors but also, in part, by the absence of strong daily competition. I have a great deal of confidence in the editors who decided not to publish the vigilante story, but I wonder if they would have made the same decision if the *Los Angeles Times* had a strong daily newspaper competitor, if the paper's editors had been worried that if they didn't publish the story, the opposition would.

Not that the *Los Angeles Times* doesn't have competition. It does. It's ringed by almost two-dozen suburban newspapers, at least five of which are large and very strong. There are also three network television stations, four local television stations, and more than seventy radio stations in the market. But the only other metropolitan daily newspaper is the *Los Angeles Herald Exam-*

iner with a circulation that was less than half that of the *Times* at the time of the vigilante story (and is now only about one-quarter that of the *Times*).

So the *Times* could afford to be responsible on that story.

I have dwelled on this example here because it illustrates an important point that is often overlooked in discussions about the state of the American newspaper today. Americans are a competitive people; everything—from our now two-year-long presidential campaigns to our belief in a capitalist system to our celebration of the Super Bowl and the World Series and the weekly wire service college football and basketball polls—demonstrates that. Competition makes everything better, most of us believe. It's our pervasive, No.-1-vs.-No.-2/if-you-build-a-better-mouse-trap/my-dad-is-better-than-your-dad/survival-of-the-fittest psychology. But competition is not, by definition, beneficent. It can be pernicious—as it could have been if the *Los Angeles Times* had used the vigilante story, and as it often has been in some newspaper (and other product) wars in which sensationalism, false claims, irresponsibility, and greed too often take precedence over good judgment.

Nonetheless, I think that all of us should be concerned about the steadily diminishing competition among daily newspapers in this country. Despite the excesses born of competition—despite all the times I have shuddered when picking up a newspaper with lurid, screaming headlines in a competitive market—I continue to believe that, in most cases, competition can (if combined with responsibility) spur newspapers to be better. And God knows they could, should, be better.

I was proud of the *Los Angeles Times* for not publishing its story on the white vigilantes in the early 1970s, but I am often embarrassed when I see other stories the *Times* doesn't publish or publishes belatedly or inadequately, in large measure because there is no daily newspaper competition pushing the *Times* to do its best every day on every story. Would the *Times* have been as indifferent to the David Begelman and Eulia Love stories as I wrote in chapter six if it had had strong daily newspaper competition in Los Angeles? I doubt it.

Shouldn't a newspaper be able to generate its own internal pressures and demands for excellence? Yes, to a certain degree. The *New York Times* and the *Washington Post* have been particularly effective at generating that kind of internal pressure. And there has been more of it at the *Los Angeles Times* in the last couple of years or so, too. But that isn't enough, not for any newspaper. Outside competition helps immeasurably. The *New York Times* and *Washington Post* make each other better by competing with each other. So did the *Chicago Tribune* and the *Chicago Sun-Times*. The *Philadelphia Inquirer* made its greatest strides from mediocrity to excellence in the late 1970s when it was battling the crosstown *Bulletin*.

But such newspaper competition is increasingly rare in our society. The *Philadelphia Bulletin* went out of business in 1982, leaving the *Inquirer* and the *Daily News* (both owned by Knight-Ridder) as the only papers in town. That same year the *Cleveland Press* and the *Buffalo Courier-Express* also went out of business, leaving monopolies in their towns, too. Last year, the *Memphis Press-Scimitar* folded, leaving Memphis with one monopoly newspaper. Over the past dozen years more than 140 daily newspapers have closed or merged, leaving city after city to be served by a monopoly—noncompetitive—newspaper.

There are eighteen daily newspapers in Rome, seventeen in Tokyo, fourteen in Paris, eleven in London. In the United States only New York and San Antonio have as many as three dailies—and 98 percent of all American cities have only one. Only twenty-seven cities in the country have truly competing newspapers—newspapers operating under entirely separate, independent, fully competitive owners. (In twenty-five other cities newspapers compete editorially but operate jointly on the business side.)

In 1900, America's 2,042 daily newspapers were owned by 2,023 different proprietors. In 1980, the number of newspapers had dipped to 1,730, and the number of owners had plummeted to 760. Chains now own 70 percent of all daily newspapers. Twenty companies now own the newspapers that provide more than half the total national daily circulation of 61 million. Among them, just three—Gannett, Knight-Ridder, and Newhouse—own more than 150 newspapers with a combined circulation of more than 11 million daily, 20 percent of the national total. Another 6 million papers (10 percent of the total) are sold by three other major media companies—Dow Jones & Co., publisher of the *Wall Street Journal* and twenty other newspapers; the New York Times Co., owner of twelve newspapers; and Times Mirror Co., publisher of the *Los Angeles Times* and seven other daily newspapers, including metropolitan dailies in Dallas, Denver, and Hartford (as well as *Newsday* on Long Island). One man— Rupert Murdoch— now owns daily newspapers in the nation's two largest cities (New York and Chicago) and in two other cities in the top twenty (San Antonio and Boston), as well.

Some newspaper chains—most notably and successfully, Gannett—specialize in buying monopoly newspapers. They don't want competition; they want profits. Other newspaper chains— most notably and successfully, Newhouse—have specialized in buying into a competitive market, then engineering a merger that leaves them with a monopoly. Again, profits, big profits, are the motive, not public service journalism of the sort that is often engendered by competition.

Many chains don't even like the sound of the word *competition*. It frightens them. When Gannett began publication of its new, national daily newspaper, *USA Today,* in the fall of 1982, the company went to great lengths to insist that the paper would not compete with existing daily newspapers. *USA Today* would be a "second or third buy" for readers of existing newspapers, Gannett said in city after city. Gannett's primary purpose in adopting this stance, of course, was to avoid antagonizing the newspaper owners in the cities where *USA Today* was to be offered. The last thing Gannett wanted was an old-fashioned newspaper war or a hostile reception when it began talking to local news dealers and setting up its local coinboxes. But Gannett was also trying to carve out a special niche for USA Today, to mark it as a different kind of newspaper—which in many ways, it is—and not competition for the local daily newspaper that would be sold next to it on the street corner.

USA Today is a flashy-looking newspaper filled with high-quality color photographs and advertisements and eye-catching maps, charts, and graphs. But its stories are almost invariably short—so short, in most cases, as to be incomplete and often misleading—and it more closely resembles a morning television news show than it does a traditional newspaper. Like most Gannett papers, it's just not a terribly good journalistic product. But that's largely because it's treated as a product—something to be marketed at a profit, without much regard for either quality or responsibility.

"Product" and "profits" are two words heard almost constantly around Gannett people, so it's no wonder that Gannett newspapers are almost invariably mediocre. Similar preoccupations render many other chain newspapers (Newhouse newspapers, for example) even worse. A chain newspaper can be good, of course. Several Knight-Ridder newspapers are very good. And a monopoly newspaper can also be good. There are still principled publishers and editors around. But there are fewer of them, and they are increasingly being squeezed by the profit demands of their chain owners (and their stockholders).

It costs a lot of money to produce a high-quality newspaper. It costs a lot of money to hire your own reporters to cover stories downtown and across the country and around the world, rather than relying on the wire services. It costs a lot of money to hire good editors to conceive and assign and edit the stories. Today, too many newspaper owners seek control of a monopoly situation, then reason: "I'm the only game in town. Why spend more money? It won't get me any more readers. It won't make me more money. Things are fine just the way they are.''

But things are not "fine" the way they are. There are too many greedy newspaper owners, and too few good newspapers, in this country. Too few readers are able to get all the information they should from their newspapers. In the political arena, this means they are more susceptible to manipulation by the political consultants, public relations men, and cosmeticians who tell their candidates how to get elected without saying anything of consequence.

What about television? Don't most people get most of their news from television these days? Yes. That's what I'm afraid of. If people vote—or make decisions on anything from abortion or birth control to buying a car or a home—based on those thirty-second local TV "news" stories and twenty-two-minute nightly network newscasts, we're all in terrible trouble. "Hi-I'm-Tawny-Tan-here-with-Tommy-Toothsome . . . Lesbian-Podiatrists-Ravage-Freeway-Orphanage. . . Film-at-eleven" is not my idea of news.

Walter Cronkite has long said that television news is just a headline service and that to be truly informed, one must also read a good daily newspaper. I agree. Unfortunately, people are so busy these days, and television has made news so easy to ingest, that many people now are content with just the headlines. Of course, so few newspapers are truly good—and most of those that are good are often unattractive to look at and impenetrably dull to read—that one cannot altogether fault either television or the viewer/reader for this lamentable state of affairs.

I don't want to be a doomsayer, a Cassandra. I said in the introduction to this book that I think newspapers are, by and large, better than they've ever been. But they've improved as medical treatment and automotive engineering and nutritional counseling and most other things in society have improved: because education and technology, evolution and progress, have made it so.

Newspapers have improved *despite* the trend toward monopolies and chain ownership—and, in some measure, *because* of television. By providing an immediacy and an intimacy that newspapers cannot begin to emulate, television has largely taken the big, breaking news story away from the newspaper and forced newspapers to become more probing, more interested in looking for the causes and effects of these stories, on both a cosmic and a personal level. But too few newspapers do those stories well. They're better than they used to be, but they're not as good as they should be.

Newspapers have problems of their own, of course. Americans do not read newspapers as avidly as do people in many other countries. Only 287 newspapers are sold per 1,000 population in the United States, according to the 1982 edition of the *World Press Encyclopedia,* and that ranks us twentieth among the industrialized nations of the world. (Sweden is first with 572 papers per 1,000 population; Japan is second with 526.)

Moreover, while metropolitan dailies in this country have less competition now from other metropolitan dailies, they have more competition from suburban newspapers, television, radio, city magazines, and a whole range of special-interest magazines. Since Americans don't read that much to begin with, something has to give. Often that something is the daily newspaper.

Increased competition for leisure-time activity—and increased demands on the family budget, especially after the inflation/unemployment spiral of recent years—have also helped make the daily newspaper an expendable option in many households. It's not surprising that the number of newspapers sold per hundred households has declined 37 percent in the last thirty years.

In recent years, yet another, and especially frightening, financial pressure has been exerted on newspapers: the threat of libel suits. For about a dozen years, from 1964 into the mid-1970s, libel law gradually expanded to provide greater protection for newspapers. Then, after a few years of mixed courtroom results, the trend began to reverse. It isn't that newspapers are losing so many libel cases but that they now have to engage in longer, ever-more-expensive battles to prevail. Many cases of the sort that were previously dismissed before trial have recently been going to trial. Trials that had previously lasted a few days now last a few weeks or a few months. Cases that previously ended in victory for the newspaper now sometimes end in victory for the plaintiff—even though many are ultimately reversed on appeal.

Fighting a lawsuit is expensive, though—even if the newspaper wins. And the threat of a lawsuit is so prevalent now that, as Benjamin C. Bradlee, executive editor of the *Washington Post,* told me one day last spring, "I've never been so aware of the problem . . . or had to spend so much time talking to lawyers every week."

A newspaper with the *Post*'s resources can survive this legal onslaught. But I worry about smaller papers and less committed editors and publishers. How many important stories—stories that generally only come to light in the local daily newspaper, stories on corruption and malfeasance, for example—are not done now because editors (especially those whose monopoly owners are obsessed with profits) just decide that the effort is not worth the risk of a costly libel suit.

When an Illinois builder won a $9.2-million libel judgment against the 38,000-circulation *Alton Telegraph* in 1980, for example, the paper—then valued at about $3 million—couldn't raise the bond required by law. Bankruptcy threatened. Finally, the *Telegraph* negotiated a $1.4-million settlement—paid with libel insurance and money borrowed from banks. The result at the suddenly financially strapped paper: Salaries were frozen, travel was limited, reportorial vacancies went unfilled, needed new equipment was not bought—and the paper had become so cautious on some potentially controversial stories that Stephen A. Cousley, the paper's editor and publisher, told the *Wall Street Journal* last year, "We're like the tight end who hears footsteps every time he runs to catch a pass."

What particularly frightens many editors is that when newspapers do lose libel judgments these days, the judgments are often for staggering amounts. From 1980 to 1982, 45 percent of all libel awards exceeded $250,000; in the preceding four years, only 17 percent topped that amount. Last October, I was told that seven of the eight most recent judgments in libel (and privacy) cases had resulted in initial awards of more than $1 million. The other award was $750,000. Six of the eight cases included punitive damage awards totaling more than $47 million—an average of almost $8 million per case.

Even worse, perhaps, on yet another legal front, prosecutors and attorneys for criminal defendants are increasingly demanding the names of reporters' confidential sources. As Jonathan Friendly reported in the *New York Times* last November, one recent study found sixty-seven such cases from September 1982 to September 1983, more than double the number for the previous twelve months. Even though reporters won thirty-seven of the cases, they are losing a greater percentage than ever before. As with libel cases, reporters may lose at the trial level and win on appeal, but the process is time-consuming and costly—and intimidating. Most journalists worry that if they are unable to assure their sources of confidentiality, many sources will be afraid to come forward with vital information on corruption and other wrongdoing.

The public would be the ultimate loser if that happened, but I don't think the public is terribly receptive these days to arguments about the important role the press plays as a surrogate for the public. If recent surveys—and letters to the editor—are any indication, a growing segment of the public sees the press as arrogant, irresponsible, inaccurate, sensational, profit-motivated, self-appointed, and (in many quarters) unwanted watchdogs of government, business, and everyone else in society. As one person wrote to John Chancellor, after Chancellors's NBC commentary criticizing Reagan administration treatment of the press during the invasion of Grenada: "What do you think we elected Reagan for? It's damn sure *you* were never elected.''

Chancellor said his mail ran five-to-one against his commentary. Peter Jennings, the anchor on the ABC evening news, said 99 percent of his mail supported Reagan's ban on press coverage of the first two days of the invasion and the restrictions imposed on the press for the next three days. An *Editor and Publisher* survey of letters to the editors of a dozen daily newspapers found a three-to-one margin of support for Reagan. Readers and viewers didn't just ''support'' Reagan; they supported him with a vengeance. One man wrote to Jack Nelson, the Washington bureau chief of the *Los Angeles Times,* ''I am sick of the press and people like you trying to always put down our government and our country. You guys sound like enemies to our country.'' Another man wrote in a *Los Angeles Herald Examiner* guest column: ''I wish some repressive political authority would shut you (the press) down. . . .''

The more loudly the press complained about being excluded from the Grenada invasion, the more loudly the public seemed to rally to Reagan's side. No wonder. The most recent finding of the National Opinion Research Center is that only 13.7 percent of the American public has ''a great deal of confidence'' in the press; that's less than half the number in 1976—and even that 1976 reading (29 percent) was not exactly encouraging.

The press seems baffled by all this suspicion and hostility—especially in the face of the Reagan administration's unprecedented efforts to deny the press (and the public) access to government information. The administration has limited information released under the Freedom of Information Act; ordered Defense Department employees with access to national security information to take lie-detector tests; and issued a directive requiring 128,000 federal officials to promise, in writing, to submit all their future writings to a review board for the rest of their lives. These are just three of thirty specific steps cataloged by the Reporters Committee for Freedom of the Press. The public should be howling with outrage at the Reagan administration; instead, they are either silent—or they are howling at the press.

Why?

Members of the print media are inclined to blame the excesses of television for giving the entire press a bad name. Surely, the sensationalism, superficiality, and what *Time* magazine last year called the "you-are-there intrusiveness and emphasis on conflict" that are endemic to television have alienated many in the general public. And just as surely, the nightly hammering away on Vietnam and Watergate and, more recently, unemployment have offended many others. Moreover, as I pointed out in my introduction, all the press—print as well as electronic—is resented in some quarters simply for being the bearers of bad news.

But the press *does* contribute to its own problems—with errors of omission and commission, of distortion and overraction and, above all, by its own arrogance.

All this brings me back, of course, to the primary point of my introduction: the necessity for self-policing in the press. If we are, on occasion, irresponsible, greedy, dishonest, lazy, or suffer from any of the other all-too-human failings, we should be mature enough to admit it and to do something about it. I just cannot understand those in the press who insist on being defensive, who refuse to say, "I was wrong. I'm sorry. It won't happen again." No one likes to admit he's wrong, of course, but I think the press has a special responsibility to say mea culpa.

That, I guess, is why I reacted so angrily in the summer of 1983 to the controversy over columnist George Will's participation in the briefing of Ronald Reagan during preparations for Reagan's 1980 debate with President Jimmy Carter. As things turned out, you may recall, Reagan's aides had access to Carter's briefing books (among other Carter records) during those debate preparations and Will knew about it. But Will didn't report this story—not in his column and not in his role as a commentator on ABC television. Far worse, in my view, after having helped coach Reagan, Will went on television and praised Reagan for his performance.

I know Will's defense—and that appalls me further. He says he's a columnist, not a reporter, and thus everyone knows he supported Reagan. True enough; their mutual admiration is no secret. He says he didn't really help Reagan all that much anyway. Probably true enough; Reagan didn't need all that much help against Carter as I recall. But for Will to insist that he didn't really do anything wrong is preposterous. As a columnist he is certainly entitled to his views and his allegiances, and if he wants to call Reagan on the phone and compliment him on his performance on television, that's just fine. But columnist or not, he should not have helped Reagan prepare for his performance—that's a job for political advisers not political columnists—and he sure as hell shouldn't have helped Reagan prepare and then gone on television immediately after the debate and praised Reagan as "quite a thoroughbred" for the very performance Will helped rehearse. That is being neither a political columnist nor a political adviser—merely a political shill.

Will is not the first political columnist to get too close to a prominent politician and to confuse his personal politics with his professional obligations, of course. In generations past, such behavior was commonplace. But Post-Watergate journalism has demanded that politicians be more open and honest than ever before, and many in government and in the general public as well are asking why the press shouldn't be held to the same standard. Good question. They, we, should be held to the same standard. We should demand no less of ourselves than we demand of those we write about—in honesty, in full disclosure, in independence from conflict of interest, in every aspect of our work.

I'll be interested in seeing if all those editors and columnists and reporters who jumped all over George Will are as critical of themselves and their own publications when they make mistakes in the months and years ahead.

I'm not holding my breath.

Index